BE WHO YOU ARE

BE WHO YOU ARE

A SONG FOR MY CHILDREN

*A Father's Empowering Message
about the Point of Life*

JIMMY BRANDMEIER

NEW YORK

LONDON • NASHVILLE • MELBOURNE • VANCOUVER

BE WHO YOU ARE
A SONG FOR MY CHILDREN
A Father's Empowering Message about the Point of Life

Published in New York, New York, by Morgan James Publishing. Morgan James is a trademark of Morgan James, LLC. www.MorganJamesPublishing.com

The Morgan James Speakers Group can bring authors to your live event. For more information or to book an event visit The Morgan James Speakers Group at www.TheMorganJamesSpeakersGroup.com.

Naomi Long Madgett, "Woman with Flower," *Star by Star* (Harlo Press, 1965). Copyright © Naomi Long Madgett. Reprinted with permission.

ISBN 978-1-68350-901-1 paperback
ISBN 978-1-68350-902-8 eBook
Library of Congress Control Number: 2017918889

Cover Design by:
Rachel Lopez
www.r2cdesign.com

Interior Design by:
Bonnie Bushman
The Whole Caboodle Graphic Design

In an effort to support local communities, raise awareness and funds, Morgan James Publishing donates a percentage of all book sales for the life of each book to Habitat for Humanity Peninsula and Greater Williamsburg.

Get involved today! Visit
www.MorganJamesBuilds.com

To my amazing wife, Paula, without whom this book wouldn't exist. Though written solely from the perspective of a father, Paula's handwriting is everywhere. Between the lines, behind the verse, and through the spaces, her voice was there—patiently waiting and helping me to find mine. The message we whittled into the wood at "the lighthouse" in Fond du Lac, Wisconsin, twenty-five years ago still says it best.

To Paula:

"I love U 4 ever!"

CONTENTS

A LETTER TO MY DAUGHTERS

Dear Jamie, Jessie, and Josie,

These pages started out as a song. I had no idea the song would grow into a book.

I began doodling the lyrics while sitting on the beach at Grandma Joan and Grandpa Harvey's beach house in Amagansett, Long Island. You were immersed in a magical day of bopping in the waves; Mom was reading and chilling under the umbrella; I was sitting next to her strumming my guitar, basking in the moment, and writing this song in my head.

I thought the right words could protect you,
Shelter you from the inner and outer storms of life.

But the love fueling my words, was more powerful, more fired, more expansive, than a foundation of lyrics alone could hold. The song took on a life of its own. Each line grew into a separate topic. The lyric spun like a thread that wove into the prose that unfolded into this book:

Be Who You Are: A Song for My Children

The song became a book; the book, a father's prayer. And my prayer—God willing—comfort when needed and shelter from the storm.

LYRICS TO "BE WHO YOU ARE: A SONG FOR MY CHILDREN"

Verse one:

Like a rose reaching through winter,
Blazing into spring,
She burst into her beauty,
Grew up suddenly.

Time will not reason,
The seasons,
Must change.

Good-bye apron strings,
I'll hold your hand, as you
Spread your wings.

Verse two:

The real journey leads inside,
I pray you'll travel far,
Your passion is a compass;
All that you love, a guiding star.

The world will come raging,
Try changing

True north.
I'm a whisper in the storm,

A voice of Love that's calling you to

Be who you are,
Time to see who you are.

Verse three: *God is in the moment,*
Live each one out loud.
Keep your castles in the air and
Two feet planted on the ground.

Your masterpiece lives complete in the stone,
Imitation is fool's gold,
To let your miracle unfold, just

Be who you are,
Go and see who you are.

Verse four: *Don't seek the soul in shiny goals,*
Behind applause that roars.
To fly beyond your wildest dreams,
Have faith, do less, be more.

Verse five: *Be kind when no one's watching,*
Sing like no one can hear,
Be bold and brave, go make mistakes,
Live to the point of tears.

The darkest night reveals the light of the stars.

Interlude: *I promise you the day will dawn,*
When Heart and Heaven beat as one,
You'll dance into your dreams,

The one destiny. My child, you'll

Theme: *Be who you are, truly*
See who you are,
You'll believe, as I believe, in who you are.

*Be who you are, and you'll
See who you are.*

*Believe as I believe in who you are.
Believe as I*
Believe in who you are.

Promise me, you'll always be,

*Be who you are!
No matter how far!*

Be who you are!

The five parts of this book are based upon the five verses of this song. Because each lyric line has a deeper meaning, wider truth, and broader picture crying out for expression from this father's heart—*the book follows the song by related subject, not line by line.*

For a free download of the song "Be Who You Are," go to
www.JimmyBrandmeier.com.

OVERTURE

When my dad died, he left his only daughter with nothing to hold on to but his blind insecurity disguised as a grudge.

Your Grandpa Frank went through life holding grudges with lots of people. In the end, it was my sister Mary's turn. Don't get me wrong, I loved Grandpa Frank, and he loved your Aunt Mary very much. He had many great qualities, but like many of us, facing problems and knowing how to express his love, weren't always among them.

His funeral was a whirlwind. Uncle Michael and I joked about our "to do" list: pick up some milk, identify Dad's dead body, clean the kitchen, break the news, write an obituary, take out the garbage, choose between a $10,000 casket or a rental, tell Dad's girlfriend he died, find her first, feed the dog, find a will, get some gas, do the laundry, pick up the dry cleaning, and oh yeah, have Dad cremated. Check! Is there really such a thing as an ordinary day?

It wasn't until we got up north to spread Grandpa's ashes around his beloved cabin that emotions hit hard, not because of his passing; I know we are infinite spiritual beings, and he's more than okay. I know with his death came the gift of awakening. I snuck off to the side of the cabin, where no one could see me, and cried deeper than I've ever cried in my life, because of how Grandpa's displaced resentment was hurting my sister, Mary, even more, after he died.

I wasn't just sad. I was mad!

After not seeing the inside for years, Aunt Mary rushed into the log cabin, in our family since 1910. Despite the one-sided quarrel, she loyally sent Grandpa pictures of her life and family along with his birthday and Christmas presents. He never responded. When I saw her scramble into the cabin, I knew what she was looking for.

My heart dropped.

Pictures of your uncles, you, and your cousins were proudly displayed everywhere. Mary flew directly to the photo albums and rifled through—nothing. She searched in the storage rafters above the kitchen—still nothing. Below the beds, nothing. Under the cabinets, but she saw nothing, nothing, nothing. None of her gifts and not one picture of Mary and her beautiful family.

I know Grandpa loved Aunt Mary. He told me so and always bragged about her. I could see the fear driving his behavior. Still, a fearful person can be a hurtful one.

I have my own fears.

As I laid my dear father to rest at his cabin in the woods, I promised myself that my fear would never become your problem. I swore that while I'm here on earth, and after I'm gone, you'll never have to scurry around searching for evidence of my love.

This book is part of that promise. It's love made visible.[1]

Know you are valued and valuable.

Feel you are safe and protected.

See you are deeply loved, even when the fear of your flawed father may be blocking the view.

Your Aunt Mary, Uncle Michael, and Uncle Johnny—looking on as I threw our father's ashes to the winds of forever, at his cabin up north.

But layers of reasons drove me to write this book.

Be Who You Are: A Song for My Children was created from my love and pulled from my pain. I was grabbed by the gut to plant a conviction like a fortress around your spirits. The creed is simple, empowering, and rare:

Be who you are, inside and out, No matter what! No matter how far!

My philosophy has always been "Use your talent to serve." You cannot use your talent to serve if you don't use your talent! You cannot love others if you don't love yourself. To love yourself you must *be* yourself. Authenticity on the outer road of life requires vision, purpose, courage, and commitment. On the inner road, it takes intention, awareness, devotion, and faith to be who you are. It seemed, at least for a while, your dad lost all of the above.

I hit rock bottom.

If you didn't understand or know about it at the time, you probably felt it. The music company I launched to secure our financial future crashed and burned. Every avenue of escape was either obsolete or closed for the recession. There was nowhere left to turn.

After throwing every ounce of my being into the ring, I crawled off the battlefield wounded and wiped out. I've lost before, been rejected a zillion times, struggled forever. But for the first time—for the very first time—something previously inconceivable seeped through the cracks of my confusion. I felt defeated, like my chances were over.

Even as my ego was flailing and wailing and trying to hold on at the surface, I did the *inconceivable*.

I quit.

And without knowing it, the "pain of events," pulled me into the inner road of life. Every day, I prayed for clarity.

It was only later, I realized an answer to those prayers was part of the guiding force pulling me through these pages.

My mother, your Grandma Hanky, was fond of saying, "God writes straight with crooked lines." Like Ray Kinsella in the movie *Field of Dreams*, who was blind to the real gift hidden in the baseball diamond he cut from the corn, I never saw it coming—the unexpected grace and surprise ending of this book—"Ease his [own] pain."

It turns out, the message I was so passionate about giving to you, was the one I most needed to hear. Live what you love.

Be who you are.

The message finally blew up in my face, and broke through my defenses, creating an opening for insight, as the company and my spirits crumbled.

Somewhere along the line, I stopped being myself, let limiting beliefs and the life-sucking cancer of "I can't" drip into my subconscious. Being a musician wasn't "normal." My friends all had "real careers" and security. I didn't accept my gifts. Instead of embracing my uniqueness and finding a way, I turned my back and lost it.

My love of creating music got lost in the business of selling music. Like a remora feeding off the reflected glory of other people's artistry, I swam next to my dream, not in it. I thought I could defer my dream, make money, and come back to it. It's the very commonness of my story that makes it so important: Compromise who you are and what you love for the sake of perceived security, status, and social approval. Thoreau was right: "The mass of men lead lives of quiet desperation."

My pain was a gift, a straight path home through the crooked lines of God Grandma Hanky told me about. As T. S. Eliot said, "And the end of all our exploring / Will be to arrive where we started / And know the place for the first time."

In the end, trying to help you, helped me; trying to guide you, guided me; trying to inspire you, inspired me. That's the beautiful nature of giving, and the irony of parenting; our children, like a mirror, show us who we are, and help us to grow up.

Now I know what I've always known.

Now the thought of feeling defeated makes me laugh. Ha! Now I know we are responsible for effort, integrity, and intention, not outcome. Now I know that every so-called defeat or failure is just gift-wrapping paper and bows unveiling the gift of clarity, and the grace of guidance, when torn from the present it conceals.

I want you to learn from my mistakes. After going through the fire, which seared through my ignorance, scorched my fear like the earth, and burned down the illusions of the ego—I can finally see. I can see the magnificent, indestructible spirit inside of you, me, and everyone. I can see the amazing power radiating with possibilities inside all of us.

I can also see the tiny tragedies, first-world problems, and itty-bitty storms in a teacup that keep us from reaching our potential. The forces that suck the smiles from our face have nothing to do with anything happening outside of us. It's our inside life that creates our outside world. I can see it now, crystal clear and true as gravity. Happiness is not an external event. Our inside life *is* life.

And I see an unrepeatable, amazing life shining inside of you.

Do you have any idea who you are and what you can do?

If you did, you'd be happy no matter what happens. You'd never cling to dream-killing comfort zones, or flatline routines. You would never seek anyone's approval but your own. You'd never bury your dream alive, leaving it gasping for air in some standardized box for the sake of perceived security. You wouldn't waste a single second on worry, want, or anger. You wouldn't need to substitute false pride for true confidence.

You would judge no one, including yourself; forgive everyone, especially yourself. And you'd love others, because you'd love yourself.

You'd be happy.

You'd be fearless.

You'd be free.

If you could look through the clouds of fear and catch even the tiniest glimpse of who you really are, living a counterfeit life would be unbearable—horrifying—like the walking dead, a fate worse than death. And no, that's not an overstatement!

Oh, I can see the so-called hardships of life. I can see the inevitable pain. So what?! Pain may be inevitable, but suffering is a choice! There is no greater pain than living a lie and missing your own life.[2]

I'm so sure of what I see in you, I wish I could just shout your wide eyes open, to spare you from the pain it may take to see it on your own. *It's true! It's true! It's true!* These are not just fluffy words on a page! You are an infinite spirit, with infinite possibilities. All this fear-based, ego-driven, programmed, cow-herd, moo-moo-moo, limiting belief, "I can't, I can't, I can't" garbage is a big, big, big waste of time!

Be—Who—You—Are!

Trust me! You don't have to let life suck the life out of you!

I—See—Who—You—Are!

I see your invincible spirit;

I see your unlimited potential;
I see your creative genius;
I see your goodness;
I see your courage;
I see your love;
I see your wings;
And—I—See—You!
But I also see fear, which is a birthstone we all share, blocking the way.
Fear—Is—Not—You!
I see standard-issue guilt, worry, want, whining, vanity, and negativity, which is all part of being born a human with an animal ego, programmed like a computer for survival and gain. The ego is not real. The layered-in, wired-on programs that evolved over time to help us survive only seem real.

I see you rising above and looking in—thanking the robot of an ego for its service, then pulling the plug—free at last from the only things that could ever enslave you.

Fear and negativity: Ignorance of who you really are.

You are a spiritual being having a human experience.[3]

And your spirit is breathtaking!

I can already see the perfect happiness, unlimited power, and natural freedom that are your birthright.

I swear, I swear, I swear, what I'm saying is true!

I am certain! I am certain! I am certain!

You are infinite! You are unbreakable! You are unrepeatable. You are awesome!

And—You—Are—Love!

And—You—Are—Loved!

Deeply, deeply loved.

My purpose, my intention, my prayer for this book is to help you see what I see.

VERSE ONE

Like a rose reaching through winter,
Blazing into spring,
She burst into her beauty,
Grew up suddenly.

Time will not reason,
The seasons,
Must change.

Good-bye apron strings,
I'll hold your hand, as you
Spread your wings.

LIKE A ROSE
REACHING THROUGH WINTER
Prelude to You

Each life touches every life.
Echoes through eternity in ways too vast to see, infinite to
    understand, and endless to imagine.
Cuts and colors a unique swath through the fabric of
    the universe,
Precious, irreplaceable, indispensable.
Every person is a crucial thread in the tapestry of the whole.
                                                        —Dad

This is big!
What could possibly compare to this! Winning lotto? A Grammy nomination? Landing that thirty-second beer jingle I was going after at the time? Fitting into a pair of thirty-two-inch waist jeans? The cable guy showing up on time?

One ordinary day, she came to me with extraordinary news.

Cue the angelic music.

Set the scene to slow motion, and cut to the deep happiness and quiet strength of my wife Paula.

"We're about to alter the universe for all time!"

Freeze-frame!

Cue the *Twilight Zone* music—Ne ne ne ne, Ne ne ne ne.

Set the scene to surreal motion, and cut to the bulging eyes and whirling thoughts of a husband taking it all in.

Alter the universe for all time? Ne ne ne ne, Ne ne ne ne.

Bigger than the cable guy showing up on time? Ne ne ne ne, Ne ne ne ne.

As the world turns upside down, his whirling thoughts spin off to the movie *It's A Wonderful Life* and Bedford Falls—a town gone bad, when one of its residents, George Bailey, gets a chance to see what the world would be like if he was never born. Clarence Oddbody, AS2 (angel, second-class), was sent from heaven to give George a simple yet profound message.

Aaaand action!

CLARENCE: Your brother, Harry Bailey, broke through the ice and was drowned at the age of nine.

GEORGE BAILEY: That's a lie! Harry Bailey went to war. He got the Congressional Medal of Honor. He saved the lives of every man on that transport.

CLARENCE: Every man on that transport died! Harry wasn't there to save them, because you weren't there to save Harry. Strange, isn't it? Each man's life touches so many other lives. When he isn't around he leaves an awful hole, doesn't he?

Fade back to an ecstatic future father coming out of his trance.

It's true!

We ARE going to alter the universe for all time!

This IS bigger than a beer jingle!

Paula told me it was time to celebrate—to give thanks and get ready. There was a miracle in the making that chose us. We were about to bring another George Bailey (in our case, Georgette) into the world. Your future mom had a new light in her eyes, gleamed from a new light within, as she calmly and lovingly whispered the words that would forever change our lives:

(Re-cue angelic music.)

"We're going to have our first baby!"

Jamie Elizabeth, April 9, 1994

(Repeat sign: segue to duet section.)

Second baby!!

Jessica Haley, May 24, 1995

(*Grand finale,* to a gorgeous trio.)

Third baby!!!

(Josie Joan, December 7, 1998)

(*Molto dolce!*)

And CUT!

Jamie, April 9, 1994

Jessica, May 24, 1995

Josie, December 7, 1998

Fade to outtakes . . .

You will change the lives of every person you come into contact with. Your irreplaceable drop of energy will forever alter the ocean of humanity. Your example, fearful or loving, will inspire and teach. Your passing comment could change a destiny—random smile, save a life. Who you are expands to us all.

Clarence Oddbody, AS2, was right. Each man's life touches so many other lives. When he's not around he leaves an awful hole.

Never let the routine of your life stamp out the miracle of your life.

You are unrepeatable. You are needed. You are infinite.

Each person's life, touches every life.

If you weren't around, you'd leave an awful hole.

SHE BURST INTO HER BEAUTY, GREW UP SUDDENLY

I'll hold your hand as you spread your wings—
Walk you through the pages of this book, and love you
through the pages of life.

—Dad

I'm giving away the punch line.

As you take your first steps out of the nest, and into the world, I'm cutting to the chase, to the back of the book—the climax of the song. Like a lighthouse blazing through the fog, I'm shooting a flare in the air, so you can see *The Point* of the journey in advance.

The framework of life is really sooo simple.

There are two roads, which layer and lead towards or away from who you are.

1. *The inner road and sole purpose of life:* Transcend the ego. Rise above fear (ego) into the essence of who you are. (Love!)
2. *The outer road and secondary purpose of life:* Make the most of yourself, your talents, your livelihood, and your life in this world. (Live!)

All you can imagine, do, be, achieve or experience is found on these two roads.

One road leads to the other.

The quality of your life depends on the relationship between them.

The framework of life is simple. There are two roads.

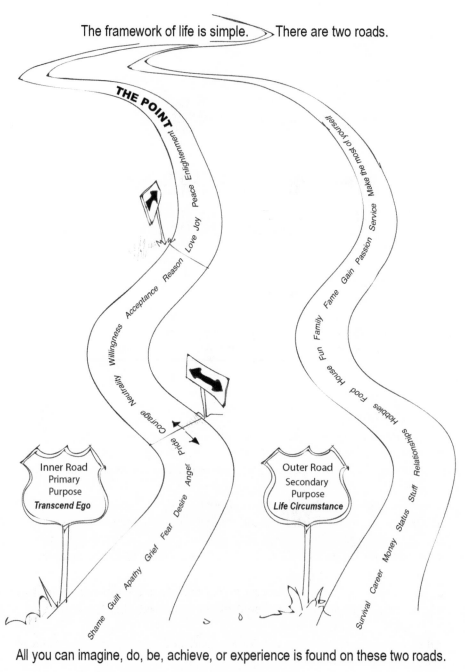

THE POINT

Enlightenment
Peace
Joy
Love
Reason
Acceptance
Willingness
Neutrality
Courage
Pride
Anger
Desire
Fear
Grief
Apathy
Guilt
Shame

Inner Road
Primary
Purpose
Transcend Ego

Make the most of yourself
Service
Passion
Gain
Fame
Family
Fun
House
Food
Hobbies
Relationships
Stuff
Status
Money
Career
Survival

Outer Road
Secondary
Purpose
Life Circumstance

All you can imagine, do, be, achieve, or experience is found on these two roads.

I wrote this book to guide you down both and to steer you away from the gravitational pull of The Big Mistake:

Believing the outer road is the only road that matters.

Believing the outer road leads to happiness.

Flip the switch.

"The ego says, once everything falls into place, I will find peace [outer]. The spirit says, once I find peace, everything will fall into place [inner]."[4]

Most people think "being who you are" means "doing what you love." They are *partly* right.

Doing what you love is a beautiful *part* of life's big picture, and *part* of the overarching message of this book. Doing what you love can also be *part* of the curriculum in the course of authenticity. It can fade the façade of appearance into an opening for your essence to shine through like the sun.

Lose your self (ego) in what you love, and you'll find your Self (essence) through what you love.

But doing what you love is only a portal to the point.

And above all,

I want you to reach *The Point.*

So what's The Point?

Buddhists call it "enlightenment." Christians call it "being born again."

I call it "being who you are" inside and out.

Perfect happiness.

Ahh.

That's The Point.

That's the purpose.

That's the punch line.

And that's what I want for you.

Fairy-tale lives filled with romance, riches, and dreams-come-true are a complete bore compared to the ecstasy of being who you are, inside and out. Buddha says, "To even hear of enlightenment is already the rarest of gifts. Anyone who has ever heard of enlightenment will never be satisfied with anything else."

Singer John Mayer's dreams came true, yet he lamented, "Something's missing and I don't know what it is at all." After actor Matt Damon won an Academy Award, he went back to his hotel room and threw it on the bed thinking, "Glad I didn't kill anybody for that." Comedian Jim Carrey says, "I wish people could realize all of their dreams of wealth and fame so they could see that it's not where you'll find your sense of completion."

The greatest material gains and achievements in the world are not good or bad, or right or wrong—they're just not enough. Like the toys we quit playing with as children, we simply lose interest as we grow up.

The further you wander outside yourself for happiness, the further from happiness you'll be. Even the noblest pursuits of this world can only take you halfway home, or

The BIG MISTAKE
Believing the outer road leads to happiness.

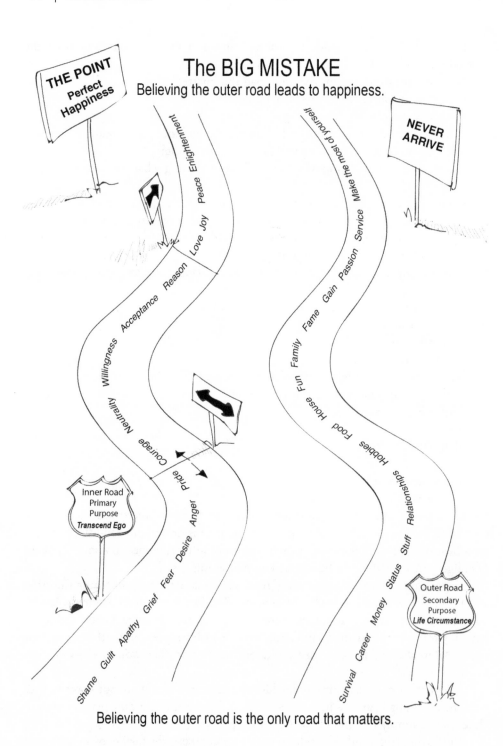

Believing the outer road is the only road that matters.

depending on motivation, halfway to hell. The journey to who you are is a "journey without distance."[5]

People who focus on the outer road only, believe happiness can be found in the bowels of a bulging shopping cart, at the center of attention, or on the shores of a far-off dream. Always in the future—never now:

This book is kicking and screaming with a simple message.

Quit looking in the wrong place for what you really want!

Quit looking in the wrong place for happiness!

Quit looking in the wrong place for who you are!

You're not out there!

You're in here!

But *out there* matters too.

Yes! Yes! Yes! Yes!

To spiritualize your life, you simply have to change your motives. You don't have to give up your dreams, sacrifice what you love, or settle for less.

No! No! No! No!

It's the exact opposite! I want you to explode into your dreams!

Dynamite the dams of fear (shame, guilt, apathy, grief, desire, anger, pride, depression, low self-worth, need for approval, worry, craving, blame, stress), and you'll blow a hole in the ego so big that happiness will come bursting through on its own. You'll create the inner conditions for your outer dreams to unfold naturally. Thoughts will soar, mood elevate, energy skyrocket. Consequently, cash will flow into the river of your potential, in any amount needed to make the most of yourself.

So how do we make the most of our limitless potential?

How do we . . .

Stay *happy* (inner) no matter what *happens* (outer)?

Imagine the life we want (inner) and live the life we've imagined (outer)?

Create wealth (inner) and financial independence (outer)?

Attain fulfillment (inner) and success (outer)?

Find our passion (inner)?

Find our Why! Why! Why (inner)!

Fuse our *what* and *why* into a rocket-launching *how* aaaand

BAM!

Live the dream *inside* and *out?*

How do we love, and love, and **love ourselves first** (inner),

So that we can love others (outer)?

How do we forgive, and forgive, and **forgive ourselves first** (inner),

So that we can forgive others (outer)?

How do we raise our consciousness level from fear to love? (And what the heck is a "consciousness level," and why should we care?)

How do we merge our, unrepeatable, unlimited, unchartered inner and outer roads, to create amazing, fulfilling, and, fun, fun, fun lives?

I'll hold your hand,
as you spread your wings.

Enlightenment

Joy

LOVE ♥

Reason

Acceptance

Willingness

Neutrality

Courage

Pride

Anger

FEAR

Desire

Grief

INNER ROAD

Apathy

Guilt

Shame

I'll breadcrumb your way up the inner and outer roads of life.

Lose your self (ego) in what you love,
and you'll find your Self (essence) through what you love.

Beep, beep, beep, beep!
(Sound of the answer truck backing up to the front of the book.)
Now that we've backed into the beginning, let's start with the basics.
Time.
As the saying goes, time is life and life is time.
To make the most of your life,
Make the most of your time.
Now, now, always now,
Let the fun begin.

TIME WILL NOT REASON

What do you want, why do you want it, and what are you waiting for?

—Dad

Time is still.

The veil between heaven and earth has lifted.

Gratitude dances in the light of silence.

Paula, or as they call her at work, Captain "Paula the Pilot" Brandmeier, is probably just landing her United 777 airplane in Hong Kong. Jamie and Jessie are nestled in—or is it stuffed into?—their college dorm room, right down the road at University of Wisconsin, Madison. And Josie has a few more hours of peaceful sleep before I nudge her into the day with those three dreaded words: "Time for school."

Awake in every sense of the word, I'm rapt in a dialog with divinity, sitting in bliss at 3:00 a.m. praying and waiting with absolute certainty for answers to my questions to boomerang through the universe and make their way home.

That's how creativity works. Spark the fuse of your focus with questions, wait for the heavens to pull the answers, light them up, and burst them into awareness like the fourth of July.

My question was simple—the answer seemingly obvious. Was I wasting my time even posing it? Ha! That was the core of my inquiry.

What is the definition of wasting time?

I knew if I stayed out of the way and listened, answers would soar my way. Still, as my empty mind stared at a blank page, certainty cracked into fidgeting; it began to feel like wasting time.

Then out of the gentle blue, it occurred to me with a chuckle. What could be more meaningful than talking to Jamie, Jessie, and Josie, and someday their children, through this book, even long after Paula and I are gone?

Time filled with meaning can never be a waste, even if no one else can see what you're spending it on. Even if you fall short along the way. Even if—wait a minute! I see what happened there! The universe just snuck one in on me.

A waste of time is time spent doing something that is meaningless to you.

The first kernel of wisdom popped, and the rest were just heating up. Soon a crescendo of lightbulbs were building into a steady stream of exploding ideas and aha moments. I could feel the universe kicking in and revving its engines, delivering what I ordered like it always does. Ah, ye of little faith.

Time was no longer still.

It disappeared behind a steady flow of answers shooting in as rapid-fire questions.

How can you know if you're wasting time, if you don't know what you want? How can you know if you're wasting time, if you don't know your outcome? How can you make time for what matters most to you, if you don't know what matters most to you?

Incoming!

Incoming!

How can you know if you're wasting time, if you don't know, or won't admit, what you love to do?

Flashhh!

Sacrificing what you love to do isn't wasting time it's killing time—pulverizing your spirit—slaughtering the unrepeatable like a pig.

Whoa! Thoreau popped in.

"As if you could kill time without injuring eternity."

Bam!

What do you want, why do you want it, and what are you waiting for?

Are you talkin' to me? (How did Robert De Niro pop into my head?)

A year from now, you'll wish you'd have started today?

I said are you talkin' to me?

What time zone do you live in—the urgent and unimportant?

Tick, tick, tick!

Do you have a last-minute lifestyle?

Shouldn't it be tick-tock, tick-tock?

Are meaningless errands, menial details, activities without aim, and poor planning spilling your time like a puzzle?

Uh-oh, here comes Socrates.

"Beware the barrenness of a busy life."

Do you live in the time zone of distraction?

Fifteen hours and thirty-three minutes per month on Facebook. Five hours and fifty minutes per month on YouTube. Two hours a day texting. Two weeks of the year surfing the net! And we also spend a week and a half per year deleting spam!

Garbage in, garbage out!

How can you switch your time zone to Important Standard Time (ISD), if you don't know what's important to you? How can you eliminate the inessential from your routine, if you don't know what's essential to you?

Bang!

John Lennon's voice joined the chorus. (Hmm, Imagine!)

"Time you enjoy wasting is not wasted time."

Boom!

Yes John, as long as you know the difference between enjoying and escaping.

Pow!

Even author Viktor Frankl's voice chimed in on the action.

"What man actually needs is not a tensionless state but rather the striving and struggling for some goal worthy of him."

Side thought off the starboard bow!

Lennon and Frankl? They'll never be as big as Lennon and McCartney.

Ping-pong! And here comes the bottom line!

You need an inspiring vision to anchor your time and life.

Thunderbolts and lightning! The good book agrees!

"Without a vision men perish!"[6]

Boom!

Without a vision, potential withers on the vine.

Crash!

Talent rots!

Bang!

Passion shrivels. Chances dry up. Fear runs over, Happiness decays, Time scatters. Without a vision, the quality of life slowly deteriorates and drifts without aim, like a tumbleweed blowing in the wind. And it's no fun!

Incoming, Incoming, Incoming! Woo hooo!

A vision is a compass, a guide, a magnet pulling you to what matters and rescuing your time from what doesn't.

Keep 'em coming!

How can you plan, if you don't know what you're planning for?

How can you get there, if you don't know where you're going?

How can you live the life you've imagined, if you haven't imagined the life you want to live?

Bing!

Bang!

Boom!

Lack of imagination is a life of lack.

And here comes Einstein!

"Imagination is more important than knowledge."

Light it up!

Imagination is a tool that builds things in heaven and brings them down to earth.

Look up.

Our vision can only reach as high our imagination.

Look in.

Our imagination can only reach as high as our self-concept.

Our imagination and lives are limited to what we think of ourselves.

You get the love you think you deserve.

Geez, how did a line from *The Perks of Being a Wallflower* get in my head?

If you don't value yourself, you can't value your time!

If you don't respect yourself, you can't respect your time!

Are you picking up what I'm putting down? Are you catching what I'm throwin'? Are you flowin' where I'm goin'?

It is impossible to value yourself, to respect yourself, to love yourself . . .

*If-you-are-not-**be-ing-your-self**!*

If you are not being who you are, you will miss your own life!

Now that-is-was-ting-time!!

Whoa! The words of your Aunt Joan brought it home.

"Be who you are, or you'll miss your own life."

Whew!

Time out!

Take a calming time capsule.

Slow it down.

Stop time tempo.

The definition of wasting time isn't as simple as I thought. There are lots of layers, which on the surface seem to have nothing to do with time.

Know what you love to do.

Know what is meaningful to you.

Know what you want and feel why you want it.

Then imagine those things into a crystal clear vision of the life you want to live.

And respect who you are.

Value who you are.

Which can only happen if you . . .

Be who you are!

Be who you are!

Be who you are!

The thing is, different things mean different things, to different people.

Wasting time is different for everybody.

I love to jam on the flute. I'm sure 99.999 percent of the world would consider that a waste of time. The thing is—for far too long, I believed them.

Learn from my mistakes. Do what you love to do, no matter what.

Don't believe them.

As the fireworks come to an end, I'll leave you with some fire-starting questions of your own.

What turns you timeless?

When does time disappear for you?

What are you doing when the shell of time breaks into infinity—when now transforms into always?

Whatever it is, do that!

Create a vision for that!

But to make it real, you must schedule that.

Now, now, now is the critical and decisive hour.

It looks like the poet Rumi is popping in with one more point of light.

"May the beauty of what you love, be what you do."

Deep breath, and exhale . . .

It's 6:00 a.m.! Three hours flowed into a single magic moment.

Time is still.

The veil between heaven and earth has lifted.

Gratitude dances in the light of silence.

Good night, Paula. (It's bedtime in Hong Kong.) I'm so lucky to have you.

Good morning, Jamie and Jessie. Seize the day, my girls. I'm so grateful for you.

It's time to wake Josie for school.

As Josie tosses and moans and fights for one more wink, I look at her and think to myself:

Treasure every moment.

What turns you timeless?

What are you doing when the shell of time breaks into the sun of infinity...
When now transforms into always?
Whatever it is, do that! Create a vision for that!

HABITS AND ROUTINES

World-class dreams require world-class routines.

—Dad

What's wildly important to you?

Think of one thing you really love to do.

Name one thing you really want.

Is there a skill you'd love to master, content you're passionate about creating, a difference you're driven to make? Name one specific outcome, big or small, that you're *committed* to achieving.

Then answer a simple question.

How much time did you spend on it today?

Yesterday?

Last week?

Last year?

Emerson said, "One of the illusions of life is that the present hour is not the critical, decisive hour." I wrote the phrase, "time will not reason," in the first verse of the song, after you leapt from the cradle to college in a blink—to show you that every second is critical and decisive. It doesn't matter what you want. It matters what you do on a consistent basis. *Your ultimate destiny is formed in your daily routine.* I never want you to blink and wake up wondering how time stole your chances.

One of my music business students came to me ready to give up. He said that despite his best efforts, his big dreams had a small chance of coming true. I didn't feed into the complaints he was programming himself with and simply asked him to describe his daily routine.

"Well," he said, "I wake up at about 10:00 a.m. and have a cigarette. Before I jump into the day, I watch a movie. After that I get dressed, eat breakfast, and figure out what to do."

Between "breakfast movies," commuting, eating dinner, and partying at night, he had about an hour left to dabble with his dreams. From a lack of vision and planning to lack of belief in himself, my student had layers of challenges. I decided to focus on one—time. Becoming aware of how he spends his time could transform his life.

"You can still achieve your dreams," I told him, "but only if you understand an immovable fact of life."

Your goals and dreams must match your habits and routines.

"Name one thing you want to do?" I asked.

"I want to write songs." An answer he seemed to pull from the air not his heart.

"How much time did you spend writing today?"

"Hmm," he grunted.

"When's the last time you sat down to write?"

"Umm, let me think." Then he blurted out, "I don't have enough time!"

I stopped him right there.

"You may not have a motivating vision. You may not have a powerful purpose you're *yet* aware of. You may not have focus. You may not have faith. You may not truly believe you can achieve your dreams, but I promise that you have more than enough time!"

And I promise you! Your purpose is already there, waiting for the right conditions and a solid foundation from which to unfold. One of those conditions is an empowering daily routine. *We are what we repeatedly do. Excellence, then, is not an act, but a habit.*[7] Your daily routine is the foundation from which your life will either soar or crumble.

But forget everything else for now. Foundations are laid one brick at a time.

Simply getting up earlier in the morning would transform your life. Waking up at 6:00 a.m. gives you another twenty-eight hours a week to write. Waking up at 5:00 a.m. adds thirty-five extra hours to your week. You would gain almost two weeks in one, simply by getting out of bed sooner. *World-class dreams require world-class routines.*

Though his story seems extreme and obvious, many of us unknowingly do the same thing. We unconsciously let the inessential suck the time out of our lives, and the life out of our time.

When you were little, I used to commute from our home in Newport Beach, California, to my office in Hollywood. On average it took about ninety minutes each way. A traffic jam on the 405 (standard procedure) bumped the time up over two hours. Your mom figured that I was spending about a month and a half a year in traffic. That wasn't productive business. That was unnecessary busy-ness.

But time isn't always wasted in large blocks; bits and minutes can add up to days and years. In my case, there were many ways I unconsciously let my time and your childhood blink by.

On any given day, I'd check my in-box compulsively or let empty conversations interrupt me. I'd take on the urgent and unimportant minidramas of others, say yes when I wanted to say no. I'd miss hidden time eaters, like a one-hour workout gobbling up two hours with prep and travel. We spend five days of our lives waiting at red lights! Whoa! I'd make a forty-five-minute phone call that could've been a five-minute email, spend hours in passion-killing meetings, watch too much cable news, focus on to-do lists instead of outcomes, and most importantly—instead of hanging out with you and Mom, to songwriting, practicing and praying . . .

I'd fail to slot what I was wildly passionate about into an unbudgeable daily schedule.
Things I care about were devoured by things I couldn't care less about.
Blink!
Days turned into decades.

Because my amazing wife (your supermom, Paula) flies Triple Seven jumbo jets around the globe for a living, I flew solo daddy duty a lot. Like a whirling dervish, I'd fly through the door after a numbing commute, head straight to the kitchen, rummage for a pot, and start boiling water. I never knew exactly what "man food" I was going to make for dinner, I just knew it would involve a noodle. Once dinner was cooking, I'd scurry next door to the babysitter and bring you home. Many nights I felt exhausted, suffering from cell phone ear and traffic trance. As I once wrote in a song—"My days are full, but my life is empty." Why?

Because I wasn't conscious of my use of time.
Because I let the urgent rob me of the important.
Because I didn't create a sacred space of time each day for what matters most.

My gnawing fear is that the frustration I had with myself rubbed off on you. I didn't need to zigzag through your early years like an over-caffeinated pinball. Simple changes in focus, planning, and priorities would have replaced chaos with calm.

I want you to learn from my mistakes, to instill in you the same lesson I learned the hard way, and I tried to teach my student—to repeat and repeat and repeat.

Your goals and dreams must match your habits and routines!
Destiny is formed in your daily routine.
Destiny is formed in your daily routine.
Destiny is formed in your daily routine.
Okay, now go to the blackboard and write that one hundred gazillion times.

I want you to have an extraordinary life vision and be aware of how your habits and routines affect it. I'm not talking about time obsession. That's just another distraction, which distorts your focus and chokes off the flow of life. I'm talking about time awareness—creating a peaceful setting that liberates your creativity and frees you to passionately dive into what you love.

Goal: Lose Weight

Your goals and dreams must match your habits and routines.

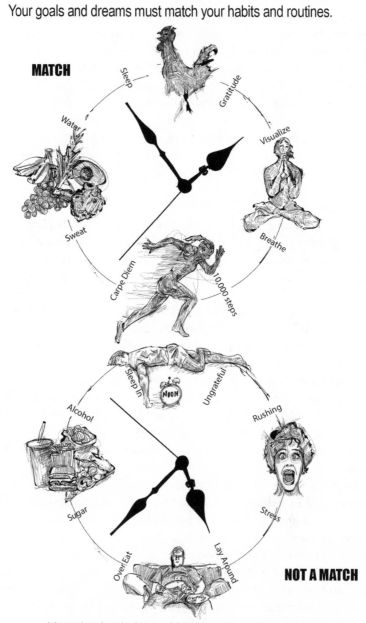

Your destiny is formed in your daily routine.

I want you to have the strength and wisdom to say "no" to the inessential—to plant a flag, like a fortress, and defend what's important to you. To boldly draw a line in the sands of time that no invader can breach—to create and defend a daily oasis of time for things that matter most to you. *To have the guts to take your time, so it cannot be taken from you.*

No matter what!

Like a tyrant plundering a rare treasure—disempowering habits will loot your potential, ransack your talent, break into your vision, and steal the sparkle from your eyes. To spare yourself from the ravages of time tyranny, you must align your goals and dreams with your habits and routines.

Focus less on things to do today and more on outcomes to achieve today—manage your *have-tos,* so you can dive into your *want-tos*—trade your *to-do list,* for a *to-be list,* knowing it's who you are that attracts or repels what you want in life.

I pray you lead a life of alignment—inner world aligned with outer world—daily duties aligned with infinite purpose—the beauty of what you love, aligned with the grace of what you do. I pray you're so engaged, in flow, on purpose, and present with life that the illusion of time disappears altogether.

To hoist your own sail and harness time like the wind, instead of letting it whirl you around like a ship in a storm, you must first be conscious of what's pilfering your time.

Though there are many ways we can loot our own fortune, most of us do not recognize two time pirates in our midst. Unaware, we leave the door to our minds unattended, letting the bandits slip through to run wild. As we're dreaming and scheming and plotting our course—*focus* and *emotion* have commandeered the vessel, and are the real forces steering the ship.

MIND SPACE IS TIME SPACE

Mind space is time space, and time space is life.

—Dad

There's a reason why Alice Herz-Sommers, the oldest Holocaust survivor and concert pianist, practiced three hours a day and flourished right up to her death at the age of 110. Even as she was ripped from her home as a child and forced into the barbaric hell of a Nazi concentration camp, her family tortured and killed, she focused on goodness.

"This is the reason I am so old, even now, I am sure. I am looking for the nice things in life. I know about the bad things but I look only for the good things. The world is wonderful, it's full of beauty and full of miracles."[8]

We get what we focus on.

Focus takes time.

Emotion takes time.

Time is life.

And empowering, disempowering, or numbingly unimportant—focus is a choice.

Aware of it or not, what we hold in mind, we attract into our lives. Focus on abundance and you'll create it. Focus on lack and you'll create it. Let your focus blow willy-nilly in the wind, and you'll create a tumbleweed life of reaction, distraction, and burnout. Positive or negative—mind space is time space, and time space is life.

How much of your mind space is being fried to a crisp by focusing on negative emotions? How much fulfillment and fun are being suffocated by downer dialog?

32

How many of your relationships are being assaulted by petty gossip and resentment? How much of your day, mood, and physical body are being eaten alive by worry?

Studies have shown we waste five months of our lives complaining.

Three and a half years of our lives feeling anger.

Two hours and fifteen minutes a day worrying. That's six and a half years in a lifetime.

Eight minutes a day moaning about bad service.

Five hours a day gossiping.

A year and four months of a woman's life is spent crying, partially because of feeling tired. And on and on and on.

Negativity is fear made visible. . .

A life-sucking ocean of gooey energy that engulfs our emotions,
kills our time, and murders our mood.

Negativity is *fear made visible.* It's a time suck, energy drain, health hazard, and dream killer—a life-sucking ocean of gooey energy that engulfs our outlook and clouds our mood.

Picture swimming in an oil spill of anger, fear, resentment, worry, stress, excuses, judgment, gossip, and guilt—polluting your life by complaining, blaming, whining, worrying, and wallowing. ("There's no time." "Things are so hard." "I'm so tired." "I don't feel good." "It's not fair." "I need absolute control over the future." "OMG, the Internet isn't working!") Being sucked under by the riptide of *I can't* instead of soaring on the wild ride of *I can!*

Like songwriter John Prine said, "There's a half an inch of water / You think you're gonna drown / That's the way the world goes round."

Negativity sucks!

It sucks our time, our health, our happiness, our creativity, our courage, our energy, our dreams, and it sucks the joy out of our day. The constant crash of negative waves also erodes our bodies, *literally* making us sick.

"A negative feeling instantly causes a loss of 50 percent of the body's muscle strength, and narrows our vision both physically and mentally."[9]

Feeling rundown? Check your emotions.

Have a backache? Check your mood.

Feel a cold coming on? Check your focus.

"Every negative feeling impairs a body organ, and as the years go by, that organ becomes diseased and eventually fails to function."[10]

Huh?

You mean focusing on how rotten someone is, not only eats away our time, it tears apart our bodies? Yes, like a pack of rabid hyenas!

According to the Centers for Disease Control and Prevention (CDC), emotions equal 85 percent of a body's health. The more you focus on negativity, the more you'll be swimming, or more accurately, drowning in it.

Everything is energy. Emotion, positive or negative, is *energy in motion.* Like a boomerang, what you send out comes flying back. What kind of energy are you sending in motion every day? How much of your time is being mangled to death by focusing on the dark cloud, instead of the silver lining?

Like goes to like.

That's the meaning behind one of the most misunderstood sayings in history! "The rich get rich and the poor get poorer has nothing to do with money"—it has everything to do with energy, attitude, self-concept, and emotional focus. The emotions that fill your mind, *rich* or *poor,* fill your time, and create your world.

Positive or negative — Mind Space Is Time Space.

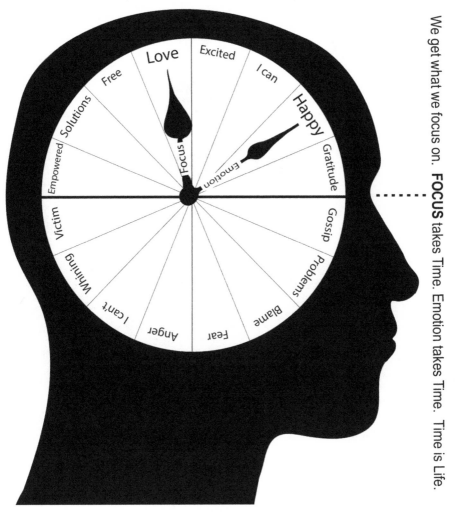

We get what we focus on. **FOCUS** takes Time. Emotion takes Time. Time is Life.

PACKAGE DEAL

Every single emotion comes ready-made with a matching set
of thoughts.
Millions of them!

—Dad

Feelings and thoughts are a package deal.

Two for one. (Each negative emotion also comes with the added bonus of a free, subconscious guilt trip!)

So come on down! Hurry on in! Shop for your favorite feeling! Buy one now, and get millions of thoughts you can't control thrown in for free.

You can choose to shop in the negative aisle!

It's filled with feelings of fear.

The hidden price—millions of me, me, me, I can't, I can't, I can't, worry, want, and anger thoughts, with guilt thrown in for free.

If you're not satisfied (you won't be; read the fine print), there is a return policy.

Fine print: You will never be satisfied with anything from the negative aisle.

Or you can choose the positive aisle!

It's filled with feelings of love!

Along with feelings of love, you'll automatically receive millions of grateful, abundant, and peaceful thoughts, with laughter, and a zest for life thrown in for free! One feeling, a million thoughts!

What a deal!

Feelings and thoughts are a package deal.

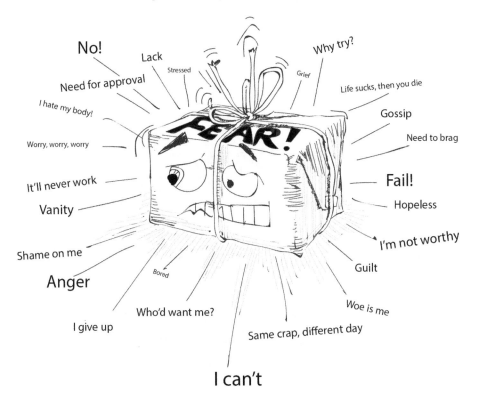

One feeling, a million thoughts! What a deal!

Plus: Free gift with purchase—
Subconscious Guilt!

If one emotion creates millions of thoughts, which affect our entire outlook on life, to change your outlook from darkness to light, simply focus on positive feelings.

Thousands and even millions of thoughts can be replaced by a single emotion.[11]

Change your focus, and you'll change your feelings.

Change your feelings, and you'll change your thoughts.

Change your thoughts, and you'll change your energy, unleash your spirit, ignite your genius, charge your imagination, and alter the course of your life.

Thousands of thoughts can be replaced by a single emotion.

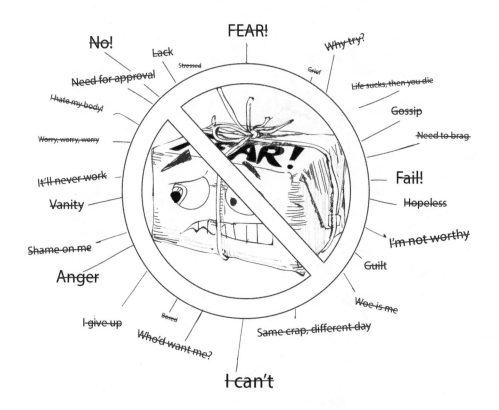

A tiny shift, of even one degree, launches the ship to a new destiny.

Small shifts equal gargantuan change!

Like Alice Herz-Sommers who saw the bad things but chose to focus on the good things, don't repress or pretend a negative feeling isn't there. You're only human. Of course it's there! Let it be what it is without judgment or guilt and simply "focus on the good things."

Are you mad at a friend?

Let it go and focus on what you want. Focus on the good and let the anger run out.
Is a nasty comment eating at you?
Let it go, focus on what you want; focus on the good, and let the grudge run out.
Focus and feeling are time. If you give them away, you give your time away.
Giving your time away is giving your life away.
Don't give someone who wronged you a piece of your life.
Don't give bad weather, bad traffic, or bad romance a piece of your life.

To change your outlook from darkness to light, focus on positive feelings.

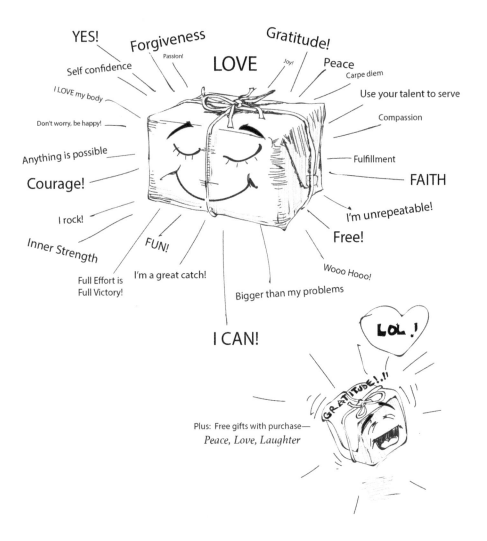

Don't let a short-circuited Internet, or "half an inch of water" drown your happiness.

Does giving your life away to gadgets, grudges, and God knows what, sound ridiculous? That's exactly what you do when you let someone barge into your brain and hijack your focus and feelings.

Emotion is energy, and energy always runs out when it is not fed.

So don't feed the fear.

Feed the love.

Like in the Indian fable of the two wolves inside each of us.

A Cherokee elder spoke to his grandson about the wolves within.

"A fight is going on inside me. It is a battle between two wolves.

One is Evil. It is fear, anger, envy, jealousy, sorrow, regret, greed, arrogance, self-pity, guilt, resentment, inferiority, lies, false pride, superiority, and ego.

The other is Good. It is love, courage, joy, peace, hope, serenity, humility, kindness, benevolence, empathy, generosity, truth, compassion, and faith."

The grandson thought about it for a minute and then asked his grandfather: "Which wolf wins?"

And the Cherokee elder replied,

"The one you feed."

PAIN JUICE

Surrender the secret "juice" you get from negativity.
Like a bad drug, kick the habit.
Don't get off on it,
Get off of it!

—Dad

It's hard to give up the sheer *pleasure* and *juice* we get from negativity.

Huh?

You mean we get off on our anger?

Get juiced from being a victim?

Get a rush from being offended?

Enjoy whining like Debbie Downer?

Take pleasure in negativity?

Yup!

Suffering, hatred, grieving, grudging, or complaining about an "owie," is the nectar of negativity, which feeds the ego.

Without its "pain juice," the ego would die of thirst.

We get off on our pain.

If you could bottle pain juice and put in on the market, it'd be a megahit. Who needs energy drinks like Red Bull, when you could have negative energy drinks like Pain Juice? Someone should pitch the pain-juicing business on the TV show *Shark Tank*.

I can almost hear the slogan now:

41

Pain Juice!
The negative energy drink!
For the life you love to hate!
Get off on it!

(Cue music.)

ANNOUNCER: Poor me, poor me, pour me a glass of grief, a shot of wallowing, or a pitcher of things to be offended about.[12] *Who needs a good bottle of wine, when you could have a bad case of whining?*

Instead of getting hoped up, get hopped up on hatred. Juice a Pint of Problems or get off on a glass of our Woe Is Me Whiskey. Grab a six-pack of Bad Childhood and milk it till the blaming cows come home, on your way home from the job you love to hate.

Critical Kool-Aid and Judgment Juice are guaranteed to artificially make you feel better about yourself. Self-indulge with a Goblet of Guilt or, if you get off on being helpless, try a Victim Cocktail, made from the lamest excuses and not-my-fault blame. And for the secretly insecure, try our Vanity Vodka in all of your Me, Me, Me Martinis.

But if you really want to pahhhdee, have a trashcan of our biggest seller, Fear Wapatuli! All fear comes as a set. We eliminate the guesswork out of which fears you get off on and mix them all together into one big Fear Wapatuli Party!

(Fear is also sold separately in a negative assortment of flavors, including anger, pride, worry, and self-loathing.)

Pain Juice!
For the life you love to hate!
Get off on it!
Dissatisfaction guaranteed, or your money back.
(And don't miss our double-bubble unhappy hour every Monday morning.)

You only have to do *one thing* to rid yourself of negativity and raise your level of consciousness.[13]

Surrender the secret juice you get from negativity.

Like a bad drug, kick the habit.

Don't get off *on* it; Get off *of* it!

Look at it and let it go!

I can see the Pain Juice Company executives sitting in front of Congress now, like the tobacco companies did in the '90s:

"There's no evidence that pain juice is addictive or bad for your mental health."

Then twenty years later:

"Oops!"

Remove the storm clouds, and the sun shines through.

Remove the secret payoff you get from juicing negativity, and the love of who you are will shine like the sun. Why choose love potion over pain juice?

It's an indisputable fact.

Love's more fun!

Pain Juice!
For the life you love to hate!
Get off on it!
(Dissatisfaction guaranteed, or your money back.)

Without its "pain juice," the ego would die of thirst. We get off on our pain.

IMAGINATION

Imagination is the wind, the sail, the compass, and the destination.

—Dad

On an empty L.A. night in 1990, struggling comedian Jim Carrey drove his clunker of a car to the top of the Hollywood Hills, and launched his imagination towards a dream.

"I wrote myself a check for ten million dollars for acting services rendered and dated it Thanksgiving 1995. I put it in my wallet and it deteriorated. And then, just before Thanksgiving 1995, I found out I was going to make ten million dollars for *Dumb and Dumber*. I put that check in the casket with my father because it was our dream together."

Carrey went on to say:

"The focus that you hold in your life determines how your reality turns out. Our intention is everything. Not one single thing has been accomplished without intention."

Hmm. Not so dumb or dumber, is he?

As I think of how Jim Carrey's imagination created a ten-million-dollar vision, a few questions come to mind. What if he wrote himself a check for five million dollars? Would the universe have sent him that instead? What if Jim Carrey didn't have ten million dollars' worth of self-worth—didn't really believe he could achieve his dream—didn't accept his unrepeatable gifts—didn't place ten million dollars' worth of value on his talent and time? Hmm.

When golf virtuoso Tiger Woods was a young boy, he wrote his dream on a 3 x 5 index card and read it every night before falling asleep. His dream was to break the world record set by golf legend, Jack Nicklaus. He even taped a list of Jack Nicklaus's accomplishments in his closet. Every time he matched one of those accomplishments, he scratched it off the list.

What if Tiger Woods never used his imagination to create a soul-stirring vision? Imagination armored him with bulletproof commitment, ironclad purpose, and launched him like a precision missile into the rarefied air of massive action. What if he had never burned that vision into his subconscious? What if he had asked a smaller question?

"How can I get a job in the field of golf that guarantees security and allows me to work next to what I love to do?"

Versus

"How can I master what I love to do, live my passion, and beat the legendary Jack Nicklaus?"

Would he have had the same meteoric career?

No!

The same wealth?

No!

The same drive?

No!

The same putt? Ha!

No!

Would his life have been different if he had asked a different question? Yes! Yes! Yes! A different question would have created a different destiny. A smaller question would have created a smaller life. Tiger who? We wouldn't even know his unique name.

The reach of our questions determines how far we can reach. The size of our questions reflects the size of our self-worth. The size of our self-worth determines the breadth of our imagination, the shape of our vision, and the quality of our lives.

Life always gives us what we ask for.

And we never ask for enough.

Actor Will Smith says we have internal command over our lives:

"The idea is that you have command over what your future, what your situation is. Whatever that universal force is that you connect to—you, in sync with that force, have command to will your future."

Will Smith didn't get where he got by accident. He imagined himself there: "In my mind, I've always been an A-list Hollywood superstar. Y'all just didn't know yet." Then he took internal command, and willed his future—or better put, he Will Smithed his future by designing his own unrepeatable life.

You, too, can take internal command and Jamie B. your future! Jessie B. your future! Josie B. your future! Design your own unrepeatable life, create your own unrepeatable career, work for your own unrepeatable dreams, or you'll end up being a slave for someone else's.

Oh, yeah . . .

One more thing.

After Will Smith used his imagination to Will Smith his future, he worked his Will Smith butt off: "I've viewed myself as slightly above average in talent. And where I excel is ridiculous, sickening, work ethic. You know, while the other guy's sleeping? I'm working."

So how do you harness the power of imagination?

Simple!

Start with the end in mind and work your butt off.

Life always gives us what we ask for. And we never ask for enough.

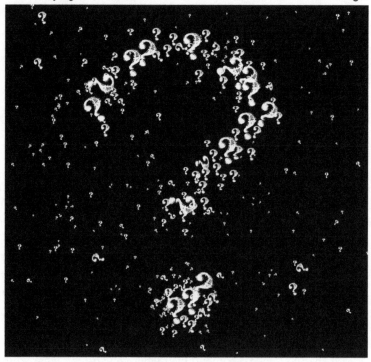

IMAGINE, AIM, FIRE, REPEAT

*Like water over rocks, imagination forms into the flow of
our habitual beliefs, actions, thoughts, and moods.*

—Dad

Aim your imagination like a bullet.

Imagine your dream. Imagine living it. Make it bright and vivid and real.

"The inner journey must never be without direction. When you take the inner road, it is to do what you did mentally before you started. You go for the prize you have already seen and accepted."[14]

Focus on your desired outcome with so much juice and passion that you
block out all other negative or wandering thoughts.

"By believing passionately in something that still does not exist, we create it. The nonexistent is whatever we have not sufficiently desired."[15] But here comes those two words again.

Habit and routine.

"Imagination has choice, but it chooses according to habit."[16]

As contradictory as it sounds, imagination must become routine; the feeling of your wish fulfilled, another daily habit. You must burn the vision of your imagination into your subconscious, or like a seed planted on barren land, it will shrivel up and blow away.

My jazz improvisation teacher at Berklee College of Music in Boston, the vibes virtuoso Gary Burton, built imagination into his practice routine. Our so-called textbook was *The Inner Game of Tennis,* which had nothing to do with music. It was about visualizing peak performance on the tennis court. It worked for tennis star Andre Agassi. He won Wimbledon 10,000 times in his head, before he ever stepped on the court. The same thing applies to making music, making money, or making cupcakes.

See it first!

Imagine your wish fulfilled.

Make it part of your routine.

Feel it as you're falling asleep.

Step into it as you're waking up.

Live it on the inside, and with consistent action—

You'll see it on the outside.

But be aware of habits driving your inner and outer worlds.

Like water over rocks, imagination forms into the flow of our habitual beliefs, actions, thoughts, and moods.

So open the floodgates.

Make room for imagination to flow.

And the current of creativity will pull you up, in, and . . .

Beyond your wildest imagination.

LOOK FARTHER

Look beyond what you think you can do.
Look beyond what they say you can do.
Look beyond the barbed fences of convention.
Let go of the rails, of fear and familiarity, and eyes open,
*   heart first . . .*
Dive in over your head!
Immerse yourself into every last drop of who you are.

—Dad

When you were babies, I gave playing the flute another crack. I started practicing, put out a CD, created momentum, and eventually found myself on stage at Carnegie Hall with singer/guitar virtuoso, Jose Feliciano, who recorded one of my songs. I imagined myself onto that stage. Though grateful for playing at Carnegie Hall and having an iconic artist perform my music, the morning after the show there was a letdown. What was the next step? What now? Then it occurred to me. *Darn! I was so busy with the details, I forgot to imagine farther than this.*

Dreams can only travel as far as you let your imagination take them.

Look farther.

Don't be afraid to take your hands off the wheel and flow into uncharted territory.

Imagination, deeply felt, will always whisk you through the riptide of fear. Dare to ignore your senses and the "you can't" people, even if I'm one of them. Like the time the three of you produced the incredible music video for your Uncle Michael's Christmas song.

Your plan was to create the entire video out of still photos. It would take over two thousand photographs to capture the flip-card feel you envisioned. To top it off, Jamie had to come home from college and get it done over the weekend. Sensing my doubt, she said, "You don't believe I can pull this off, do you Dad?" Though I never doubted you, I did have doubts about your time and resources. But after seeing your passion I realized I was breaking my own rules.

With a powerful why, and unbending commitment, you can achieve anything.

You stuck to your guns, imagined a vision, and brought it to life. (To view the J-girls' Christmas video, go to www.JimmyBrandmeier.com.)

Once again, the parent learns from the child.

Like you did with the Christmas video, make a habit of boldly declaring what you want, and simply ignore the life-sucking contagions of other people's doubts.

Reach past what others say is realistic. Shoot beyond what they say is practical. Look farther.

Whenever you hear the red flag of a phrase "You have to be realistic," just reply, "I am realistic. I expect miracles, because that's how the universe works!"[17]

Tell them it's the creative nature of *reality* to grant our wishes like a genie in a bottle. The power to imagine (im-a-genie) puts the magic lamp of creation in our own hands—and the greatest minds in history agree.

Einstein: "Everything is energy and that's all there is to it. Match the frequency of the reality you want and you cannot help but get that reality. It can be no other way. This is not philosophy. This is physics."

Heisenberg: "Our mere conscious act of observing a thing affects and changes it. Thoughtful intention increases the probability of affecting physical matter."

Jesus Christ: "Whatever things you desire, when you pray [visualize, imagine], believe that you will receive them, and you shall have them."

Point out that the power of focused imagination, vision, and prayer is based on quantum physics—that what they're really saying when they tell you to "be realistic" is *their* perception of reality is limited, bound by the small view of their own experience, distorted by fear, and projected out from their lower level of consciousness.

Skeptics define themselves, not reality.

I still shake my head in disbelief when I think of advice given by guidance counselors, trying to standardize your genius and stuff it back into the bottle:

"No one from our area of the state goes to Ivy League schools. Aim for a community college. You can try plan A, but make sure you're realistic. Have a plan B to fall back on. Be safe. Be practical. Be realistic."

How about this advice from Will Smith instead?

"NEVER have a plan B. It distracts from plan A."[18]

Or this advice from dear old Dad?

Master what you love to do, and someone will pay you for it.

It's better to be among the living so-called failures than the living dead.

There's only one possible failure in life—the failure to be who you are.

Be careful who you listen to.

Never let someone else's fear become your own.

Look farther.

Stretch your imagination beyond your comfort zone.

Look farther

Take baby steps into the infinity of your ability by reaching beyond your grasp again and again—one project, one class, one Uncle Michael music video at a time.

Look farther.

What do you really want? Don't be afraid to admit it to yourself and the world.

Look farther.

How much money do you expect to make? Reboot your program. Expect more.

Look farther.

What kind of job fulfillment do you expect? Expect more.

Look farther.

What kind of health and physical shape do you expect to be in? Expect more.

Look farther.

How much love do you think you deserve?

How much happiness do you expect?

Where do *you* impose boundaries on your boundless self-worth?

You are in charge of setting your compass.

You get to choose the heading.

You get to decide how far.

Look farther.

So when you arrive on the shores of a dream, like I did after reaching Carnegie Hall, you won't say, "Darn, I should have imagined farther than this."

"The greater danger for most of us lies not in setting our aim too high and falling short; but in setting our aim too low, and achieving our mark." [19]

You hold the key that liberates your spirit from the tyranny of aimlessness.

Imagination!

Imagination is a real thing! It's an invisible quantum divining rod, not a shiny, fluffy Hallmark card. It's bigger than your senses and bigger than knowledge.

"Truth cannot be encompassed by facts." [20]

The size of who we are stretches far beyond the understanding of what our programmed minds believe is possible. So look farther and look in.

What you see on the inside is what will be on the outside.

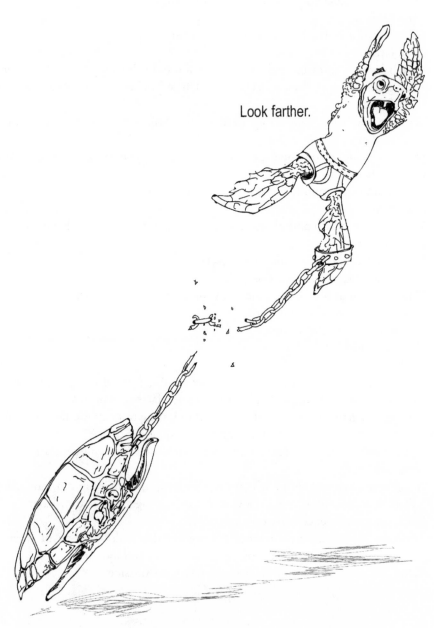

Look farther.

Stretch your imagination beyond the chains of your comfort zone.

FUN

Life should be fun!
Imagine that!

—Dad

LARRY DALEY: Why did you become a pilot?
AMELIA EARHART: Honestly, Mr. Daley? For the fun of it. Why else would
anyone do anything?

There's sage wisdom in that scene from the movie *Night at the Museum*.
I dare you to face it—dare you to admit it—dare you to live it!
Life should be fun!
Imagine that!
The average child laughs about 400 times per day; the average adult laughs only
15 times per day. What the heck happened to the other 385 laughs!?
We quit having fun, that's what!
And what can be more fun than creating a vision that frees you from the bondage
of boredom? Imagine brushing off the dead dust of a life-sucking *rut*-tine and feeling
alive again, liberated from the quicksand of money problems, rocky relationships,
career confusion, and bad moods.
Imagine a vision that saves you from a flatline, fitting-in, walking dead, just
existing, just showing up, just getting by, escaping through TV and food and booze
and buying stuff you can't afford, living from check to check, dying in bits and pieces,

and going through the same crap different day after day after same-dull-day, all over and over and over again, kind of so-called life.

Yuck!

Unnecessary!

Unnatural!

Un-*You!*

LIVE!!

IMAGINE!!

Imagine doing what you love to do.

Imagine doing what you want to do.

Imagine having fun doing what you really love and want to do!

Life is not a prison sentence to be endured; it's a gift to be opened—a hands-in-the-air freedom ride to the promised land of your own soul, forever calling you home.

Walt Disney, who literally created his own world with imagination, said, "Doing the impossible is fun!"

Making the most of your life is a blast!

Settling for the least of your life is a soul-sucking bore.

"God is happiest when his children are at play."[21]

So play!

Play!

Play!

I dare you!

I dare you to create a soul-stirring, gut-busting, hoopla of a vision, and *have fun* bringing it to life.

I dare you to break out of your comfort zone, bust through limiting beliefs, and expand your self-concept to create a "new normal," new vision, and a new life.

Just imagine!

I'm happy! Yes!

I'm whole! Yes!

And I'm having a blast! YEEESS!

I dare you to expand the reach of your questions by freeing the unlimited reach of your self-worth.

I dare you to ASK!

And ask BIG!

Expect miracles!

And expect BIG!

Laugh!

And laugh BIG!

I dare you to take internal command of your compass and design your own life. To imagine your wish fulfilled—make it part of your routine—feel it as you're falling asleep—step into it as you're waking up! I dare you to throw away plan B, and commit, commit, commit to plan A—to turn your invisible wishes into your visible life—to start with the end in mind and work, and work, and work your butt off.

I dare you to strike the power chords of your imagination and write your dreams like a song in the key of living, living, living—to play your life like a virtuoso plays a rare and precious instrument—to compose your vision with the notes of what you want, the beauty of what you love, and the soaring melody of who you are.

Just imagine!

I dare you!

LIFESTRINGS

When a guitar string is out of tune, the guitar is out
      of tune.
When a lifestring is out of tune, life is out of tune.

—Dad

How in the heck do I compose a vision for my entire life and play it like a song?
My ultimate destiny?!
My life's passion, purpose, place, and point of it all?!
Overwhelming!
My big picture?!
I can't even picture what I want for lunch, much less envision what I want for my whole-entire-life! Umm . . . right now, my big vision is more like a blank stare.

It's hard to create the big picture for your life, until you see the small pictures that make up the scene. Designing a vision is easy, exhilarating, and fun! Life wasn't meant to be so serious and drab! Let me walk you through it.

Picture your life as a guitar, strung with the lifestrings of who you are.

Huh?

Stick with me now!

Imagine that each lifestring represents a different key center of importance *to you*—tuned to the music of what you want and what you love most.

Instead of the strings of a real guitar, which are

E,

A,

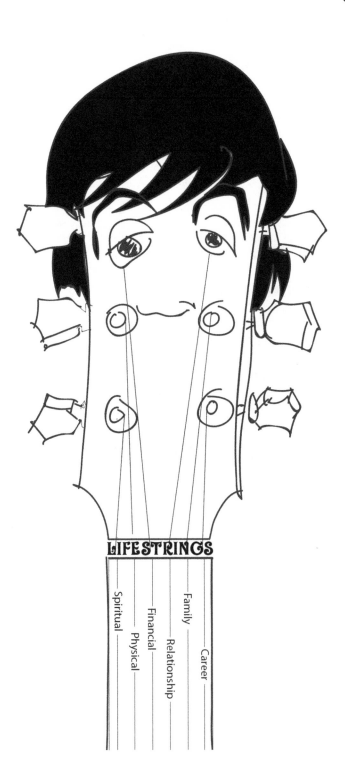

D,
G,
B,
E;
Your life guitar may consist of lifestrings such as the
Spiritual string,
Physical string,
Financial string,
Relationship string,
Family string,
Fun string.

Everyone's guitar is different; everyone cares about different things, so everyone has different lifestrings. Some have more, others less. It doesn't matter how many. A four-string ukulele is just as amazing as a forty-string harp. It only matters that the strings are authentic and playing in harmony.

When a lifestring is out of tune, life is out of tune.

If your financial string is flabby, career string wound too tight, or spiritual string missing, your life is hard to play—leaving only discord filling the gaping void where music might have rung. Your unrepeatable song, which can only resonate from an instrument in harmony with itself, will be lost.

Ahh, but a life in tune is a celestial choir, reverberating through the world like voices of light, expanding the chorus of the universe, enriching the lives of us all.

To be who you are is music.

Like ex-bond trader Brandon Stanton, who lost his job and found himself in his blog *Humans of New York,* inspiring millions of people worldwide. Or Malala Yousafzai, the seventh grade girl from Pakistan who survived being gunned down for standing up to the Taliban demanding that girls be allowed to have an education. Or trumpeter Louis (Satchmo) Armstrong whose authenticity and music were so magnetic, we named our dog after him.

Play your lifestrings like a symphony, rock them like the Stones.

Beauty rings like a bell in the night, from the chords of who you are.

Let it ring.

Let it sing.

Let it rock!

But like any unrepeatable artist about to hit the stage in the concert of life . . .

You must first tune your strings.

HOW DO YOU TUNE YOUR LIFE?

You can't know if you're in tune until you know what you're tuning.

—Dad

To put a handle on the guitar of life, so it's easier to pick up and carry around—to frame your life into a picture you can clearly see—answer a natural question. How do you tune your life?

You can't know if you're in tune, until you know what you're tuning.

I repeat. It's easy to create the big picture for your life, when you can see the small pictures that make up the scene. Creating a vision for each of the lifestrings representing the key centers of importance to you, is how you create the ultimate vision for your life.

So the first step in creating your ultimate life vision is simple and fun.

Name your strings.

The lifestrings of a typical college student may include the

School string,

Mastering what you love to do string,

Self-discovery string (trying on different things to see if they fit),

Friends and relationship string,

Extra-curricular clubs and activities string,

Fun string,

Money string,

Real-world projects/professional experience string,

Lifestrings of a typical college student

Networking string,

Living space and roommate string,

Spiritual growth (everyone must focus on this string),

Physical health (everyone must focus on this string).

This student is a twelve-string guitar. Everything she could possibly spend time, energy, emotion, and focus on in life falls within twelve key centers of importance.

So how do you tune your life?

Which lifestrings make up your guitar? What are the key centers of importance in *your life?* To string your own guitar, fill in the blanks. I'll give you some lifestring examples only, to get you started. But *you* are the only one who can name your strings.

Spiritual string: What's your vision?

Physical health string: What's your vision?

Classwork string: What's your vision?

Internship string: What's your vision?

Money string: What's your vision?

Dream string: What's your vision?

Fun string: What's your vision?

_____

_____

_____

_____

_____

_____

_____

Everything you could possibly spend time, energy, emotion, and focus on in this world falls within the key centers of whatever you listed above.

To know if your life is in tune, you must know what you want for each string. Once you name them, the second step is to

Create a vision for each lifestring.

1. Specifically, decide what you want for each string.
   Write it down.

Which Lifestrings make up your guitar?

2. Know why you want it. Feel why you want it. See why you want it. Write it down.

3. Create a soul-stirring vision, which pulls you out of your comfort zone, stretches your ability, and propels you heart first into what you want. Write it down.

To stop the endless loop of thoughts in your head, to strain out the noise and capture the whispers of your soul seeping toward your heart, *you must write it down.*

The truth of who you are and what you want is already there.

Creativity is listening.

Mining for truth is taking dictation.

Asking for clarity on what you want, and writing down the answers you receive, is the first step in making the invisible, visible.

Don't worry about not knowing exactly how your guitar is tuned. As life unfolds you'll remove strings that no longer ring with your calling and discover new ones that do.

"Restring This Thing" is a tune everyone plays, and something that always happens when jamming on the song of life.

THE GAP

Being out of tune is the difference between what you want,
and where you are.

—Dad

W hat's the difference between your inner vision and your outer reality?
How far in or out of tune are you?
Once you know where you're going, know where you are.

And you'll know if you're flat or sharp. Be specific.

Let's use money as an example.

Say you want to earn $100,000 per year within three years of graduation. Let's assume you have a powerful, energizing *why*, and of course you've written it all down.

Let's say you're earning $2,000 at your part-time college job. In this case your money string is about $98,000 out of tune with what you want.

How about your physical string?

What would a powerful vision for your body look and feel like for *you*?

Endless energy, bouncing vitality, powerful strength, flowing flexibility? Pain-free, guilt-free, and fat-free? Do you want to lose weight, clean up your diet, sculpt six-pack abs?

Why?

How would the perfect vision for *your* body and health affect *your* life?

Let's say your goal is to simply lose ten pounds. In that case, your physical string is out of tune with what *you* want by ten pounds.

Being out of tune is the difference between what *you* want, and where you are.

64

Being out of tune is the difference between what you want and where you are.

WHAT U WANT? WHERE U R?

Want: $10
Have: $5 =

_____

$5 out of tune

Money $5 out of tune

Weight 20 lbs out of tune

Want: weight 180lbs
Weigh: 200lbs =

_____

20lbs out of tune

Now that you have

1. Named your strings
2. Created a vision for each key center the strings represent
3. Clearly seen the gap between where you are and where you want to go . . .the next step may not seem easy, but it's simple.

And taking it will make you feel more alive than ever.
Tune your life.
Is your money string a little flat? Tune it up!
Is your physical string a little loose? Tone it up!
Is fear consuming your dream string? Tune it down!
Is your professional experience outside of the classroom flabby? Tune it up!
Like the leader of the band, you're calling the song.
Tune in to what you want.
Tune up what you love.
Tune out what you don't.

HARMONY

Once each string is in tune with itself, make sure it's in tune with the others.

—Dad

Sometimes we tune one string too tight, or too loose, at the expense of the others. Buddha gave the answer, "not too loose, not too tight," to a lute player struggling for inner peace.

"What happens when you tune your instrument too tightly?" the Buddha asked.

"The strings break," the musician replied.

"And what happens when you string it too loosely?"

"When it's too loose, no sound comes out," the musician answered.

"Then know you are like the strings of your lute. When your effort is too strenuous it leads to strain and discomfort. When your effort is too loose it leads to slackness and laziness. In neither case are you able to accomplish your goal.

"Practice the middle way, and you will produce the results that you desire."

Are you focusing on career at the expense of your friends? Fun at the expense of school? Work, work, work at the expense of your body? Perceived security at the expense of who you are?

It took a near-death accident for author Stephen King to realize that focusing on one string at the expense of the others—even the writing string he passionately loves—can pull your life out of tune:

Sometimes we tune one string too tight or too loose at the expense of the others.

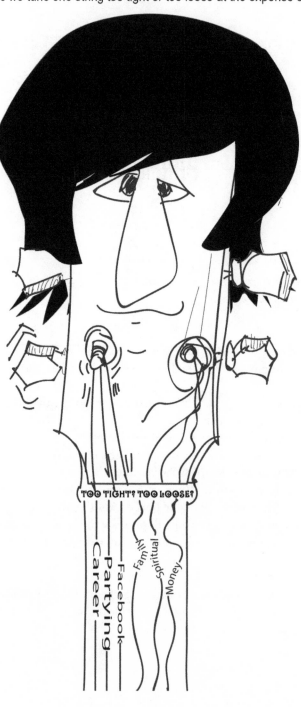

"It starts with this. Put your desk in the corner, and every time you sit down there to write, remind yourself why it isn't in the middle of the room. Life isn't a support system for art. It's the other way around."

The same thing applies to any string on the guitar of life.

Life isn't a support system for your goals; your goals are a support system for life.

For well-being.

For spiritual growth.

For the most important thing.

For climbing the ladder of consciousness from the dungeons of fear

To the heights of who you are.

For Love.

If your dream string is plucked from the ego, change your motivation, or cut it. If it strums from the chords and chorus of who you are, let it ring.

The world wants to hear your song, not the "look at me chorus" of the ego, not the distortion of a life out of tune, not an Elvis imitator, Frank Sinatra knockoff, or autotuned pop star.

Finish *your* unfinished symphony.

Jam on *your* passion,

Strum us *your* heartstrings,

Play us *your* soul,

Sing us *your* love,

And write us *your* life.

Like Brandon Stanton, Malala Yousafzai, and Louis Satchmo Armstrong, release the music of who you are to a world in need of who you are.

And a grateful world will tip its hat and cheer . . .

Sing!

Sing!

Sing!

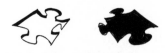

TRAPDOORS

The future doesn't exist and never will.

—Dad

Beware the trapdoors through which many fall prey on the road to their vision:

1. Big is better
2. Wanton desire
3. Waiting for someday to live

Yes, I want you to create a magnificent life vision, one that's so *crystal clear* and energizing that you're chomping at the bit to dive into it every morning. One that clearly and powerfully pulls you to any life you can imagine. One that guides you through the freedom gates of self-reliance to any destiny you choose.

But don't get jammed up in door number one by mistaking big for better.

One size does not fit all.

You don't have to create some huge, world-shaking vision to justify your life and be happy. Your outer vision may be to create a simple lifestyle that bypasses busyness, making room for who and what you love, giving you the freedom to enjoy the day. Like Thoreau at Walden Pond: "My greatest skill in life has been to want but little."

To have more, desire less.

To steer clear of trapdoor number two, stay carefree and detached from the outcome of your efforts, free from the jailors of a dream—wantonness and desire.

Beware of the trapdoors through which many fall prey, on the path to their vision.

"Satisfaction lies in the effort, not in the attainment. Full effort is full victory."[22]

And we're all falling through trapdoor number three.

Waiting for someday to live.

Waiting for the vision, job, money, relationship, or dream to come true to be happy. The last time I checked, "Someday" wasn't a day of the week.

Don't let visions of tomorrow rob you of today. The best way to create an amazing future is to live an amazing present.

The future doesn't exist and never will.

The fullness of life is now.

VERSE TWO

The real journey leads inside,
I pray you'll travel far,
Your passion is a compass;
All that you love, a guiding star.

The world will come raging,
Try changing
True north.

I'm a whisper in the storm,

A voice of Love that's calling you to

Be who you are,
Time to see who you are.

YOUR PASSION IS A COMPASS; ALL THAT YOU LOVE, A GUIDING STAR

Passion is a compass.
It guides us towards our dreams.
Passion is also a magnet.
Being passionate,
Bringing passion to "everything" we do,
Pulls our dreams to us.

—Dad

H ow do I find my passion?
How do I "know" what my true passion is?
And who says I have one passion—playing hide-and-seek—I must somehow find?
I hear you! Cookie-cutter cliches about finding your passion can leave you feeling confused. When it comes to finding your passion(s) (or letting who you are unfold naturally), one size, or one cliche, does not fit all. So start by asking more empowering questions. You've heard these prompts before. But did you ever *really* think about them—and turn *thinking into action?*
What do you really love to do?
Crush your fear: What would you do if you weren't afraid?
Forget about money: If money were no object, how would you spend your time?
Use your imagination: What would you do if you knew you couldn't fail?
True passion has its own demanding question:

75

What do you have to do, no matter what—even if you knew you could "fail"?

And when you ask, "What do I want to do with my life?" look to the source of your yearning and add, "What does life want to do with me?"

Passion is what we *must* dive into, heart first, regardless of the outcome. It's the music we compose though no one may ever hear, the company we start though the odds are slim, the portrait we paint though no one may ever see it, the work we love though it may never pay, the play we write simply because we have to, the search for spiritual truth though society considers God a side job.

You already know your passion. You just don't know you know. As Chinese philosopher Lao-tzu said, "At the center of your being you have the answer; you know who you are and you know what you want."

You know what gets you excited and what numbs your brain. You know which song lyrics move you, lines from movies that made an impact, classes you hate, classes you love. You know which passing comment from a teacher *stuck* with you. You have friends with similar interests whom you love to be around, and people that make you want to run for the hills.

What about mentors and models from the past and present who inspire you?

Charlie Chaplin? Rosa Parks? Jane Goodall? Viola Davis? Grandma Hanky?

Do you think it's a coincidence that your airline pilot mom relates to the adventurous spirit and moxie of Amelia Earhart? Do you think it's a coincidence that I get emotional about the creative struggles of Van Gogh? There are subjects you're naturally curious about, and subjects you couldn't care less about.

They say when your attention wanders, there's someplace it wants to go.

You know where your attention likes to wander off and hang out, don't you? You know what's fun for you and what bores you to death. As the great philosopher "Uncle Johnny" once said, "Follow the fun!"

Listen to the guiding voice in your daily routine.

It speaks to you in the language of enthusiasm, curiosity, or a piqued interest.

It feels like time standing still, ideas flying, life flowing.

It sounds like fun, looks like success, smells like Christmas, feels like crazy new love.

Life is not a jail sentence to be endured; it's an adventure to be lived.

What makes you come alive?

"Ask what makes you come alive and go do it. Because what the world needs is people who have come alive." [23]

ACTION

You can't think your way to finding your passion!

—Dad

There's wisdom in the whispers calling from your soul.
Take time to listen.
But don't take too much time.
Don't stop to think and never start acting.
Why?
Because the only surefire way to learn what fires you up, is through action:
You can't think your way to finding your passion.
Empowering questions!
Yes.
Focused thinking!
Yes.
Blood-stirring visualizing!
Yes.
All mandatory first steps, which lead to clarity.
But there's only one way to know for sure.
Act!
Action is a teacher.
Finding your passion is like dating. You can't find the right one by thinking about the right one; you have to go on a date. And you may have to date a lot of duds before the sparks fly.

77

Like dating before marriage, action paints a crystal-clear picture of what you love and what you just like, what you want and what you don't, who you are and who you are not. Instead of clinging, wallowing, and wondering about what you want, start dating.

Make a decision.

The prelude to every action is a decision. The formula is simple.

Decide!!

Take action.

Learn from your actions.

Adjust accordingly.

Embrace uncertainty.

I am certain that if you *use uncertainty as a tool* of self-discovery—a doorway to self-knowledge—your passion (or passions) will unfold. Step through the doorway. Let go of control. Make a decision and take action, especially when you're uncertain, and I promise you, certainty will emerge.

Do your best at what you do best.

Author Anthony Robbins says most people are best at one of three gifts.

1. Talent
2. Management/leadership
3. Entrepreneurism

Blink don't think!

Which one immediately resonates with you?

You may be good in all three areas.

Blink don't think!

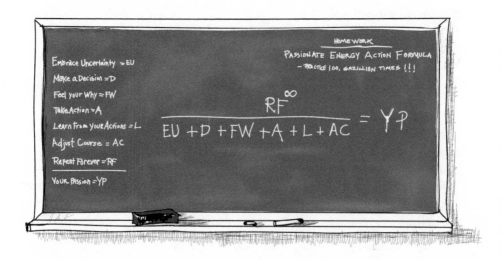

But which gift brings you a deep sense of fulfillment

Survival demanded that I become an expert entrepreneur, which led to honing my management, marketing, and leadership skills. But mining the depths of my talent is what truly strikes the gold of my essence. For me, making the invisible visible—using my talent to serve—is deeply and powerfully fulfilling. That's why I like business. Starting a business is a creative act. But the seeds of greatness can only grow from being who you are, and who I am is talent. Don't mistake the business of your passion for your passion. Just because you're good at something doesn't mean it's your full calling. Just because you *can* do something doesn't mean you *should*.

DREAM MAGNETS

The magnetic energy of who you are attracts or repels what you want.

—Dad

Bring passion to everything—and I mean everything—you do.
Cleaning cat poop? (That's my first album.)
Clean with passion. Overdeliver.
Grunt work at an internship?
Grunt with passion. Overdeliver.
Saying hello?
Greet with passion. Overdeliver.
Why?

Passion is a magnet that draws in unexpected opportunities, pulling your dreams to you. The magnetic energy of who you are attracts or repels what you want.
How?

The answer speaks to the overarching message of this book, and leads full circle back to the overarching purpose of life. For most people . . .

Raising your level of passion raises your level of consciousness.

Consciousness is energy, or "mojo," as I like to call it. Like the sea, consciousness has different levels. Each *mojo level* is a measurable, magnetic energy field that attracts more of the same. We each vibrate at a certain level. Weak or strong—the magnetic *power of pull* is determined by our energy/mojo level. Remember what Einstein said,

"Everything is energy and that's all there is to it. Match the frequency of the reality you want and you cannot help but get that reality."

Like goes to like.

To be laser-beam specific versus self-help cliché, Hallmark card fluffy or New Age nutty, see the following "mojo map" of consciousness levels.

Mojo Levels
Above 200: Upper levels are bursting with magnetic POWER that PULLS.

Enlightenment	1,000
Peace	600
Joy/Unconditional Love	540
Love (**Gratitude**)	**500**
Reason	400
Acceptance	350
Willingness (**Passion**)	**310**
Neutrality	250
Courage	200

Below 200: Lower levels are dead with FEAR, requiring FORCE that needs to PUSH.

Pride	175
Anger	150
Desire	125
Fear	100
Grief	75
Apathy/Hatred	50
Guilt	30
Shame	20

Each level is a measurable energy field, attracting more of what it is.

An in-depth discussion on consciousness levels is included later in this Verse.

Based on Dr. David R. Hawkins's Map of Consciousness: www.Veritaspub.com.

Passion is a powerful rung on the ladder of consciousness (energy), calibrating in the 300s. Most people are stuck on the weak energy rungs below 200.

Below 200 are force, falsehood, and fear.

In the lower levels you have to force everything to do anything.

Above 200 are power, truth, and love.

At level 300, passion naturally gathers energy, takes on a life of its own, and begins attracting your wishes like a magnet.

Passion pulls.

Fear pushes.

Bringing passion to everything you do, charges the magnet of your being, raising your mojo level from weak to strong—from push to pull—from force to power.

To find your passion, live with passion.

And your passion will find you.

Same goes for the magnetic power of love:

Do what you love, and turn what you do into love.

When legendary music producer Quincy Jones was asked about the secret to his massive musical and financial success, he gave a powerful one-word answer:

"Love!"

Like singer Tina Turner, you may be asking, "What's love got to do with it?"

Love is a powerful rung on the ladder of consciousness (energy), calibrating in the 500s. It has even more magnetic power to draw in your dreams than passion, which calibrates in the 300s. As Dr. David Hawkins says, "A state of lovingness is the most powerful of all survival tools."

Pour love into everything you do—no matter what you're doing—and you'll attract the things you love into your life.

Love is a magnet. It attracts what it is.

Being love,

Bringing love to "everything" we do,

Pulls our dreams to us.

Bring gratitude to everything—and I mean everything—you do.

Cleaning cat poop? Be grateful!

Clean with gratitude.

Grunt work at an internship? Be grateful!

Grunt with gratitude.

Saying hello! Be grateful!

Greet with gratitude.

"It is necessary, then, to cultivate the habit of being grateful for every good thing that comes to you, and to give thanks continuously. And because all things have contributed to your advancement, you should include all things in your gratitude."[24]

Gratitude is an aspect of love, which hums in the powerful mojo levels of the 500s. Like goes to like. We don't attract what we want; we attract what we are.

Gratitude is a magnet. It attracts what it is.

Being grateful,

Bringing gratitude to "everything" we do,

Pulls our dreams to us.

Discovering who you are doesn't have to be some deep gut-wrenching drama.

It's simple.

Live with gratitude.

Live with love.

Live with passion . . .
And your passion will find you.

The magnetic energy of who you are attracts or repels what you want.

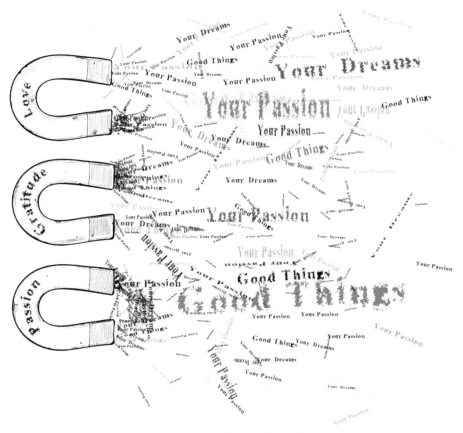

Live with love. Live with gratitude. Live with passion. . .
And your passion will find you.

E PLURIBUS UNUM

Out of many [interests], one [passion].
—Dad, variations on a U.S. theme

Who says everyone has one designated passion? Who says everybody was born to do one thing? Who says we have to choose one thing to do forever? Who says we have to choose one thing over the other?

What if I want to do more than one thing? What if I'm passionate about lots of things? What if I'm not all that passionate about anything?

What if my passion isn't a thing to *find* but an unpredictable combination of interests and experiences that *unfolds* over time—a composite of curiosities, likes, and attractions fused to form a purpose and place, impossible to see in advance?

Someone pleeeze . . .

Cut the switch on the programmed clichés, pummeling my brain since birth!

CLICHÉ: *What are you going to be when you grow up?*
YOU: *What if there's no category for that? And is that be or do?*
CLICHÉ: *What's your major?*
YOU: *What if what I want doesn't fit into the 4-Cs (cookie-cutter college curriculum)?*
CLICHÉ: *What's your one passion? One love? One thing?*
YOU: *But—I—love—lots—of—things!*

CLICHÉ:	*Sorry! There's no major for that. So put your unrepeatable spirit into our college cage and sign here. Then sign the student loan papers to ensure the cage stays locked.*
YOU:	*I need to know my future now! I need control!*
CLICHÉ:	*If you'd like to get a master's degree in predictability, just lop off all but one of your interests. (Prereq: Thinking something's wrong with you for pursuing too many things.)*
YOU:	*Well, I've already completed the prereq!*
CLICHÉ:	*Way to go! Great job!*
YOU:	*Oops. You mean, "Average job," don't you?*
CLICHÉ:	*Yes, I'm sorry. We strive for mediocrity at 4-Cs University and exclamation points are banned. I meant, "Way to look like you're going. Average job."*
YOU:	*Phew. Now that I have fake control, over my fake future security, I feel fake better. This unfolding stuff is just tooo uncertain.*
CLICHÉ:	*Thanks for omitting the exclamation points.*

Some people are born to specialize in one thing.
That's great *for them!*
But downright unnatural for others.
There's nothing wrong with you if you are what author Emily Wapnick calls a multipotentialite. *(Multi-potential-ite)* Her definition:
"A person with many different interests and pursuits in life."
The traditional term is Renaissance man. Webster's definition:
"A person who has wide interest and is expert in many areas."
Some people either love, like, or simply have small interests in many things. Why lop off any of them? The garden of who you are can only blossom if all of who you are grows together. A single bloom would look kind of sad in a field of hacked-up flowers.

Instead of searching for one ready-made passion, *multipotentialites* intuitively blend their interests into a surprise passion potpourri.

Like my friend Jeremy, whose *multi-interests* in law, business, entrepreneurism, music, and event planning blended into a career as an A-list music supervisor in Los Angeles. (A music supervisor oversees all music-related aspects of a film and television production.) His master's degree in percussion performance from 4-Cs University was only a piece of what naturally unfolded into a new and unexpected passion.

So how do you blend many interests into one? First thing: Quit forcing! Quit controlling! Quit trying to create an entire masterpiece with one stroke of the brush. An unfolding canvas of passion is painted with the colors of patience and faith.

If you don't know what you love, follow what you're drawn to. There's a message and map—a pathway unfolding inside the things drawing you in. Slight interests

The garden of who you are can only blossom if all of who you are grows together.

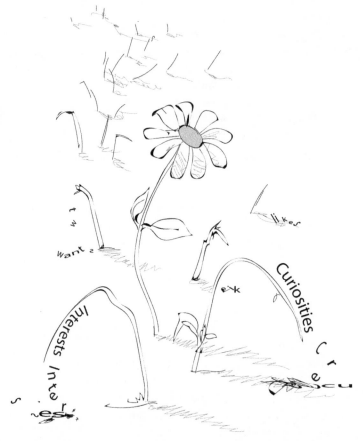

A single bloom would look kind of sad in a field of hacked-up flowers.

or mild curiosities may be breadcrumbs leading to the wider road of an emerging destiny.

You girls are interested in lots of things. The arts, languages, animals, books. You're drawn to social issues, environmental causes, people who make a difference. Jessie loved the idea of joining a program that cares for sea turtles between semesters. Jamie loves to travel, write, and play piano. Josie loves all of the above. Who knows how all of these things will blend together?

But I do know one thing about one thing. For some, it's made up of many things. (*E pluribus unum—out of many* [interests], *One* [passion])

I don't want you to lock yourself in a cage, simply because . . .

You majored in it.

Spent money or time on it.

Think you're supposed to.

Or think it fits into the media family profile.

Be who *you* are—not who your uncles, aunts, cousins, or parents are.

You can't grow up if you close up.

Stay open.

Stay empty.

And leave room for *all* of who you are to fill your cup.

I know one thing about one thing, for many, it's made up of many things.

E pluribus unum. . . Out of many [interests], One [passion].

WATERING BUCKETS

A field of multidreams is watered with decision, action, timing, flexibility, and faith.

—Dad

What's *your* obligation?

What does life ask of someone whose passions come in many shapes and sizes? What does a field made up of many different flowers need to blossom? To grow your field of multidreams into the garden of who you are, sprinkle in waters from four magic buckets.

What Bucket: Decision, meaning, commitment, action.

When Bucket: Timing, priorities, and patience.

Learn Bucket: Listen to the feedback of your actions. Look for merging ideas.

Adjust Bucket: Follow the feedback. Be flexible. Adjust course.

So, what about the *What Bucket*?

Even if you don't know exactly *what* your *what* is, decide, commit, and take action on one *what* at a time. And know *why* you want your *what*. If there's no *why*, there's no *what*.

What?

Decide and commit to one *outcome*. Committing to an *outcome* leads to new insights and ideas, which expand into new *outcomes*, which over time mix and merge and unfold into a *never before, never again* passion surprise. All motivation is derived from meaning, so fuel your *what* with a powerful *why*.

How about the When Bucket?

What would happen if an air traffic controller tried to force every plane to take off and land all at once?

Gridlock! Kah-boom!

Everything would crash!

The same goes with your goals, likes, inklings, dreams, and schemes.

Life wants you to be the air traffic controller of your passions, even if your passions are currently preferences. Guide them in one by one with precision and timing.

Prioritize what to focus on now, next, and later?

Choose one outcome for takeoff.

Be patient.

Give it time.

A blended passion unfolding from many things needs time to bloom into view. Decide and commit to the plane you want to land first, and put the others on a holding pattern until the runway clears.

Learn Bucket:

In the bird hunting days of my Wisconsin youth, my dad taught me how to flush out a partridge hidden in the brush: Walk slow and steady through the woods. Be patient. They're out there. You just can't see them. Then every once in a while

Stop,

Look,

Listen, and without warning . . .

Woosh, woosh, woosh, woosh, woosh!

The partridge will pop out of the brush, sending your heart to the races.

The same thing applies to every outcome you set.

There are winged ideas, waiting in the woods of your actions, but to flush them out you've got to act. As you move slowly and steadily towards your outcome, every once in a while . . .

Stop,

Look,

Listen to the feedback of your actions, and out of the quantum blue . . .

Woosh, woosh, woosh, woosh, woosh!

Merging ideas and cross curiosities will send your heart to the races.

Try this! How about that?

Woosh!

Connect this old dot, to that old dot, and voila—a new un-dot.

Woosh, woosh, woosh!

This intersects with the other thing you love. That blends the other thing you like into a brand new thing!

Adjust Bucket:

Flushing up an idea bird is like a living map that unfolds as it's followed.

Go this way. Turn that way.

Move forward. Fall back.

Mix, merge, or meld.

End, mend, or blend a whole new plane onto the runway. (Or is it a partridge?)

Aaaaandddd wooosh!

The wings of your passion are unfolding, woosh by unflappable woosh.

Oh. And one more thing . . .

It's a watering bucket unto its own, which nurtures all of life.

Faith

Have faith in yourself.

There is greatness in you. This is not philosophy or fatherhood speaking—this is fact. Your masterpiece will emerge step by shaky step, with every firm decision you make.

Have faith in God.

Trust that the same force and source nurturing the unfolding of every single thing in the universe is nurturing your unfolding as well.

"Behind every blade of grass is an angel whispering, 'grow, grow.'"[25]

Trust me.

I can see the power of your essence, pulling you home, as it unfolds from bud to bloom. And the view is amazing! If you could see what I see . . .

You'd be fearless.

You'd do your best, forget the rest, and enjoy the day.

You'd rest in faith.

Faith that your unforeseeable passion, purpose, and place will unfold in time, if you're strong enough to surrender to uncertainty, until certainty—and the unrepeatable glory of who you are—burgeons into view.

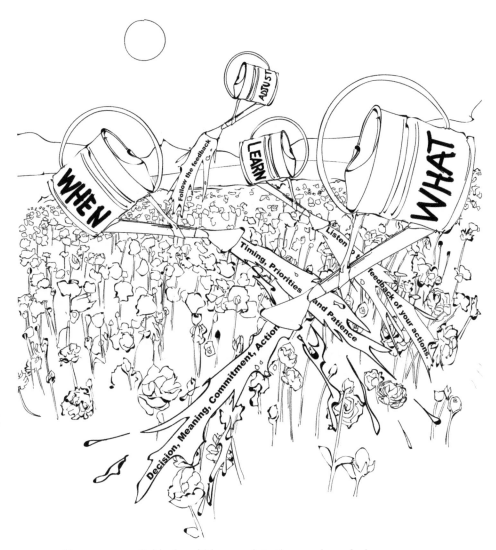

To grow your field of multidreams into the garden of who you are. . .
sprinkle in waters from four magic buckets.

UNUM PASSIO

The hunter who chases two rabbits catches neither.

—Confucius

*If you're pulled by one passion (unum passio), focus on
   nothing else.*
Master it!

—Dad

S ome people *are* born to do one thing.
   Some are a mix of many.
   Both are beautiful.
   Both are needed.
   And both are bound by one, nonnegotiable rule . . .
   Be who you are.
   As I watched a *60 Minutes* special on jazz virtuoso Marcus Roberts, I wondered
out loud—"Did I break the rule?"

   Roberts focused on one thing, stuck to his guns, and played piano. He didn't
wander down a million rabbit trails, circling around his passion, but never to it. His
story touched a nerve.

   In my early days, music was my driving force. Along with spirituality and family,
it still is. But life has a way of stealing the wheel if you let it. Did I veer from my one
thing, race down too many rabbit trails, drive by my dreams on the way to paying
for my dreams?

   Hmm. Maybe?

Or maybe I just tried to do too many things at once.

At times I bit off more than I could chew—lost focus of what I loved by focusing on making money to support what I loved.

They say, "Do what you love and money will follow." *NOT TRUE!*

The truth is . . .

Master what you love and money will follow.

Mastered passion pays.

Marcus Roberts focused on one thing and mastered it,

And the money followed.

But there's a rule of nature, built into the art of mastering anything.

You can't master what you don't love.

Why would you want to?

No matter how offbeat, impossible, or totally crazy your *unum passio* seems . . .

Master it, and the universe will take care of you.

It worked for Adam Winrich. He focused on one thing:

Snapping a whip.

Huh?

He's a professional whippersnapper.

After seeing Harrison Ford wielding a whip in the movie *Indiana Jones Raiders of the Lost Ark* the nine-year-old Winrich focused on one thing—the art of whip cracking.

I'm sure Winrich was jeered by the herd when he graduated from college with a double major in math and physics and chose to face the danger of his passion, instead of the safety of a *real job*.

"Grow up!"

"Whip cracking is a hobby, not a living."

"Show me the money!"

But after becoming a world champion whip cracker, setting sixteen Guinness world records, the jeers turned to cheers. Mastered passion not only flows smoothly on a steady financial current (currency), it creates the wave it's riding.

Offers flowed in from around the globe. He has multiyear contracts with Renaissance fairs nationwide. His DVDs sell for $30.00 a pop. Appearances on radio and TV, including *Conan,* are standard procedure. Winrich travels the globe cracking the whip of nonconformity worldwide. But most importantly . . .

He's doing what he loves.

Winrich wouldn't be experiencing the richness of life, and having so much darn fun, if he chased two rabbits instead of mastering one.

So don't waste your time on things you don't care about, or things the world says you're supposed to care about.

If there's no motivation, there's no meaning.

If there's no meaning, it's not your mission.

If it's not your mission, it's not your monkey.

If you don't know what your one thing is, *do one thing at a time until you do.*
If you do know what your one thing is, *master it.*
And sure as a sunrise, who you are will blossom into view.
Failure is impossible.

If you're pulled by one passion, focus on nothing else. Master it!

The hunter who chases two rabbits catches neither. Confucius

WOUNDED PASSION

Accept your gifts. Do not apologize, compromise, or doubt.
Respect yourself. Forget fitting in. Toss your fear. Never play
* small.*
Let yourself Love what you Love.
Listen to the ring of your passion. Answer the call.
Accepting your gifts is accepting yourself.
　　　　　　　　　　　　　　　　—Dad

Passion's call demands to be followed. You did not choose it so much as it chose you. Squelching true passion is like force-quitting your heart and trying to stay alive. I've learned this the hard way. It's impossible!

I played the flute. I mean *really*? What red-blooded male growing up in Wisconsin plays the flute? What kind of oddball, dead-end thing is that? Loved it! *I stopped playing.*

I wrote music. I'm more passionate about writing music than *ever*! Loved it! *I stopped writing.*

I played the guitar religiously. Teaching at good ole Stan's Music store by ninth grade: Loved it! *I stopped playing guitar.*

I used to sing. Your uncles and I started singing together when I was five. Loved it! *I stopped singing.*

I stuck to my guns for a while though. I moved to California after high school, practiced all day, took embarrassing odd jobs to pay rent on a ramshackle apartment, and lived on four-for-a-dollar boxes of macaroni and cheese.

Loneliness was a painful way of life.

Something that I didn't quite understand had a deep, driving pull over me. It didn't matter what I was going through on the outside, the fire never stopped burning on the inside! I was deeply passionate, deeply driven, deeply determined, and deeply broke.

All I knew was I loved music, and I loved to create, to make the invisible visible. Music was what I was supposed to be making and selling and living. But I couldn't make a living so *I stopped making music.*

I put on my business suit of armor and told myself it was time to get a *real job.* Or turn what I love into a business, become respectable, accepted, and fit in! As the old saying goes, "When I write a good song, it makes me cry, but when I write a good jingle, it makes me buy real estate." And so my company *Jingle Jams* was born, along with a slew of Polly Pocket, bug killer, strip mall, and car dealer masterpieces. Who could forget this jingle gem? Sing along with me now!

We really, really, really want to buy your car, truck, or van!

I didn't accept my gifts or let myself love what I love.

You can't defer, deny, ignore, shrink, or shadow who you are. Passion will never leave you alone. It demands attention.

You may have to live in a ramshackle apartment, dining on macaroni and cheese while mastering your calling. To others it may look like the pieces of *normal* existence you've hobbled together to hold your dreams are the sign of failure. But you'll know better.

Passion is oxygen. All it really needs is space to breathe. When your passion is gasping for air, nothing else can possibly matter. You can't love, live, or laugh while holding your breath. It would feel empty, sound shallow, and ring false—smiling while groping for breath—life would be a lie!

An ignored passion will creep into every area of your life and scream for attention! It will show up as . . .

Sickness in your body.

Tension in your home.

Frustration in your work.

Anger in your relationships.

Ache in your back.

Emptiness in your days.

Distance in your stare.

Restlessness in your sleep.

Gnawing in your heart.

Like a dam filled to the point of bursting, repressed passion will sooner or later cause something to break.[26] It will plow through your family, job, health, and relationships, hurting those you love the most. The flailing energy of choking passion will go wild and express itself any way it can to survive. Like a wrecking ball, it will crash into your life through:

Alcohol
Drugs
Overeating
Underperforming
Watching TV
Medications
Internet
Busyness
Laziness
Drama
Avoidance through any means possible.

Like Al Pacino said in the movie *Scent of a Woman*, "I have seen boys like these, younger than these, their arms torn out, their legs ripped off—but there isn't nothin' like the sight of an amputated spirit. There is no prosthetic for that."

True passion cannot be tamed or caged.

Wounded passion, like a wounded bear. . .
will lash out and maim, as it wails for its last breath.

True passion cannot be tamed or caged. Passion is powerful and must be expressed—it can never be repressed. Wounded passion, like a wounded bear, will lash out and maim, as it wails for its last breath. The pressure of quiet desperation will mount into an explosion of frustration. Innocent bystanders will be caught in the crossfire. When the dam finally bursts and all inner hell breaks loose . . .

Someone's going to get hurt!

TRUTH IS PAIN BEFORE IT'S PEACE

Always!
Be careful with whom you share your dreams.
Someone will always feel threatened.
Someone will always try and burst your bubble.
Someone will always say you can't.
Always!

—Dad

I n the movie *Dead Poets Society*, Neil Perry was forced into a life he didn't want. His sentence was to start with four years at the prestigious Welton Academy for boys, followed by four years of hard time at Harvard—then on to life without parole in the "real world" as a wealthy, status-symbol doctor.

To most people, an Ivy League education and life as a big-shot doctor may look like success—but so-called success without authenticity is a façade.

Neil didn't want to put on an act—he wanted to act!

So he stuffed his passion for acting into a gilded cage of conformity out of fear of his father, where it seethed and boiled in a stew of quiet desperation until his English teacher blew the lid off. *Carpe diem!* "Seize the day" was the call that liberated Neil from his private prison.

Giddy with excitement, he told his roommate, Todd, about his revelation—how he's finally found what's inside of him—what he wants to do— about trying out for the school play—how he's always been passionate about acting, and always afraid to tell his father.

Todd burst his bubble with a dose of reality.

"How are you gonna do the play if your father won't let you?"

Like a time bomb ticking,

You can't,

You can't,

You can't . . .

His years of silent anguish were creeping to a dangerous edge. The best thing and the worst thing happened.

Neil won the lead part.

For the first time ever, he believed living his passion was possible. For one brief shining moment, he was happy; there was hope. Then his father stepped in with a wrath-filled ultimatum to quit the play and drop "this absurd acting business" or else!

Caged and confused, Neil sought advice from his English teacher, Mr. Keating, who told him to tell his father about his passion for acting.

NEIL: I can't talk to him this way.
MR. KEATING: Then you're acting for him, too.[27]

Liberating who you are takes courage.

The sword of Truth will sever imitation foundations, cut open hidden wounds, and expose the raw nerves of sick relationships.

Like any healing crisis, *truth is pain before it's peace.* That's why many people remain stuck. They won't face the storm before the calm. Your growth can be a threat to those around you. They will *always* fight you. But it's your life—you're the one who has to live it. You're the one who has to take a stand. You're the one who has to believe. You're the one who has to take the leap of faith. You're the only one who knows the truth. Saying "yes" to someone else is saying "no" to yourself. You're the one who has to live with the consequences. It's not easy, but the alternative—the slow death of living a lie—is utterly unbearable!

Neil dared to lift his passion out from the shadows, igniting a blow back of fury from his father, whose tyrannical response was to yank him out of Welton and sentence him to military school.

Crushing his free-range spirit into a gilded coop was more than Neil could take. Drained of all hope—he whimpered what would be his last words to his mother . . .

"I was good. I was really good."

Cut to Neil's final scene.

Neil holds a key in his hands. He unlocks a drawer in his father's desk and pulls out a pistol wrapped in cloth . . .

And the curtain falls . . .

And the light goes out . . .

Cut.

Neil was but a walking shadow, a poor player, who strutted and fretted his fourteen minutes upon the stage, and then—was heard no more.[28] In the end, trying to exhume a truth buried in the dirt of family dysfunction was too much. The slow death of living a lie was utterly unbearable. Instead of being who he was, no matter what, Neil took the fast way out.

I do not exaggerate the dangers and darkness of living a fake life!

I repeat! I repeat! I repeat!

The pressure of quiet desperation will mount into an explosion of frustration.

Innocent bystanders will be caught in the crossfire.

When the dam finally bursts and all inner hell breaks loose,

Someone's going to get hurt.

Some things are going to die.

Worse yet . . .

Some things will have never been born.

Liberating who you are takes courage. Like any healing crisis. . .
Truth is pain before it's peace.

That's why many people remain stuck.
They won't face the storm before the calm.

WRONG SIDE OF THE LINE

There's a line.
It stands between the power of passion and the poison of
wanton desire.
On one side you have Freedom; on the other, Enslavement.
On one side you have Love; on the other, Fear.
On both sides, what you see is what you get.
                              —Dad

Wait a minute!
Is being too passionate keeping me from my passion?
Too desiring keeping me from my desire?
Too wanting keeping me from getting what I want?
That doesn't make sense!

I thought passion and desire were good things. I thought if you weren't hungry, you didn't want it; if you didn't care enough to freak out and worry, you didn't care enough. No pain, no gain! No suffering, no validation! Stick the Rocky Balboa soundtrack on, and put your nose to the grindstone! That's what you were supposed to do! Sacrifice is a badge of honor!

But then again, at times, when intense passion started to kick in, I'd sometimes catch myself and try to keep it at bay. I was secretly afraid that being passionate about getting something would keep me from getting it. At least it seemed to work out that way sometimes. Maybe it's better not to want it so bad.

Hmm.

Ahhh.

Naah! That can't be right.

Is the energy of desire truly a "denial that what we want is ours for the asking, without all the effort, without all the trial and error, and without all the hard work?"[29]

C'mon! That's upside-down!

What we want comes into our lives "in spite of desire not because of desire?"[30]

Ask Horatio Alger!

That doesn't make any sense!

The "Desire Loop" is another top forty hit.

Constant craving for what you want creates more constant craving for what you want.

Wanton desire cuts and pastes wanton desire into our lives, like a drum loop into a hip-hop song. Instead of simply choosing and surrendering the outcome, the desire becomes so intense it crosses the line into an unhealthy attachment—burning a subconscious loop into your being, which says . . .

"I'm incomplete → I'm incomplete → I'm incomplete → Boom, chicka boom, chicka boom boom boom."

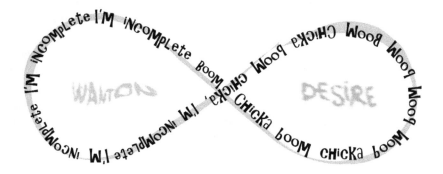

How do you break the loop?

Keep the desire, without crossing the line into wanton desire.

Desire and wanton desire are two different vibrations.

One is fear.

One is love.

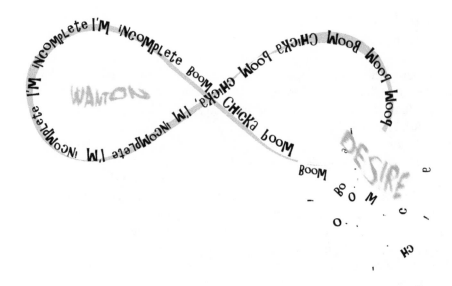

FEAR: *I'm obsessed with success. If I don't get that job, I'll be devastated.*
LOVE: *I'm on fire with enthusiasm! Win or lose, I'm passionate about going for it!*
FEAR: *I crave money. People will look at me differently when I have money.*
LOVE: *I desire wealth to liberate my potential and make the most of myself.*

"Wanton desire creates the fear of not getting, which always blocks receiving."[31]

I ran into a friend who was passionate about opening a coffee shop. As he was sharing his plans and excitement, I witnessed his passion decay into anxiety:

"I've got to make this happen, if I don't I'll be crushed." (The fear of not getting is an attachment to outcome.)

"But *I can't* find the money." (Focusing on lack attracts it.)

"I can't find the perfect location." "Saying something isn't ours puts a psychic distance between ourselves and what we want."[32]

My friend crossed the line of passion, into the loop of wanton desire, right before my very eyes. He may get what he wants *in spite of his desire, not because of it.* But the satisfaction of achieving his goal will be eclipsed by the fear that motivated it.

What begins as passion can end up as an obsession, which is just another word for fear, only with more syllables! Ha! The way to get what you want is to simply choose, take action, and surrender the outcome. Worry is a lack of faith that has never helped anyone; not to mention, it isn't any fun.

I was happy for my friend's new passion to open a coffee shop, and sad for the desire that may end up keeping the doors closed.

I want to spare you from the pain of being on the wrong side of the line, by shouting as passionately as I can.

Suffering is an unnecessary choice!

There's a line between passion and wanton desire.

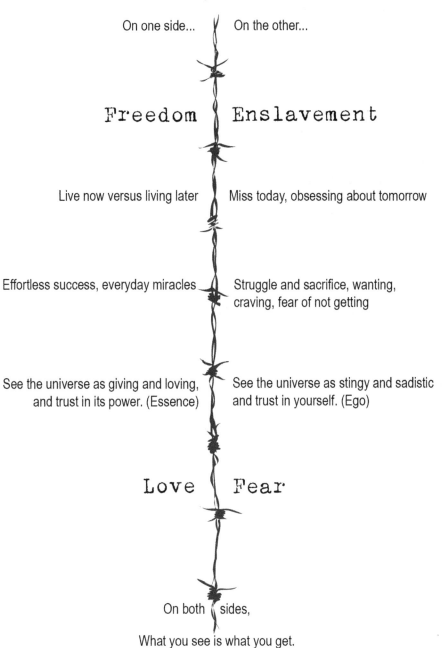

On one side...   On the other...

Freedom   Enslavement

Live now versus living later   Miss today, obsessing about tomorrow

Effortless success, everyday miracles   Struggle and sacrifice, wanting, craving, fear of not getting

See the universe as giving and loving, and trust in its power. (Essence)   See the universe as stingy and sadistic and trust in yourself. (Ego)

Love   Fear

On both sides,

What you see is what you get.

Suffering is an unnecessary choice!
Suffering is an unnecessary choice!
"Why should we go through any cost of pain and suffering to achieve anything in our life? Isn't that a rather sadistic view of the universe?"[33]

Einstein said, "The most important decision we make is whether we believe we live in a friendly or hostile universe."

Please trust me on this because it's ab-so-lute-ly truuue! We live in a friendly universe. The air and essence of the universe is unconditional love. What you naturally want most—which is different than the cravings of the ego—the universe wants for you. And it's yours for the asking!

Yes! Never ever stop living with passion!
Yes! Bring passion to everything you do.
Just make sure you know where passion ends and fear begins.
And stay on the passion side of the line.
The point is not to quit trying and living passionately,
The point is to quit craving and enjoy the ride.
Miracles are effortless.

PASSION AND PRIDE

You can do what you love, and turn what you do into love.
Or
You can use what you love to feed the ego and fill the holes
forged by fear.

—Dad

've always loved music.

How did your Grandma Hanky and Grandpa Frank put up with the nonstop noise of six kids? Your uncles and I never stopped singing, and at the top of our lungs! Besides being completely wacky and wild, your Uncle Johnny liked to bang on the drum all day. Uncle Michael sang more than he talked. I remember using croquet mallets for air guitars and harmonizing Beatles songs when we were around five years old. I remember the utterly magic effect music had on me in the rare moments we sounded good. I couldn't imagine anything better. We gave air guitar concerts in our garage on Bragg Street in Fond du Lac, Wisconsin, to all the neighborhood kids. Aunt Mary was CEO of concessions. As she sold Kool-Aid for five cents a glass, the feeling of being the *cool kid* seeped through my raw passion for music and into my ego.

Passion and pride:

There's no way I could understand it at the time, but two different motivations were growing at once.

Fast forward to seventh grade. I remember playing at the Y-Dance (YMCA) with your uncles in our band Stone Quarry. I remember feeling transfixed and transformed one night as my lead guitar solo blended perfectly with the chords to the song "Million Years." I loved that feeling! But besides loving the music, I remember loving the attention, the cool factor, the girls, and the applause drowning out my middle school insecurity and inflating my fragile ego.

Passion and pride:

Again, two motivations growing at once.

Though I didn't get it at the time, one was raising my level of consciousness to *courage, willingness,* and *love,* and one was bringing me down to *fear* and *desire.* And more often than not, when a wrong note threatened my contrived identity, I was pulled under to *grief* and *guilt.*

I remember bursting through the door after school in ninth grade and yipping with excitement to Grandma Hanky about the magical "new song" we played in band that day.

"Mom, Mom, Mom! You won't believe this new song we learned. It was mesmerizing! It took me away to another world! I lost myself in the melody. It was dripping with beauty. You probably never heard of it. The song is called 'Stardust!'"

Grandma Hanky laughed and said, "That's not a new song, my dear boy. I listened to 'Stardust' when I was your age. Hoagy Carmichael wrote it before I was even born." Then she said, as she often did through the years, to both Uncle Michael and me, "I'm grateful that you love music."

I asked why. "Because I love what music does to you" was her loving answer. She saw the passion; she didn't see the pride—or maybe she did and knew that someday I'd grow out of it.

When I graduated from Saint Mary Springs High School, a sweet nun said much the same. She wrote in my senior yearbook, "When I see you in band, you're like a different person." (Translation: not a loudmouthed, obnoxious, class clown.) Sister Irene and Grandma Hanky only saw half of what music did to me. They saw the innocent passion of a boy motivated by a love for music, but they didn't see the ego and insecurity creeping in from behind.

Passion and pride. Mix in a little fear and poof, out pops the ego!

The lower levels of consciousness were circling the wagons of what I naturally adored. As I grew into my teenage years, insecurity, desire, false fronts, and false pride also crept in. Music quit lifting my soul. I needed it to inflate my ego.

Unknowingly, I flipped my motivation and flipped the point.

I went from

Doing what I love, and turning what I do into love

to

Using what I love to feed the ego and fill the holes left by fear.

One brings happiness and freedom, the other dissatisfaction and want.

One empowers.

One enslaves.

I didn't understand this for years. I was locked in the jaws of desire, trying to fit in by standing out. I wasn't free, and you can't be happy if you're not free.

Free from needing to look cool, free from seeking approval, free from needing a prefabricated identity, free from seeking validation, free from fear in all its socially expected forms. What if I suck? What if I can't keep up with my friends? What if I don't make it? As Uncle Michael recently reminded me, when I told him I was experiencing a creative block, "You have everything to share, and nothing to prove." [34] He should have told me that when I was sixteen. I want to save you decades of unnecessary frustration.

What you naturally love can deform into the cancerous twins of pride and desire if you cling too tight. Clinging to even the worthiest dream is a form of slavery.

"If you can dream, and not make dreams your master," as Kipling said, you'll stay free, even as you throw every ounce of your being into the ring.

Pride is an intruder, breaking and entering into the sanctuary of what you love. Desire is its accomplice, fear its base.

And liberating yourself from fear is the only reason you're here.

Every self-help book in the world is screaming,

"Follow your passion, follow your passion, follow your passion!"

I'm saying, it's better to not follow your passion if it leads to pride, or desire, or anger, or any of the other standardized faces of fear.

The only thing that raises your level of happiness is raising your level of consciousness anyway.

Nothing, nothing, nothing matters more than transcending the ego.

So wear your passion, your dreams, and all of the truly amazing things of this world like a loose garb. Enjoy! Have a blast! But be in the world, not of it. [35]

True passion leads you to who you are, which is love.

If passion is leading you anywhere else but home, change course, reboot, or quit.

What good is it for someone to gain the whole world, and yet lose or forfeit their very self? [36]

Pride is an intruder, breaking and entering into the sanctuary of what you love.

Desire is its accomplice - fear its base.

THE REAL JOURNEY LEADS INSIDE, I PRAY YOU'LL TRAVEL FAR

Outside in? The "real world" has it exactly backwards.
The only way to a happy life leads from the inside out!
Your inner world determines the outer.
Happiness is not an external event.

—Dad

A vision is like an ecosystem in nature. Remove any of its layers and everything collapses. Take away the bees and even the most thriving ecosystem will crumble. Albert Einstein said if bees disappeared, "man would have only four years of life left."

Deceptively unrelated events cause drastic disturbances to ecosystems worldwide. Like in these headlines:

"Shark Population Collapses on East Coast, Causing Other Species to Vanish."

"Alaska's Sea Otter Decline Affects Health of Kelp Forests and Diet of Eagles."

"Moose in Minnesota are Roaming out of Existence, Because It's Not Cold Enough." And ecosystems are more than meets the surface.

If you were able to hover above the world, and all at once behold the radiant beauty of every meadow, mountain, and stream, you'd only see half the glory. "What we see above ground is only the outer margin of an ecosystem that explodes in intricacy and life below."[37] The full picture emerges underground, where seed and soil shape its destiny.

It's the same with your vision, dream, or goal:

It cannot bloom on its own.

It's part of an interactive ecosystem.

And what happens above ground is dependent on what happens below.

Like interdependence in nature, no part of your vision can be isolated from the other and still thrive. There's an interconnectedness between your . . .

Self-concept and life circumstances.

Self-worth and level of expectations.

Inner speech and outer world.

Subconscious beliefs and level of achievement.

As naturalist John Muir says about unity in nature, "When we try to pick out anything by itself, we find it hitched to everything else in the universe." The interconnection in the ecosystem of your vision and your quality of life can be no different.

When we try to pick out any piece of our vision, dream, or goal by itself, we find it hitched to everything else in our subconscious and conscious universe.

Ecosystem of a Powerful Vision
The Soil
Consciousness: Soil from which all of creation is cast.

Consciousness level: Quality of soil from which your vision can grow.

The Seeds and Roots
Imagination: Molds consciousness into anything you want.

Intention: Activates and directs consciousness to manifest what you've imagined.

Subconscious beliefs: Boundaries of your imagination and limits of your vision.

Self-concept: Shapes your imagination.

Self-worth: Determines the reach and power of your imagination.

Habitual thoughts and mood: Channel through which vision flows, veers, or dams.

Inner speech: Creates feelings, which program the subconscious, which designs your life.

Feelings: Programs your subconscious to manifest what you feel.

Subconscious mind: Controls creation. Commands your life.

The Water and Sunlight
Meaning: Source and fuel of motivation.

Motivation? Love or fear? The blessing or curse of your vision fulfilled.

Clarity: Triggers the power of specificity, igniting the creative forces of the universe.

Decision and commitment: Sparks a new destiny—power to stay the course.

Strategy: The map.
Action: The teacher—creates momentum, energy, and excitement.
Surrender: Freedom from the prison of vision—wantonness and cravenness.

The Bloom
Your vision fulfilled.

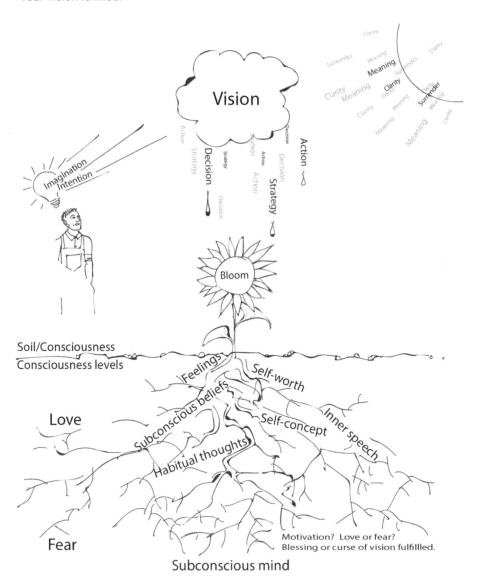

SELF-CONCEPT LAYER

Your life cannot be any different than your self-concept.

—Dad

Many people can't break the dream barrier because something in the ecosystem of their vision—above ground or below—is out of alignment.
Like self-concept.

The collapse of your self-concept will pull your vision out of alignment and cause your dreams to disappear; just like the collapse of the shark population caused other species to vanish on the East Coast. As author Neville Goddard says:

"If a man's concept of himself were different, everything in his world would be different. His concept of himself being what it is, everything in his world must be as it is."

The circumstances of your life are a reflection of who *you* think you are—of what you tell yourself you can or can't do. "Your concept of yourself is all that you accept and consent as true,"[38] even if all you accept and consent as true is dead wrong!

Somewhere along the line from Mequon Avenue in Fond du Lac to the 405 freeway in Los Angeles, my self-concept expanded from "I really don't think I can" to "Yes I Can! Really!"

The music industry seemed a long way off, when I was growing up in small-town Wisconsin. Los Angeles was a distant, scary, and unknown place, seen only on TV, not in the mental Midwest perception I held of myself. Big-time musicians, big-time music execs, and big-time super freeways, were bigger than my small-town self-concept. But *a blood-stirring vision is stronger than illusions of limitation.* So I let go of my comfort zone, blindsided my fear, and moved to L.A. in spite of my insecurities.

I was scared all the time.

I leapt anyway! I met who I needed to meet, pursued what I needed to pursue, dove in over my head, worked with great musicians, rubbed shoulders with top executives, and white-knuckled my way down the 405 freeway even though driving in L.A. freaked me out.

Then one day, as I was cruising down the 405, I thought, *This freeway doesn't bother me anymore.* I was recording with some of the greatest musicians in the world and realized, *These musicians don't intimidate me anymore.* I was working with some of the top music executives and thought*, Though there's much to learn from everyone, I'm just as smart and talented as anyone around here.* Then it occurred to me with a chuckle,

This town doesn't scare me anymore.

By leaving my comfort zone, breaking through my small-town self-image and facing the *risks of my passion,* I created a *new normal.* I expanded my self-concept by daring to think bigger and plunge through my fears.

I dare you to *design your self-concept in any area of your life.*

It's as easy as one, two, three!

1. Choose a self-concept/vision that forces you out of your comfort zone. Live it on the inside as if it's already true.
2. Let go and leap through your fears.
3. Keep going until you reach a *new normal.*

Change your self-concept and you'll change your life.

"You are free to choose the concept you will accept of yourself. Therefore you possess the power, which enables you to alter the course of your future."[39]

I'm the poor boy, the rich girl, the fat one, the failure, the smart one, the dumb one, the winner, the loser, the leader, the follower, the outcast, and on and on.

I've known virtuoso musicians who've seen themselves as average and lived down to their self-concept. I've known average musicians who've seen themselves as virtuosos and lived up to their self-concept.

I've taught music business students who were part of the alternative education program while in high school. The "alt-ed" program was designed for students with low grades and low expectations, symptoms of a sick self-concept.

One of the students told me how she and her mom lived in a car for much of her childhood. When her mom had a boyfriend, they had a roof over their heads. When she didn't, they had a dashboard over their heads. "Self-concept is your reaction to life."[40] So how would you expect someone who spent their childhood living in a car to react to life?

This student was as smart, talented, and as promising as anyone! Because grit and the ability to persevere through a struggle are key factors in achieving success, she had an advantage over students who have never been challenged by life. The only thing that stood between her and living any life she imagined was her distorted self-concept.

I'm the outcast! I'm not as good as "normal" people. I'll never fit in.

I've seen severely overweight people lose a hundred pounds of fat without losing their "fat self-concept," and gain it all back. I know people who were programmed to just get by financially, by growing up in families that struggled to pay the bills. Buried beneath their dreams of abundance were the bones of a "just get by" self-concept. The result:

Their financial self-concept being what it is, everything in their financial world must be as it is. The same goes with every area of life and each layer in the ecosystem of your vision.

Your life circumstance is a reflection of who you think you are.

You are free to choose the concept you will accept of yourself.
Therefore you possess the power, which enables you to alter
the course of your future. Goddard

SELF-WORTH LAYER

Your vision is worthless,
Your dreams are worthless,
Your potential is worthless,
If below ground, you believe they're worthless.
And worst, worst, worst of all . . .
If you believe you are worthless.

—Dad

One of my dearest friends moved to Los Angeles to become an actor. Though he had several major auditions he couldn't close. Tired of sleeping on the floor, routine rejection, and telemarketing flare pens to pay the bills, he once lamented to your songwriter Uncle Michael, who was sharing the floor with him, "Why am I living in a town I'm never going to work in anyway?" Though he was making progress and doing all the right things, something in the ecosystem of his vision was out of alignment. Deep down—below ground—he thought his acting dreams were worthless.

The idea that you are unworthy and powerless to live the life *you* want to live is . . .
Utter crap!
Flush it!
The idea that you are less than anyone, ever, is pure garbage.
Toss it!
How do I know, know, know this?
A one-of-a-kind gem is invaluable.

You are the only one of *you* who will ever exist! And you are sacred.

When you were born, your work or place was born with you.

No one can take your place but you.

Denying the worth of what you love, no matter how different, impractical, crazy, or insecure it may seem, robs you of happiness and the world of your unrepeatable gifts. How would I know this, if I didn't experience it myself? An experience that is part of the genesis and essence of this book and one that I want to spare you from having:

The world needs you to take your place.

Not mine. Not Mom's. Not a place that sounds good and looks good . . . *yours!*

I don't care which broken mirror of fear may have distorted your true reflection— like seeing yourself through the eyes of the warped media, celebrity culture, or comparing yourself to the airbrushed body images Madison Avenue programs us with. I don't care what feedback you may have received from peers with *normal* career paths, assembly-line teachers, or misguided family members.

You are powerful beyond measure, but only if *you* know how powerful you are.

You don't need to take swag lessons like Justin Bieber did to be cool. That's not cool—that's cliché. Just another way of trying to fit in, conforming in the guise of rebelling! And as they say, "Nonconformists are all alike."

I'll tell you what's cool.

Cool is being comfortable enough in your own skin to be who you are.

If you don't fit in to who you are, you can't fit in to anything.

Rudolph the Red-Nosed Reindeer and Hermey the Elf didn't fit in. (Ha! I just love that Christmas special!)

Like people whose calling breaks from the herd, Hermey and Rudolph were misfits. The elves shunned Hermey, and as for Rudolph, "All of the other reindeer used to laugh and call him names."

ELVES: *Hermey doesn't like to make toys. Hermey wants to be a dentist. Oh shame on you! You'll never fit in.*
OTHER REINDEER: *Hey, fire snout! Rainbow puss! Red schnoz!*
COMET THE COACH: (Scolding Rudolph's, uh, nonconformity) *You should be ashamed of yourself. What a pity. He had a nice takeoff too.*

Whether it's a friend, teacher, coach, or worse yet, one of the people we love most, there's a Comet in all of our lives. Forgive me the times I've played the role of Comet the critical reindeer in yours.

But notice it was the misfits who went on to do great things in the story of Rudolph. We'll never know the names of the average elves, or all of the other reindeer who used to laugh and call him names. But Rudolph not only stood out— sing along with me now—"He went down in his-tor-eeeee!" Like Columbus! Ho, ho, ho!

So when any of your fellow elves or reindeer snub their brown noses at who you are, just remember . . .

Your value doesn't decrease based on someone's inability to see your worth.

Though it hurts when those closest to you can't see you, it doesn't matter. The only thing that matters is what you see.

The size of your expectations, accomplishments, and net worth cannot be any different than the size of your self-worth. It doesn't matter how fantastic your vision is.

You get the life *you* think you deserve.

No one can take your place but you.

INNER SPEECH LAYER

VISION: I'm going to be wealthy!
INNER SPEECH: People like me don't become wealthy.
   And money is evil anyway!
VISION: I want to enjoy the day.
INNER SPEECH: The Internet is down and it's raining!
   OMG! I can't live like this!

If your inner speech does not match your vision, it won't
   come true.

—Dad

For most of us, every idea, dream, or decision to change is tethered to a wounded little subconscious voice saying, *No you can't.*

VISION: I'm going to lose weight and get into world-class shape.
INNER SPEECH: No you can't. That's who you are; you're the fat guy!

I'm going to start my own company and become wealthy.
Broke is your self-worth. Your net worth can't be any different than your self-worth!
I'm going to make it in the movie business and work with the best there is.
Yeah, right! Sounds good, but deep down, you don't really believe it.
I'm going to use my gifts to change the world.
World-class gifts don't stand a chance against your second-class opinions of yourself.

121

DREAMS: You can't!
GOALS: You won't.
IDEA: Never work!
VISION: Who am I to think I can achieve this?
HAPPINESS: You don't deserve it! You don't deserve it! You don't deserve it!

Beneath the best-laid plans of mice and men, stands a subconscious heckler screaming . . .

You suck!

We are all orators to a captive audience, hanging onto our every word, feeling the intensity of every phrase, sharing the emotion in every thought, believing in every message, and acting automatically on all that is heard. The orator is you. The audience is your own mind. The message is your constant inner speech, forever preaching, programming, and defining the quality of your life.

Align your inner-speech with the life you want.

"It is our inner conversations, which make tomorrow's facts."[41]

Think how inspiration stirs your blood when hearing a great orator give a moving speech. It can awaken tired dreams, jar emotions, and change lives.

It's the same with inner speech.

Most people let what the Buddhists call "monkey mind" direct their lives. They're unaware of how their inner monkey is mindlessly swinging from thought to thought, attracting whatever it's "ooh-oohing" and "aa-aahing" about.

Monkey-minded inner yipping creates monkey-minded lives.

Not fair! I don't feel good! I hate my hair! Ooh, ooh, aah, aah! I'm too busy, too tired, too broke. Yip, yip, yap, yap. I want a banana. Look, a bird! I hate this weather.

Empowering inner speech creates empowering lives.

With a powerful reason, I can find a way to achieve anything. It's never too late. I expect success.

If the movie of your life is directed by your inner speech, why not fire the monkey and write your own script? Like the old showbiz adage says—"If it ain't on the page, it ain't on the stage." Start by watching the inner movie that's showing right now. What's currently playing in the theatre nearest you, or should I say, the theatre within you?

Is it a love story or a horror story, light inspiration or dark drama, thriller or downer, comedy or tragedy, independent or formula, action-adventure or boring documentary?

Who wrote the script?

You or your family,

You or your guidance counselor,

You or your peer pressure,

You or your fear pressure,

You or the manic monkey?

Take creative control of your vision!

The circumstances of your life are the solidified sounds of your own inner dialog.

Like it or not, the movie playing inside is the same one showing outside.

Be the playwright and director—the Stephen Spielberg of your inner blockbuster.

Make it extraordinary! Make it powerful! Make it *you*! For whatever *you* make it, makes it real!

Ready on the set.

One: *Imagine it.*

Two: *Watch it inside.*

Three: *Live it outside!*

Aaaaannnddd ACTION!

INNER SPEECH:	*I can't! I can't! I can't! Ooh, ooh, ooh . . . aa, aa, aaaa!*
DIRECTOR:	*CUT!! I SAID, FIRE THE MONKEY!!!*

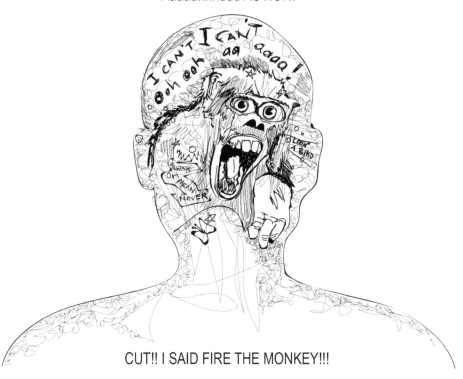

Aaaaannnddd ACTION!

CUT!! I SAID FIRE THE MONKEY!!!

SUBCONSCIOUS LAYER

The mission statement of the subconscious reads as follows:
"Your wish is my command."
The fine print:
Be careful what you wish for.
And be aware of programmed wishes you never knew you
wished.

—Dad

We are unaware of the absolute power the subconscious has in programming our dreams and controlling our lives. Everyone is hacking away at effects on the surface when they should be cultivating the field of all cause and creation below.

To achieve any wish, you *must* achieve it in the subconscious first.

If the picture hidden in your subconscious is out of alignment with the picture in your conscious mind, the ecosystem of your vision will collapse.

All change, all dreams, all visions live or die based on *ideas*, which have grown strong enough to harden into *feelings* buried in the subconscious.

Impress an empowering idea (feeling) on your subconscious, and your subconscious will bring it to life. Impress a disempowering idea (feeling), and it will do the same. An idea or vision with no feeling will blow away like seeds in the wind. That is why the *reasons* behind your vision are so important. Reasons fuel feelings, and the magnetic glue of commitment. Feelings direct the subconscious, and the subconscious creates the circumstances of your life.

To command your life, command your subconscious.

To command your subconscious, command your feelings.

"A change of feeling is a change of destiny."[42]

You have been given a great gift.

"Through the power to imagine and feel, and the freedom to choose the idea you will entertain, you have control of creation."[43]

SUBCON STUDIOS
Conscious to Subconscious
Interview Series

*The subconscious is the cradle of creation. But in order to
understand how the subconscious works, you must first
understand how the subconscious and conscious minds
work together.*

—Dad

CONSCIOUS MIND: *Testing, testing, one, two, three—is this microphone on?*
SUBCONSCIOUS MIND: I'm like an "emotional" recording and production
studio. I'm always on.

What do you record and produce?
I record your every feeling and produce your every wish. I put the power of creation
at your fingertips. But to be in control of creation, we must work together.

Why? Does Subcon Studios charge by the hour?
To create the life you want, you must create it in me first. I'm the root. The
circumstances of your life are the bloom.

So what's your job and what's mine?
You generate ideas through the vibration of feelings and impress them upon me.
I receive your ideas and give them form. You're the singer. I'm the tape.

So I can sing any note and you'll play it back?

As long as you sing it with feeling! No feeling, no playback.

I give orders and you take orders?

You can sing me a love song, or sing me the blues, plant weeds or flowers, poison or power.

Poison or power? That's my fourth album!

I accept any idea you impress upon me as true, and bring it to life.

Can you fulfill my deepest wish?

Together, we can move mountains. "When you make the two one [subconscious and conscious], if you say mountain move, it will move."[44]

But I didn't wish to be broke all the time.

Yes you did. Every time you complained, worried, or whined about money you impressed a vibrational message upon me, which the world calls a "feeling," saying you wished to be broke.

So if I feel lack, I'll get lack back no matter what I say.

If you're not feeling it, you're not saying it, and I can't hear it.

Okay, record this! I'm rich, I'm rich, I'm rich! Abracadabra! Am I rich yet?

All I hear is I'm rich. I'm scared!! I'm rich. I'm scared!!

But I didn't say I'm scared!

No, but your feelings did. And true or false, good or bad, constructive or destructive, the dominant of two feelings is the one I'll express.

So constantly worrying about money makes a stronger impression on you than an occasional, timid wish for wealth.

The "worry wish" is an all-time greatest hit! I call it the "worry inversion." You wish and worry at the same time. Instead of getting your wish, you get your worry.

Now I'm worried that I worry too much.

"Never dwell on difficulties. Never wallow in the imperfections of yourself or others. Be careful of your moods and feelings, for there is an unbreakable connection between your feelings and your visible world."[45]

Bummer.

There you go again, wishing for something to be bummed out about!

I am just sooooo grateful!

Now you've got it. More to be grateful for is on its way.

CONSCIOUSNESS LAYER

The subconscious is a part of the ecosystem of consciousness
itself . . .
The omniscient, omnipotent, omnipresent source of all
power, some call God.

—Dad

Consciousness is the ocean.
  We're the fish.
  We're swimming in it.
Like the ocean, which takes on different characteristics at different sea levels, consciousness takes on different characteristics at different consciousness levels.

Your perception of the world, field of thoughts, and quality of life are spawned from the consciousness level you're swimming in.

There are two things to consider when picturing the one reality of consciousness:

1. Consciousness
2. Consciousness level

I can hear you now. "Uh-oh! Dad's getting too deep. It's time to act like I'm listening and check my texts!"

I remember the three of you girls playing games with your friend Kelsey as children. Kelsey said, "The loser of the game will be tied to a chair and forced to listen to your dad's deep thoughts." The ocean of consciousness is not that deeeeeeep!

Consciousness is the ocean. We're the fish. We're swimming in it.

ALL is consciousness. Consciousness is ALL

You don't need to know a million things about spirituality, quantum physics, or psychology, yada, yada, yada. I don't know how texting works, but I text every day. So turn off your cell phone, put down Kelsey's rope, and stick with me now.

Consciousness is the one thinking substance that makes up all of existence.

Picture this one substance as invisible Play-Doh. You can mold it into anything you want with your thoughts. (As long as your thoughts have grown strong enough to form feelings!)

A thought impressed upon the Play-Doh of consciousness creates the thing imagined by the thought.[46]

Your subconscious is part of consciousness like a drop of water is part of the ocean. What you hold in mind, melds with the creative mind of the universe.

Okay! Now that I've explained the power of consciousness, and how you can mold it into anything you wish, with your intentions . . . could you please have Kelsey untie the loser so we can move on to the subject of the different consciousness levels?

And don't worry!

Because repetition is the mother of learning—rope or no rope—I'll repeat this hoity-toity sounding stuff until it's as familiar as texting.

LEVEL OF CONSCIOUSNESS LAYER

Our consciousness level is the root.
Feeling is the branch.
Thought is the bud.
Our life circumstance is the bloom.

—Dad

T he greatest thinkers in the history of mankind have all told us the same thing. Our inner thoughts create the outer circumstances of our lives.

"For as he thinks in his heart, so is he."
—Proverbs 23:7

"The world we have created is a product of our thinking."
—Einstein

"We are formed and molded by our thoughts."
—Buddha

"A man is but the product of his thoughts. What he thinks he becomes."
—Gandhi

"Wealth is a mindset. It's all about how you think."
—Schirmer

131

"Man can alter his life by altering his thinking."
—William James

"I get what I think about, whether I want it or not."
—Dyer

And my personal favorite . . .

"Did you ever stop to think, and forget to start again?"
—Winnie-the-Pooh

Each one of these great thinkers is right, and in my case, even Winnie-the-Pooh.
But there's a *but*.
And I say this with humility, respect, and a little nervousness.
These incredible minds are only half-right.
Stating *a* truth, not *the* truth.
They didn't look far enough.
They only described the branches not the roots.
Yes! Your thoughts do create your world.
But it is your consciousness level, which determines your field of thoughts.
To truly change your thoughts, you must change your level of consciousness.
I know!
Level of what?
There are seventeen levels of consciousness attainable in this world.[47]
Huh?
Aware of it or not, each one of us is living at a certain level.
Each consciousness level comes with an attractor field of corresponding feelings.
Each feeling creates thousands, even millions, of "involuntary" thoughts.
Since our thoughts create our world,
And our consciousness level creates our feelings, which creates our thoughts,
It is our consciousness level that determines the quality of our lives.
Phew!
I know what you're thinking!
Huh?
To change your consciousness level,
Therefore your feelings,
Therefore your thoughts,
Therefore your life,
It'd be helpful to know specifically what the heck a consciousness level even is!
To help you understand, let's eavesdrop in on another conversation. This time,
one between the Self, which is the real you—the spiritual you with a capital *S*—and
the self, which is the ego—the animal you—the illusionary you with a small *s*.

Each level is a measurable energy field, which. . .
Colors your outlook and paints your reality.

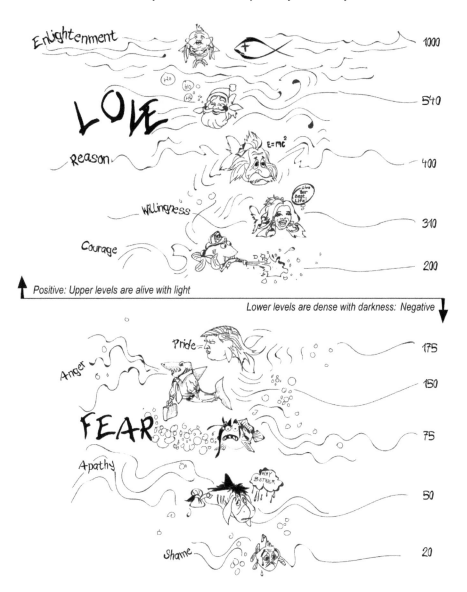

SELF-TO-selfie TALK

SELF: *Consciousness is the one substance, which makes up all of existence.*
Consciousness is the ocean. You're the fish. You're swimming in it.
selfie: *I know! You said that already! I'm a fish swimming in the ocean of*
consciousness. Geez!

—Dad

SELF (real you): Now that you understand the universal electromagnetic energy field and matrix of all existence called consciousness, let's move on to the subject of the different consciousness levels.

selfie (ego):   Am I a carp or a tuna?

Like the ocean, which takes on different characteristics at different sea levels, consciousness takes on different characteristics at different consciousness levels.

You can tune a ukulele, but you can't tuna fish. Lol! Maybe I'm a clown fish?

The bottom of the ocean is darker and deader than the top. Same with consciousness: the upper levels are alive with light; the lower levels are dense with darkness.

A carp is a bottom feeder. I'm top of the heap! Of course! I'm the kingfish!

Consciousness is energy. Use the two words interchangeably. Each level is measurable energy field, which colors your outlook, and paints your *perception*. Like the different sea levels . . .

Apathy is an energy level.

Guilt is an energy level.

Fear is an energy level.

Desire, anger, and pride are negative energy levels at the bottom.

Likewise, courage is an energy level.

Willingness is an energy level.

Acceptance is an energy level.

Joy, reason, and love—all the way up to enlightenment—are positive energy levels at the top. Each level attracts more of the same into our lives.

Like schools of fish, each level comes with schools of feelings, which in turn, spawn gigantic schools of thought, all swimming together.

Millions of thoughts? Like the schools of krill fish in the movie Finding Nemo?

Yes! One feeling creates thousands of thoughts. You can replace thousands, even millions of thoughts with a single, feeling.[48] If you're swimming at the consciousness level of fear, you'll have more fear feelings, which create more fear thoughts, and consequently, more things to be afraid of in your life.

Looky there! I just hooked a stress bass, or is that a worry walleye. It could be an anger fish, pride perch, or a sad and blue gill. Whoa! There are millions of them!

Throw it back. Fear fish are poisonous.

So if you're swimming in pride, you'll attract schools of self-fish. Get it?

I get it, "selfish."

How does pride taste?

It's hard to swallow. Gets stuck in your throat.

If you're swimming in joy, you'll attract more thoughts and things to be joyful about. If you're swimming at the level of love, you'll be surrounded by love.

Like goes to like.

So the question you might want to ask yourself before diving into your dreams is—what conscious level am I swimming in everyday? Are you submerged in anger?

I'M NOT ANGRY!!

Or floating in peace?

I SAID I'M NOT *#%@ ANGRY!!

Drowning in fear?

I was afraid you were going to ask that.

Or bathing in love?

Yes! That's me! Like the David Cassidy song, "I Think I Love Me." (Or was it "I Think I Love You"? Nah! I'm the ego. It's love me, me, me!)

The levels of consciousness progress like a ladder from weak to strong. Each rung on the ladder has an innate level of energy, which is literally measurable on a logarithmic scale from 1 to 1,000. Guilt is a life-sucking energy, which calibrates at 30 on the scale of consciousness. Love is a life-giving energy, which calibrates at 500.

Who do you think has more built-in power to charge up their vision, someone whose batteries are drained at 30 watts, or someone who's buzzing with magnetism at 500 watts? Who would draw you in, and who would you avoid like the plague? Positive or negative, the magnetism you're throwing out pulls both ways.

Okay, so what exactly is the ladder of consciousness? What are the seventeen rungs, and why do I have the sudden urge to sing "Stairway to Heaven" by Led Zeppelin?

As you've already seen, Dr. David R. Hawkins developed a practical map of the energy fields of consciousness, which outline the levels from weak to strong. It's Hawkins who calibrated the power (or lack of) of the different consciousness levels on a logarithmic scale of 1–1,000.

Here is a CliffsNotes version of his map, which represents the entire spectrum of consciousness levels, and correlating energy from weak to strong, attainable in this world.

Consciousness Level	Energy Level
Enlightenment	700–1,000
Peace	600
Joy/Unconditional Love	540
Love	500
Reason	400
Acceptance	350
Willingness	310
Neutrality	250
Courage	200

Level 200 marks the demarcation line of integrity, between truth and falsehood.

Pride	175
Anger	150
Desire	125
Fear	100
Grief	75
Apathy/Hatred	50
Guilt	30
Shame	20

Above 200 is positive, below is negative. Above 200 is power, below is force.

So this is the stairway to heaven Led Zeppelin was singing about!

The map of consciousness is the stairway to heaven within. When your father wrote the lyric, "The real journey leads inside, I pray you'll travel far," this is what he was singing and praying for—that you *travel far* on the journey from fear to love.

Maybe we could turn Hawkins's map into a song too? Hmm . . .

What rhymes with consciousness?

HAPPINESS LEVEL = CONSCIOUSNESS LEVEL

*Our level of consciousness colors the perception and
experience of our everyday lives, which determines the
happy or sad of our everyday lives.*

—Dad

SELF: Your happiness level equals your consciousness level. To be happy—raise your consciousness level by removing fear and negativity.

selfie: What's the rate of happiness for someone engulfed in desire?

Ten percent.

Courage?

Fifty-five percent.

Why?

Desire is an energy of grasping and wantonness, which says, "I'm incomplete. If I don't win *The Voice*, I'll die!" Whereas courage is a can-do energy—the level of empowerment, accomplishment, and determination.

How about pride?

Twenty-two percent.

So being an ego that depends on people to notice my greatness won't make me happy?

Pride depends on external events, not internal confidence for its fragile payoffs. A puffed up self-image is vulnerable and weak. If you're always on guard, you're living in fear.

What's the rate of happiness for the upper levels of consciousness such as . . .

Willingness?
Sixty-eight percent.
Acceptance?
Seventy-one percent.
Reason?
Seventy-nine percent.
How do you know this?
Hawkins! Consciousness research.
How about the level of love?
Eighty-nine percent.
Unconditional love?
Ninety-six percent.
Enlightenment?
One hundred percent.
You are only happy to the same degree you are enlightened.[49]
Not only does our level of consciousness determine our rate of happiness, it determines how we perceive the world and experience everyday life.
Why?
Because we don't see the world as it is, we perceive the world as we are. We view life and the world from the vantage point of our level of consciousness.[50]
Someone viewing the world from the consciousness level of apathy will see the world as hopeless.
It's kind of hard to design a life and enjoy the day when everything looks hopeless!
Someone viewing the world from the consciousness level of guilt will see the world through a lens of self-blame. Someone at the level of pride will see only social rank and status. Someone at the level of anger will see an angry, competitive world.
They are all illusions! Someone like Grandma Hanky, who views the world from the consciousness level of love, will see goodness in everything. That's real power!
I thought I was power.
You're force.
Only when we rise to the level of courage at 200, can truth and power emerge. Below 200 is nothing but falsehood and force.
Hawkins again?
Yup!
He's going to be the death of me.
Now you're getting it.

Your level of happiness stems from your place on the inner road. . .
No matter what's happening—"good or bad"—on the outer.

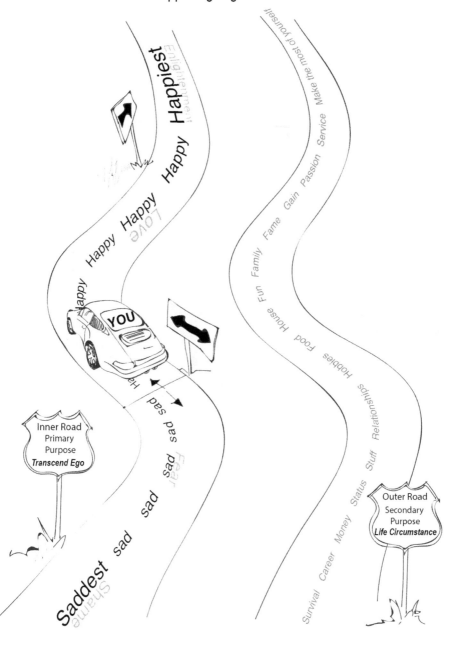

A TALE OF TWO MOTIVES

The blessing or curse of your vision fulfilled is a matter of motivation.

—Dad

W hat's the difference between Bill and Bernie?

Bill is one of the richest men on earth. His motives were to change the world and use his imagination to innovate; stretch his own capabilities, better people's lives, expand our thinking, and broaden what's possible.

Bernie was also one of the richest men on earth. He too used his imagination to create unprecedented wealth. But his motives were greed, pride, extreme narcissism, and lust for power.

Bill's life was good.

Bernie's life looked good.

Bill's life was fulfilling.

Bernie's life was filled with lies.

Bill's life had challenges, but they were meaningful, thus worthy of his efforts.

Bernie's life "was a nightmare, living with this axe over your head."[51]

Bill's work has left the world a better place.

Bernie's work has *left a legacy of shame.*

Bill Gates made his fortune serving the world by revolutionizing computer software. His estimated worth is sixty-five billion dollars. He's now doing his best to heal the world with his fortune, through the Bill and Melinda Gates Foundation.

140

Bernie Madoff made his fortune through a Ponzi scheme. He stole an estimated sixty-five billion dollars from his clients. He's now doing 150 years behind bars at a federal prison in North Carolina.

Bill cares about others. His philosophy: "Pair the self-interest that is the hallmark of capitalism with interest in the welfare of others."[52]

Bernie cares about himself. His philosophy: "F--k my victims. I carried them for twenty years, and now I'm doing 150 years."

Bill's fortune, and Bernie's misfortune, stemmed from the inside out.

If Bill never revolutionized computer software, his higher consciousness level would have found another way to create a fulfilling life for himself and others.

If Bernie never hatched his infamous Ponzi scheme, his lower consciousness level would have found another hell for him to learn from.

What's the difference between Bill and Bernie? Two things:

1. Consciousness level: We attract what we are, not what we pursue.
2. Motivation: Blessing or curse is a matter of motivation.

AS WITHIN, SO WITHOUT

The Kingdom of heaven is within you.
Look closer at what lies below.
It is the heaven within (or hell within), which Jesus
spoke of.

—Dad

To sum it up: Like an iceberg, you can look at the ecosystem of your vision, and your life, from the viewpoint of what lies above and below—without and within.

Above
Bloom of your vision fulfilled
Action
Strategy
Below
Consciousness
Consciousness level
Imagination
Intention
Meaning
Motivation (love or fear?)
Self-concept
Self-worth

Habitual thoughts and mood
Inner speech
Subconscious mind
Subconscious beliefs
Feelings
Decision and commitment
Clarity
Surrender

Most of the ecosystem of your vision lies below and within.

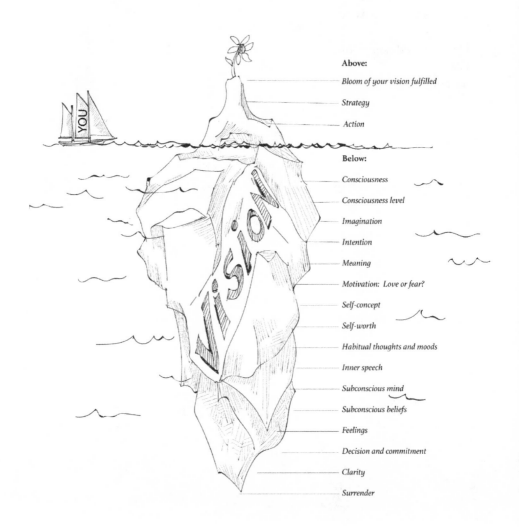

Above:

Bloom of your vision fulfilled

Strategy

Action

Below:

Consciousness

Consciousness level

Imagination

Intention

Meaning

Motivation: Love or fear?

Self-concept

Self-worth

Habitual thoughts and moods

Inner speech

Subconscious mind

Subconscious beliefs

Feelings

Decision and commitment

Clarity

Surrender

No part of your vision can be isolated from the others and still thrive.
What happens above is dependent on what happens below.

Notice most of the ecosystem of your vision is below the surface.
As Jesus said, "As within so without. The Kingdom of heaven is within you."[53]
Look closer at what lies below the tip of the iceberg.
It is the heaven within (or hell within), which Jesus spoke of.

I repeat and repeat and repeat . . .
Your inside life *is* life.
Your inside energy, positive or negative, creates your outside world.

And your inside energy also includes a force fueling every vision—one that provides the current (currency) from which all ideas, creativity, and yes, even *love* grows and flows . . .
Can you guess?
It's not bigger than a breadbox, but it is our bread and butter.
To *coin* a phrase ~~buy~~ by Eric Butterworth (LOL!):
"It's God in action."
Huh?
That's right.
Cash$$$
(And I don't mean Johnny.)
Yeah, you heard me.
Money!
Your inside life determines your financial life too.

BIG HEART, SMALL PAYCHECK

Mindset: *A fixed attitude or state of mind; an inclination or a habit.*
Mechanics: *The details about how something works or is done.*
Wealth *= 80% mindset + 20% mechanics*

—Dad

Grandma Hanky was brought up in a small midwestern town where good people worked hard, sacrificed for their kids, and proudly stood on their own two feet to just get by. Though she always worked hard for her money, she was never taught about, and never thought about, how to make her money work for her. No one ever told Grandma Hanky (or me) about passive income, compound interest, investing, paying yourself first, and basic financial literacy.

The cycle stops here!

Combine an abundance mindset with the simple mechanics of growing money, and you'll be as wealthy as you want to be.

But what if you're not called to be an entrepreneur, not cut out for starting companies, not interested in creating your own job, not a mover, shaker, or part-time rainmaker?

Grandma Hanky was a nurse for forty-two years! She was *paid to be a nurse*, but there is no doubt that this rare, loving soul was also *made to be a nurse*.

Think about the conversation your Uncle Joey captured on video with her before she died. Grandma welled up with tears as she reminisced about the thousands of

146

patients she was honored to serve. Joey asked her why that memory made her cry. She said, "because they helped me more than I helped them." Obviously, Grandma Hanky did not choose the profession of nursing for money. It was her calling. It was her passion. In a very real sense, nursing chose her.

There's no need to choose between your profession and wealth—between your heart and your wallet. I repeat. So-called success without fulfillment is failure. I've never met a more successful person than Grandma Hanky.

Many of your friends have chosen important professions like nursing and teaching that will never pay a lot of money. I can't think of people with a more important job than the amazing hospice workers who took care of Grandma in her last days.

How does someone like Grandma Hanky use their small wage to grow great wealth? The first answer to that question is foundational—mindset. They have to believe they can, and they have to release any negative judgments they may have about money. The second answer is they have to educate themselves. And the third is they have to focus! To turn their wages into wealth, they must *consistently focus* on turning their wages into wealth.

Grandma Hanky's financial focus was laser-beam sharp for the things she deeply cared about, such as the magic of Christmas for her six crazy kids. I could never figure out how she conjured up the money for the magic.

Each year she giddily showered presents on her six children, cousins, coworkers, janitors, doctors, patients, friends, neighbors, mailman, garbageman, milkman, strangers, the homeless, shut-ins, teachers, relatives, not to mention the backyard birds.

I found out later in life that starting December 26, a large portion of her small nursing check went into a savings account for building next year's Christmas memories (mechanics). Grandma knew what she wanted, she knew why, and she focused on the outcome (mindset).

Every Christmas of my childhood was magical.

Well done, my dear mother! Thank you from the bottom of my Christmas heart!

If Grandma had known about the nuts and bolts of wealth, that same driving purpose—*love of her children*—that same spiritual meaning—*give and you shall receive*—that same Christmas reason, which her beautiful life personified—*unconditional love*—would have made her a millionaire mom.

Of course, she would have given the money away.

But that's what *she* loved to do.

I really miss her.

I try every day not to focus on that.

MONEY IS . . .
The Mindset of Making Money

*Your financial life cannot be any different than your
financial self-concept.*

—Dad

Money is . . . an effect of our self-concept, not the cause.

Being broke is a financial statement. Being poor is a frame of mind. I've been broke but never poor.

Poverty or abundance is a reflection of who we think we are. Many people have a poverty consciousness. They may have been brought up in a poor, fearful, or negative family, and conditioned to believe poverty defines who they are.

Fear ran their finances.

One of my music business students showed me his three-year financial dreams. Year 1, make $2,000; Year 2, $3,000; Year 3, $100,000. His self-definition of a realistic income was $2,000. His idea of being wildly successful, like winning the lotto, was $100,000. Putting aside the fact that his low numbers were not backed up by a specific plan, his projections revealed his low self-concept.

The universe will give whatever we ask of it. Why do we ask such small questions of an infinite universe? The answer is simple—a low self-concept and ignorance of how to access the miracles at our fingertips. Limiting beliefs are lies, which if persisted in, harden into facts.

My student defined himself.

His self-definition of poverty would determine his income.

The same conditioning applies to a self-concept of abundance.

While delivering antiques to a wealthy family in the Hamptons, Grandpa Harvey was telling one of the children about his illustrious career as an airline pilot. The boy was so excited by his colorful stories that right then and there, he decided what he was going to be when he grew up. Grandpa thought he was going to say, "I wanna be a pilot too!" Instead the boy confidently said, "When I grow up, I want to own an airline!" He was conditioned to think of owning versus working by the family and surroundings he grew up in. There was not a speck of ego involved. His large expectations were completely natural. The boy was conditioned to think bigger, ask bigger questions, and *expect abundance.*

I asked Jessie to vacuum the kitchen and she kiddingly replied, "How much is it worth to you?" I knew she was joking, but saw it as a teachable moment. I told her, "Life will pay whatever price you ask of it." Her reply, "Okay, twenty bucks!" Ouch! To get my point across I paid her the $20 for five minutes of work. That was either great parenting or the worst ever. To this day she razzes me about taking advantage of my "teachable moment." Maybe somewhere inside, the message got through.

You don't have to be brought up in a wealthy East Hampton family to have an abundance consciousness. You just have to be aware of your limiting beliefs and reject them. They are lies! They are garbage! Remove the garbage!

In their place substitute anything you want.

Anything you love.

Anything that matters.

Life will pay whatever price you ask of it.

So name your price.

It worked for Jessie!

Money is . . . releasing your negative judgment about money.

Many people feel guilty for wanting to be rich. Unconscious guilt and negativity about money will keep them poor.

"You can make the most of yourself only by getting rich, so it is right and praiseworthy that you should give your first thought to the work of acquiring wealth. It is the desire of God that you should be rich."[54]

If that statement by Wallace Wattles bothers you, you may have a negative judgment about money.

The urge to play the piano, the passion to start a business, the call to grow at anything you love is the natural urge of life seeking its own fulfillment and expression. The reason to become wealthy is not to hoard trinkets and show off; it's to free your life force to bloom into full beauty.

There's a big difference between lust for money, and the natural urge for well-being.

Greed cuts off the current of life.

Making the most of yourself increases the flow.

The two sides of the coin confuse people into believing the natural desire to acquire wealth is unspiritual. Do you really think that all rich people are unspiritual and all poor people are holy? Gandhi—one of the holiest men to ever walk the earth said, "Capital as such is not evil; it is its wrong use that is evil. Capital in some form or other will always be needed." Rid yourself of the false belief that money is a necessary evil! Money is neutral. It follows your lead.

I want you to stand up and shout it,

Sit down and write it,

Lie down and envision it,

Just admit it!

"I want to acquire all the wealth I need to make the most of myself!"

Believe it!

"I have all the wealth I need to make the most of myself!"

Live it like it's already done. Lemme hear you now!

"I have acquired all the wealth I need to make the most of myself!"

Remember! *The most of yourself* is unlimited.

The unlimited wealth of the universe is ready to take your order.

Money is . . . an investor mindset.

Shift your mindset from earner/consumer to that of an investor.

I am an investor!

I am an investor!

I am an investor!

How do you change your mindset from consumer to investor, and transform yourself into a virtuoso investor *right now?!*

The formula is simple.

"Spend less than you make.

"No matter what your finances, invest every month, starting *now*.

"Reinvest returns."[55]

Voilà!

You're an investor.

You can't earn your way to financial freedom with a paycheck alone. But you can use your paycheck, no matter what the size, to build financial freedom.

And with patient and consistent investing,

You won't be just any ol' hit and miss investor . . .

You'll be a wealthy investor.

Money is . . . a service mindset.
The bigger the difference you make,
> The bigger the money you make.
> Use your talents to serve.
> Even if you're serving fast food at McDonald's. When asking the customer, "Do you want fries with that?" along with the fries, ask yourself, *How I can serve them?*

Look at every job, big or small, as an opportunity to make a difference. The bigger the difference—the bigger the money: Cultivate a "service mindset" no matter what, and your money, position, and *disposition* will increase.

I was hired to compose a low-budget jingle for a local L.A. car company called Dale's Auto Mart. The jingle didn't mean much to me, financially or creatively. But here's the bottom line—it meant a lot to Dale! So I used my talent to serve and gave Dale my all.

Big budget, low budget, or no budget doesn't matter. View each project as a gift—another chance to serve. Doing great work (service) no matter what, leads to greater work (service). Cutting corners cuts off the flow of opportunity and cash.

Give the world the best you have to offer, and it will always give back.
Use your talents to serve, and you'll have all the money you need to keep serving.
Oh, and one more not so little thing . . .
I call it "heart payment."
The smile on Dale's face made me smile as well.
☺
"You want fries with that?"

Money is . . . a mindset of value, value, value!
Focus on creating value,
> And you'll create wealth.
> Duh!
> I wish I had learned this sooner. Creating wealth is sooo simple.
> Create value!
> Create value!
> Create value!
> Snooze. What does that boring word "value" really mean?
> It means . . .
> Help people!
> Help people!
> Help people!

"The only way to become wealthy and stay wealthy," says Tony Robbins, "is to find a way to do more for others than anyone else is doing in an area that people really value."[56] As Einstein says, "Try not to become a man of success, but rather a man of value."

Focus on creating value first, and you'll make money. Making money is a by-product of helping people (creating value), not the other way around. The more people you help, the more money you make. How perfect is that?

Creating wealth by helping people is built into the business plan of the universe.

Is there a group of people you can help with your talent, idea, skills, or interests? Think BIG!

Help as many people as you can, and you'll not only make money, you'll be wealthy. It's as simple as that. No MBA required.

Duh!

Money is . . . a mindset of high standards.

If you want to raise your income,

    Raise your standards!

Standards determine how high you will climb.

To paraphrase author Tony Robbins,

Poor standards get no financial rewards (poor pay, no pay, or fired),

Good standards get poor rewards (good is the new below average),

Excellent standards get okay rewards (excellent is the new average),

Outstanding gets all the rewards.

"Excellence sucks!"[57]

It's no longer enough.

Who won fourth place in the Olympics? They attained world-class excellence, but Outstanding received all the rewards.[58]

The Buddhists say, "There's a half an inch between heaven and hell." The same applies to standards and rewards.

Outstanding is a rarefied state located half an inch above excellent. Think of it! Half an inch is the difference between a life of untold rewards or just getting by.

Stand out!

Half an inch is a journey worth taking.

Money is . . . a mindset of ideas *and* execution.

I hear a million brilliant ideas from a million different people. Not one in a million commits, starts, and executes. If they did, they'd make millions.

I never worry about people stealing ideas. They'd have to steal the commitment, purpose, and passion it takes to execute along with it.

Once you have an idea, focus everything you've got on its execution. People worry about getting it perfect, so they never start. Perfection is a low standard that creates nothing but wasted time.

Embrace imperfection. It's a sign that you're taking action.

"Start before you're ready."[59]

Start before you're ready.

Start before you're ready.

Muddle through until muddling bursts into momentum.

And muddle your way to clarity.

The greatest idea in the world is nonexistent without execution.

Money is . . . a mindset that's laser-beam specific.

Don't send the universe the alphabet and ask it to write a story for you. Write the story first and make it crystal clear.

Order up the

Specific,

Detailed,

Outcome of the income,

You wish to bring into your life.

No amount of money will make you wealthy.

There's a big difference between wealth and financial independence.

True wealth (well-being) means each of the inner and outer strings of your life are in tune and harmonizing with each other, *including* the financial string.

The parts are integrated (integrity) with the whole (holy).

Financial independence is freedom to live what you love without *needing* to work.

Though I want you to be financially independent . . .

I never want you to pursue financial independence at the expense of wealth.

But a specific amount of money, which is different for everyone, can create a foundation for wealth. According to Tony Robbins, there are three financial buckets you can choose to fill or not. I want you to take the time to visualize a specific number and timeline for each of these buckets. Talk to Mom, talk to me, or talk to an expert who can help you determine what *your* numbers might be.

Financial security for life: Housing, car, food, basic entertainment: $_____

Financial independence for life: Everything covered: $_____

Financial freedom: Anything you can think of is covered:[60]$_____

You choose the lifestyle. You choose the dream. You choose the number.

Visualize.

Form a clear picture of what you want, take action with faith and purpose.

And truly, truly, truly

Believe!

Money is . . . YOU being YOU!

Be who you are!

If you are not, nothing else matters, and nothing else works.

You can't have outstanding standards.

You can't provide indispensable value.

You can't make money making a difference.

You can't master anything you don't care about.

There'll be no passion driving you further. Your self-concept will be weak, confused, and worst of all, you will never be happy. As you blame and play the victim, your outer world will reflect the inner.

Money is the effect, not the cause.

There's only one way out and one way up.

Be Who You Are!

If you are not, you may survive, you may even make lots of money . . .

But you will NEVER thrive!

IMPOSSIBLE!

MAILBOX MONEY
Money Making Mechanics 101

*I don't want you to spend a lifetime working hand to mouth
for money. I want you to learn how to make your
money work for you.*

—Dad

Make money while you sleep!
They call it passive income.
I call it "mailbox money."
What's that?

mailbox money /ˈmālˈbäks/ /ˈmˈnē/ : Income received on a regular basis, with little time or effort required to maintain it once the initial work and foundation have been laid. (Magic mailbox required. Construction and content of magic mailbox vary.)

Most college and high school students, the ones with the greatest potential for checking the mail for a living, are financially illiterate and know nothing about passive income. They're herded like sheep into whatever field or major they're interested in without any advice on how to use their wages to create real wealth. No matter what you're majoring in, the first step is to focus and learn all you can about finances and the wonders of passive income. Become a mailbox money virtuoso.

155

The next step is to create a vision, commit, plan it, and schedule it into your day. Once that's done, add the not-so-secret sauce . . . work and work and work and work! *Passive income does not mean passive effort.* It requires energy, enthusiasm, and hard work to build a magic money mailbox that keeps on delivering while you sleep.

Ideas to create mailbox money are as infinite as your interests. You already have an abundance of ideas and interests that could help others. Start there. Use them to create real value, and you'll create real money. Is there an uncommon approach to a common practice or problem you could update? How can you use your field of passion to create mailbox money above and beyond your salary?

Ryan Seacrest had a master plan: "The plan is to build something that doesn't require me to stand there and do it." He started his own company that produced hit TV shows such as *Jamie Oliver's Food Revolution, Keeping Up with the Kardashians,* and many others to build his mailbox. This is above and beyond his day job as radio host of American Top 40, KIIS FM morning jock, and E! channel series producer.

Are you a freelancer who works from project to project? Instead of charging a fee for your various services, ask for a piece of the equity on projects you believe in.

Are you a singer? There are jingle singers earning seven figure incomes by stacking up royalties on three-hour recording sessions done years earlier. Are you a photographer? Create an online site where people could license your photos while you sleep. Are you an aerobics instructor? Put out a series of your own workout DVDs. (That's what I'm going to do—*Belly by Brandmeier*—it's going to be big! The belly, not the DVD.) Are you good at real estate? Buy a property and rent it. You could create an app, write an e-book, start a blog, and on and on and on and on. Yes, there may be a lot of people doing things like this, but there is only one you. *You* are the unique selling proposition in any business you start.

Dig into the toolbox of your resourcefulness, which is much more important than your resources. You've already got the raw materials of imagination and talent. Transform them into a clear outcome, purpose, and plan.

"You're like an eighteen-wheeler filled with lumber. What are you going to build, man?" That's how John Mayer challenged students at Berklee College of Music. What's your answer? How will you use the lumber of your ideas to build your magic mailbox? Which business planks will lay the foundation? Decide! Start building! Now!

Make money while you sleep.

To build a magic money mailbox, create a vision, commit, plan it, schedule it. . .
and work, and work, and work, and work!

COMPOUND INTEREST

Like gravity, an almost magical force of nature exists, so
powerful, so life changing, yet so unassuming, nobody
pays attention.
Albert Einstein called it "the eighth wonder of the world.
He who understands it, earns it; he who doesn't
pays it."
You'll be paid royally for paying attention or pay dearly for
ignoring it. What did Einstein call the most powerful
force in the world?
Compound interest.

—Dad

D o not moan and complain about not making enough money to get rich. That's garbage-in that will create garbage-out. It's possible to become a "minimum-wage millionaire" by harnessing the power of compound interest. It's a financial tool that any wage earner can use to use to create wealth.

If I told you that I could turn one penny into five million dollars in a month, through the magic of compound interest, would you believe me?

If I presented you with two choices: give you $1,000,000 today or give you one penny today, and compound its value by doubling it for 30 days, which would you choose?

Go ahead! Make a choice, and see if it was the best one.

Behold the power of a single penny and the magic of compound interest.

Day 1: $0.01
Day 2: $0.02
Day 3: $0.04
Day 4: $0.08
Day 5: $0.16
Day 6: $0.32
Day 7: $0.64
Day 8: $1.28
Day 9: $2.56
Day 10: $5.12
Day 11: $10.24
Day 12: $20.48
Day 13: $40.96
Day 14: $81.92
Day 15: $163.84
Day 16: $327.68
Day 17: $655.36
Day 18: $1,310.72
Day 19: $2,621.44
Day 20: $5,242.88
Day 21: $10,485.76
Day 22: $20,971.52
Day 23: $41,943.04
Day 24: $83,886.08
Day 25: $167,772.16
Day 26: $335,544.32
Day 27: $671,088.64
Day 28: $1,342,177.28
Day 29: $2,684,354.56
Day 30: $5,368,709.12

Did you choose the million dollars or the penny?

Don't tell me you can't become a millionaire! Don't tell me you can't become anything you want to become!

So what's in the pixie dust that gives compound interest its sorcerous bang? Mix the magic potion of time, patience, consistency, and compounding in any amount, and almost without notice, untold riches will appear.

The same two magic words that lead to the mastery of anything are the two words that lead to mastering the forces of compound interest.

Patience and consistency.

The secret is starting early, and letting *time build wealth for you.* The later you start, the less time can work for you, and the more you have to work against it.

Rachel Cruze, author of *The Graduate's Survival Guide,* gives a great example of letting time and money work for you.

Ben invested $2,000 a year at 12 percent interest, or $167.00 per month, starting at age nineteen. He stopped investing after eight years, at age twenty-seven, and let time and his $16,000 work for him. His brother Arthur did the same thing, but didn't start until he was twenty-seven. To make up for lost time, he continued investing for thirty-nine years.

Ben saved for eight years and let time do the rest. Arthur saved for thirty-nine years but gave his employee of time the first eight years off. Who do you think ended up with more money?

Due to the magic of compound interest, Ben came out $700,000 ahead.

Ben's eight-year, $16,000 investment: $2,288,996

Arthur's thirty-nine-year, $78,000 investment: $1,532,166

The difference: *Time and an early start.*

The strategy: *Patient and consistent investing.*

Patience and Consistency.

Mix the magic potion of. . .
PATIENCE, CONSISTENCY, COMPOUNDING.
Untold riches will appear.

DEBT OR DREAMS: YOU DECIDE

The "dark magic" of compound interest in reverse: You can either let compound interest grow your money while you sleep or—like a mob loan shark—let it extort your money and break the legs of your dreams.

—Dad

When Einstein said of compound interest, "You either earn it, or you pay it," debt is what he was talking about. *The interest on what you owe compounds just like the interest on what you save.*

College seniors graduate with an average of nearly $27,000 in student loan debt.

The average senior will graduate with $4,100 in credit card debt; 7.2 percent of students drop out of college due to debt and financial pressure; people ages eighteen to twenty-four spend nearly 30 percent of their monthly income on debt.

They lose their dreams to debt!

You must choose between two lifestyles. One liberates your potential. The other makes you an indentured servant. The choice is serious and obvious.

Debt or dreams? You decide.

Instead of paying interest on student loans, use that same money and make interest pay you. For example . . .

DEBT:
Student loan: $10,000
Monthly payment: $115.59 for ten years

Interest paid over ten years: $3,871
Break even total paid: $13,870.80

DREAM:

Instead of borrowing, invest that same money over ten years, and you'd be $40,165.96 richer versus scrimping and scrapping for ten years to *break free* from a $13,870 debt.

Debt or dreams?
It's a decision that will affect the rest of your life.
Choose thoughtfully, choose wisely, choose powerfully!

Debt or Dreams?

Compound interest can either grow your money while you sleep, or. . .
like a mob loan shark–extort your money and break the legs of your dreams.

PAY YOURSELF FIRST

It's not what you earn, it's what you keep. Instead of buying
mall drugs, take that same money and invest. Repeat
after me!
Pay yourself first.
Pay yourself first.
Pay yourself first.

—Dad

Get rich slowly!
So how do you do that?
Follow the Warren Buffett rule.
Don't save what's left after spending; spend what's left after saving.
Turn your paycheck into an employee of YOU Inc. regardless of profession, calling, work, or lack of work.
How?
Pay yourself first!
And repeat Tony Robbins's formula 100 gazillion times.

1. Spend less than you make.
2. Invest every month starting now.
3. Reinvest returns.

Decide and commit to exactly what you want to invest each month and NEVER waver. *Forming the habit of paying yourself first* is a routine that will set you free. Like every area of life, your financial destiny is formed in your habits and routines.

Though everyone's dreams are different, everyone needs the same thing to make them real.

FREEDOM!

Mailbox money is freedom. It gives you the freedom to spend time the way you'd like and the freedom to make the most of yourself.

What kind of mail are you sending out? (Energy, actions, routines?)

Junk mail finds its way to the addresses of junk habits, junk spending, and junk thoughts.

Bulk mail finds addresses of the nonfocused, mediocre herd. Moo!

To change your address . . .

Change your habits.

Change your focus.

Change your mindset.

Pay yourself first.

Harness the power of Patience and Consistency.

Unleash the forces of compound interest—"the eighth wonder of the world. "

Just say no to debt—the dark magic of compound interest in reverse.

Raise your standards.

Master what you love, and the universe will pay you. (And you can't master what you don't love.)

Be who you are, and you'll have true wealth, which really means *well-being*.

Forget about overnight mail—there's no quick fix, no free lunch.

Trade express mail for expression mail.

Your ideas are the package.

Your execution is the postage.

Your dreams are in your hands.

Choose hand delivery over hand-to-mouth delivery.

Build your magic mailbox, and check the mail for a living.

Be free!

Have fun!

Start now!

VERSE THREE

God is in the moment,
Live each one out loud.
Keep your castles in the air and
Two feet planted on the ground.
Your masterpiece lives complete in the stone,
Imitation is fool's gold,
To let your miracle unfold, just
Be who you are

GOD IS IN THE MOMENT

Every moment was counted.
We were timing her every breath, never knowing for sure
which one would be the last. The nurses told us that a
pause of forty-five seconds between breaths meant she
could die at any moment. For reasons that God only
knows, my mom held on.
—Dad (watching over Grandma Hanky at hospice)

t was almost Christmas! We were driving through Lakeside Park, laughing like children, oohing and ahhing over the decorations, and singing Grandma's favorite Christmas song, "Away in the Manger," at the top of our lungs. On the way back, we had to stop at Tuckers Toofers drive-in and pick up a cheeseburger before calling it a night. She loved this time of year.

But Alzheimer's snuck in at light speed.

Three weeks later, as Grandma slipped into a coma, she uttered what would turn out to be her last words to your Uncle Michael. Staring straight ahead, and mustering up all the strength she had, Grandma managed a final, "*I wuv you.*" Her speech may have been broken by the impending coma, but the message summed up everything she stood for, everything she wanted her life to say.

For eight more days, the family stood and watched as Grandma slipped deeper into another world—somehow very real—one we could feel, but not see or truly understand. It's hard to explain, but as she lay there, mystical things seemed to be happening all around us.

167

Like the infamous angel picture your Uncle Michael caught outside the hospice. After snapping pictures in rapid style, one of them, unlike the others taken a split second before and after, appeared to catch the image of an angel. Though I joke with Michael about capturing a nice shot of fog, or exhaust from a car—because of his unwavering conviction, and my own intuitive knowing—I do believe it's the real thing. In a hospice setting, where people go to transition from the physical to the spiritual, it only makes sense that angels would be there, to help ease the way.

Like Clarence Oddbody, our favorite movie angel from *It's a Wonderful Life,* said, "Don't they believe in angels? Then why are they so surprised when they see one?"

After seeing an angel, Michael heard a voice. When he prayed, *Why are you letting her suffer, why don't you take her home now?,* he received a crystal-clear, two-word answer: *for you*. It seems the angels and Grandma Hanky were giving us time to adjust, and also liked to chat with Uncle Michael in very short phrases.

The incredible hospice workers—the ones who comfort the dying for a living— had stories of their own. They told us, "Mystical moments are routine at the hospice. Patients usually look at the upper corner of the ceiling when talking to deceased loved ones, angels, and anyone else that may be flying by." I witnessed Grandma talking to my deceased Dad (Grandpa Frank), friends who have passed, and someone named Edna? I still can't figure out who Edna was.

And here's the craziest one. The nurses told us that whenever the front doorbell rang—and no one was there when the bell was answered—someone in the twelve-patient hospice died within forty-eight hours. I jokingly replied, "You mean there are angels playing ding-dong ditch with the hospice?" With the nonchalance of someone describing any old job routine, every worker there, from the cook to the CEO, said,

"The doorbell has been preparing us for years." So, to insert a bit of comic relief into our vigil—every once in a while I'd sneak out and ring the doorbell to freak everyone out. One night the doorbell did mysteriously ring. The next day the patient across the hall from Grandma passed away.

Angel picture your Uncle Michael caught outside Mom's hospice room.

After snapping pictures in rapid style, one of them, unlike the others taken a split second before and after, appeared to catch an image of an angel.

LIVE EACH ONE OUT LOUD

There we were, six kids, gathered around a mother we adore, who was in an Alzheimer's induced coma, who could literally die at any moment, and in the moment we chose to express our deep love for Grandma, each other, and life, through gut-splitting laughter.

—Dad

After the last legion of visitors left, we were finally alone with Grandma. All of her kids, Johnny, me, Mary, Michael, Joey, and Jeffy were shooting off story after story as we sat around her bed. Stupid jokes were flying around the room. Goofy zingers were bouncing off the walls. Your Uncle Johnny was on fire with wacky one-liners. People were stepping on each other's punch lines, and a few comments were crossing the line. (Joey! Okay, maybe it was me.) I was laughing so hard it felt like I was getting an ab workout.

In the midst of the absolutely crazy family banter, I've come to absolutely treasure, the profound gravity of the scene hit me. I contained myself for a second and asked, "Is this what most people would do in this situation? Shouldn't we be a little more serious? Mom is near death, and we're making jokes and laughing hysterically?" After a brief moment of guilty silence, we all looked at each other and said, "Nah! There's plenty of time to add more tears to the ocean we've already spilled. Mom wants us to celebrate!"

I have no doubt that Grandma was laughing with us, although I'm sure she was also trying to tell us to keep our voices down so we don't bother the neighbors.

169

Why do we spend a lifetime showing up for church on Sunday, reciting rote prayers, giving lip service to faith, talking about spirituality, the unconditional love of God, espousing belief in an eternal spirit, then get so shocked when it comes time for our bodies to die? Do you believe this stuff or don't you? It's either real or it isn't. Life is 100 percent fatal, which makes every moment 100 percent precious. Grief and wallowing are two different things. The former is a natural part of loss, which should be allowed to run its course. The latter is narcissism—"vanity in rags instead of robes."[61]

Never let worrying about tomorrow ruin today. If we could find beauty and laughter in a moment as intense as Grandma's last moments on this earth, we can prevent any workaday worry from poisoning the day. As the Buddhists say, to learn to live, you must learn to die. As country singer Tim McGraw said, "Live like you were dying," because we all are. The death of our bodies is not the end. The "fact" is "death is not a possibility. Life itself is supported by its eternal Source, from which it cannot be separated."[62]

The greatest gift you can give to Grandma Hanky is to be happy.

Make the most of yourself.

Forgive yourself.

Forgive others.

Love yourself.

Love each other.

And live now!

God is in the moment! Live each one out loud.

But not so loud that you bother the neighbors.

FLY ME TO THE MOON

*Frank Sinatra was her Justin Bieber. She's the happiest
person I know, because she has everything she needs:
love and a good Sinatra song.*
—Josie, excerpt from her tribute to Grandma

Flash back to Wednesday night, 1947: sixteen-year-old Grandma Hanky is running home like a lovesick teenager late for a date. As president of the S.S.S.S. fan club (Swooning Souls Searching for Sinatra), there was no way she was going to miss the weekly radio broadcast of her lifelong lover, Frank Sinatra. She *loved* Sinatra!

Flash forward to her oldest son's radio show some forty years later. Your uncle Johnny is on the air with Sinatra's longtime opening act, comedian Tom Dreesen. They're arranging to have Grandma meet her idol for the first time at an upcoming concert outside of Chicago. Good things happen to good people.

Tom Dreesen rolled out the red carpet. He escorted her by limo to the concert and personally walked her backstage to meet "ole blue eyes" five minutes before he was to perform. As she approached his dressing room, the sounds of Sinatra doing vocal exercises and warming up for the show grew louder and louder. (Can you imagine that? Listening to Sinatra warm up!) Her swooning soul that had been searching for Sinatra was finally about to find him. After all these years, there he was, waiting to meet her on the other side of his dressing room door.

She wasn't disappointed. "The chairman of the board" couldn't have been more gracious.

"So, I hear you, we're the president of the Swooning Souls Searching for Sinatra fan club—thank you!" He asked what life was like in Fond du Lac, Wisconsin, about her family, how she liked being a nurse. Sinatra treated her with the respect due royalty. After posing for a picture, he bid her a warm good-bye and jumped on stage. The picture of Grandma and Sinatra stands like a shrine in the family. It was one of the greatest nights of her life.

The Picture of Grandma and Sinatra stands like a shrine in the family.
The biggest "fan girl" night of her life.

Grandma's Swooning Soul Searching for Sinatra finally found him...
Thanks to Uncle Johnny and comedian Tom Dreesen.

But it didn't end there.

Tom Dreesen had so much fun watching Grandma light up like a schoolgirl—he was so taken with her genuine kindness and class—he invited her to be his guest at Sinatra's upcoming seventy-fifth birthday party and concert in New York!

She was to stay at the Waldorf hotel and be driven in a VIP bus with a cast of Sinatra's celebrity cronies to the show at the Meadowlands Amphitheatre. On the bus, she sat behind an up-and-coming singer she wasn't yet familiar with. Grandma couldn't believe her ears when she heard him say, "I'll be bigger than Sinatra someday." She didn't like hearing that! "Well, I never! There's only one Sinatra. A lot of talented people try to copy him, but there's only one." It turns out, the singer was Harry Connick Jr. I love your passion, Harry, and think you're a great artist, but my mom's right, there's only one Sinatra. (And one Harry Connick Jr.)

But, the concert and bus ride were only the first act!

Sinatra's wife, Barbara, threw a private party for a hundred people at the Waldorf after the show. And of course, Grandma was invited to the invitation-only birthday bash.

Picture this. An unassuming small-town Wisconsin girl—a simple nurse, mother, and grandmother—sharing a table and dinner conversation at the Waldorf with Secretary of State Henry Kissinger, movie star Robert Wagner, actress Stephanie Powers, and of course, Tom Dreesen. They loved her! She never thought about glamour, limousines, and fancy parties. She often said, "My talent is admiring the talents of others." So why did everyone at the mother of all fancy parties genuinely love her company? Here's the lesson I want you to learn from Grandma Hanky.

None of the world leaders or big-time celebrities cared what she did, because in her presence they could sense who she was. Her class came from her natural goodness. Her nobility stemmed from her natural humility. Her magnetism stemmed from her natural kindness. Her conversations flowed from a natural interest in *others*. People were drawn to her because of her natural lovingness.

She stood higher than the crowds of posers, wannabe's, and look-at-me's. Aware of it or not, people could feel her authenticity. She was comfortable in her own skin. She didn't need any big hoity-toity worldly position or acclaim. She personified the rarest trait of all, and the simple message of this book, *be who you are*. People love being around those who are and avoid being around those who are not.

And one more lesson: She didn't like to talk about her trip when she returned home because she thought it would sound like bragging. She didn't want to make people feel uncomfortable. I didn't even know she had dinner with Henry Kissinger until much later. Who would you rather be around—someone who uses every pause in a conversation to say "I, I, I," or someone who doesn't need anyone's approval and is secure enough to listen?

The former fan club president of the S.S.S.S. had her wildest teenage dreams fulfilled. I'll be forever grateful to Tom Dreesen and my brother Johnny for giving Mom such unforgettable life moments.

Years later, the music of Frank Sinatra helped Grandma fall asleep when Alzheimer's relentless gnawing made it hard for her to sit, sleep, or do anything. When agitation and frustration grew into quiet suffering, I'd pull out the secret weapon—*love and a good Sinatra song*. I'd ask, "Hey Mom, wanna hear a lullaby?" As if grabbing for a lifeline that could pull her from the pain, she'd hold my hand and wait for a song. I sang the same one every time—"Fly Me to the Moon"—one of her all-time favorites.

"In other words, hold my hand" . . .

The moment she heard that melody, she peacefully fell asleep, holding my hand all the while. It worked every time, and every time it worked was a moment I'll cherish forever.

Uncle Michael took a picture of me holding Grandma's hand while sleeping in her hospice room.

I remember thinking. . .

HOLD HER HAND NOW

*I couldn't have known that the routine of holding
Grandma's hand until she fell asleep, along with her
lifelong ritual of making the sign of the cross when
saying good-bye, would be part of our final moments
together.*

—Dad

Whenever we'd head home from visiting Grandma, she'd stand in the doorway, signal to us to make the sign of the cross, and watch until we drove out of sight. It has been a ritual since we've learned to drive. The one time she didn't do this, when Alzheimer's made it hard to find her way back to her room after standing at the door, she'd call our house, worried sick because we didn't make the sign of the cross.

It had been eight days since she slipped into a coma. We were about to perform that good-bye ritual for the last time.

Your Aunt Mary, Uncle Michael, and I slept at Grandma's bedside the night before. It seemed we had been sleeping there long enough to develop a morning routine. I was putting the pullout bed back in place, Michael and Mary were tidying up, taking care of Grandma, getting dressed, and getting ready for the day. After the chores were done, we took our places. I sat on one side of the bed, Michael on the other, and Mary sat on the bed, next to Grandma.

175

Her breathing was perfect. Unlike the false alarms and ups and downs of the previous seven days, she seemed more peaceful and comfortable than ever. There was no sense of emergency or sign that anything would happen soon.

I knew Grandma was tired of suffering. I knew she wanted to go *home.* I also knew she may have been hanging on out of love for us—out of worry for us—out of a sense of responsibility for us. We had been telling her it was okay to leave all along, but it didn't seem to register. I also knew that the last thing she'd ever want is to inconvenience her children or anyone!

As I was sitting at her bedside, thinking about how to communicate that it was okay to move on—out of the blue something compelled me to blurt out, "Hey Mom, if you don't go home, we can't go home."

The second those words left my mouth she switched from peaceful to restless like a jolt. My words struck a nerve. Michael realized what was happening. *That's it! Of course! She doesn't want to inconvenience us.*

Mary chimed in, "It's time to go home now, Mom. I'm making the sign of the cross and backing out of the driveway." Michael played along. "We'll see you soon, Mom. Make the sign of the cross, time to go home; call me when you get there." As my sister and brother were helping my mom let go—as surreal emotions flew around the room—as I was sitting by Mom's bedside witnessing her last seconds on earth, I quietly had my own "angel moment."

I heard a voice.

It was friendly. It was not only cheerful, it was downright playful, and it was as clear as a bell.

Hold her hand now.

That's all it said. *Hold her hand now.* I calmly answered inwardly, *Okay, okay,* and I held my mother's hand like I did when singing her to sleep with Sinatra.

Then, in what seemed like a moment suspended in time, she took her last gentle breaths and finally flew to the moon, peacefully drifting off to sleep, holding my hand all the while. I made the sign of the cross as she left, and I still call her every day to tell her we're okay.

On December 30, 2012, at 7:02 a.m.—with Aunt Mary, Uncle Michael, and me by her side—Frances (Hanky) Brandmeier finally let go.

As time stood still, as I watched Mary and Michael sobbing in slow motion, the veil between perception and reality lifted like a light, shining the essence of my mother's rare soul, into a luminous inner view. As her body died, the soothing love of her spirit came alive in the room. Like energy emanating from the voice heard moments before, I could feel her playful spirit, comforting, loving, somehow more than ever . . .

Free and alive.

Then, and now, even as I write these words, all I could do was smile.

A soft, quiet, *knowing* smile.

For the first time, I experienced something I've heard about many times before, but never truly understood.

God is in the moment . . .

And the moment is eternal.

Don't worry about calling, Mom. I made the sign of the cross.

I know you made it home okay.

THE SUN

The sun that helps us grow,
into blooming flowers,
in summer.
You shine brightest of all,
a golden gem.
Your warmth reaches everybody.
Trees couldn't touch the sky, without you.
You hold everything together.
You do your job silently, but not unnoticed.
For your inner light is impossible to miss.
And when it's time for the sun to set,
Night won't be so bad,
Because the stars were left,
with some of your light,
to lead the way back home.
In the morning you'll be above us,
Watching,
Making sure we're okay.
And we'll smile back,
Doing the sign of the cross,
Because we are.

   —Josie Brandmeier, eighth grade, poem about the
   unfathomable influence of Grandma in our family

KEEP YOUR CASTLES IN THE AIR, AND TWO FEET PLANTED ON THE GROUND

Don't be a stand-in-place dreamer! Standing still is moving backwards.

—Dad

Most people talk, talk, talk about their dreams for so long, they can't see them wilting in the hot air! Most people think, think, think about their dreams so much, they don't notice them slipping away. We're good at building castles in the air, but not in laying the foundations on which they must stand.

So what's a castle in the air anyway? Here's what Webster's dictionary says: "A hope or desire unlikely to be realized: An impractical notion or daydream."

With all due respect to Mr. Webster, I have this to say about that:

Wrong!

Building a castle in the air is not only practical, it's mandatory. You must first see the invisible before you can make it visible.

It is only an *impractical daydream* if you fail to take the second step.

Henry David Thoreau agrees.

"If you have built castles in the air, your work need not be lost, that is where they should be." (First step.)

But he goes on to say,

"Now put the foundations under them." (Second step.)

179

So why is the dreamer considered foolish by the so-called practical?
One reason:
Dreams aren't enough!
You must put the foundations under them.
To bring your castle in the air down to earth and make it real, you must . . .
Schedule it!

> If you have built castles in the air, your work need not be lost. . .
> That is where they should be. [First step]

Now put the foundations under them. [Second step]

FROM SOMEDAY TO NOW

To turn someday into now . . .
Schedule it! Schedule something! Schedule anything!

—Dad

"Talk about it and it's a fun *someday* dream,
Create a vision and it gets more exciting,
Plan it and it's possible,
Schedule it and it's real."

This empowering quote by author Tony Robbins contains the secret sauce for taking your dreams from someday to now.

Schedule it and it's real.

"Someday" is a word that keeps our dreams safely in the clouds, off in the distance and away from our daily life. The trouble is, clouds always dissipate and *daily life is life.*

To turn your daydreams into daily routines . . .

Schedule something!

Scheduling anything!

No matter how grand or far away your dream might seem,

There is always an action you can schedule now!

Always!

The second you schedule even the smallest action, such as a phone call, or even looking up the number to make the call, the universe literally shifts. That five-second phone call is a brick in the foundation of your destiny. Brick by brick

181

builds a career, skill, or business, and with it, the power of momentum, whisking your dreams into reality.

Josie and I were chilling in the backyard, daydreaming about all of the fun *someday places* in the world we'd like to live *someday.*

"The village of Roses, Spain, would be magical," Josie riffed! "We could live by Julia and Carlos, our friends we met through Jessie's student foreign-exchange program. How about Rome? We could eat those fancy pizzas with the egg in the middle like we did on our vacation there!"

I jammed along, "I'd love to live on a Greek island in the Mediterranean, like the one in the *Mamma Mia* movie, nothing but room to write and think and pray and eat falafel."

As we were riffing on a daydream, an opportunity for one of those Daddy teachable moments dawned on me. Hmm.

I could use our Greek island daydream to demonstrate what it *feels like* to turn someday into now—to show how scheduling a tiny action makes it real. So I started laying the foundation for our island in the air.

DAD: *Okay Josie, let's put finding a Greek island paradise on our schedule. How does five minutes from now sound?*

JOSIE: *Why five minutes?*

DAD: *I'm trying to teach you about making an appointment with your dreams—about scheduling your castle in the air. We should probably wait five minutes for the sake of this mock exercise—plus I have to go to the bathroom.*

JOSIE: *Eeeewww!*

DAD   *(five minutes later): Time for our appointment. Small talk first:*
        Man, the traffic was terrible, nice weather, how 'bout them Packers. Okay, let's get down to business.
        First step: Google "real estate in the Greek islands." Let's find out how much our dream island would cost.

Josie tapped into the cloud of Google servers so we could take our heads out of the clouds and have a closer look.

There was land for sale with amazing views of the Aegean Sea on Serfios Island. If we really needed more space to think and eat falafel, there were entire private islands available for purchase. The 1,112-acre island of Omfori was available for a mere $61 million, or we could pick up the 54-acre fixer-upper island of Stroggilo for only $5.5 million. No problem, piece of cake—or should I say, piece of baklava? I have a two-for-one coupon. We'll take two![63]

The point of googling the Greek islands with Josie was to get her familiar with the shift—the *feeling* that comes from moving *someday* to *now* through scheduling small actions. If she learns to schedule her somedays into a *routine* of simple actions—then as Thoreau also said—she'll "meet with success, unexpected in common hours."

So what are you daydreaming about? Whatever it is, schedule it!

Do you daydream about getting in world-class shape? Schedule a workout routine.

Developing a world-class skill? Schedule a practice routine.

Landing the perfect internship? Schedule a time to research potential companies.

Starting your own business? Schedule a meeting with a mentor.

Producing a TV show? Schedule creative time to write a one-page brief.

Do you daydream about the perfect, job, relationship, income, or lifestyle?

Schedule it! Schedule something! Schedule anything!

To Turn Someday into Now. . .
Schedule it! Schedule something! Schedule anything!

Schedule it and it's real.

YOUR MASTERPIECE LIVES
COMPLETE IN THE STONE

To master anything on the outer road,
You must chisel away the chips of raw talent,
Until you strike the vein of gold,
Buried beneath the green of budding skills and
*   inexperience.*

—Dad

Your outer *masterpiece lives complete in the stone* beneath 10,000 hours of practice.[64] Your mission is to chip away the hours and set it free.

I had a music business student who wanted to be a hip-hop writer and producer. Though I knew his nascent writing skills were still in the process of developing, I thought with the "write" guidance (bad pun intended), he could chip away at his layers of inexperience and free his budding talent. So I called a hip-hop producer friend of mine about becoming his musical mentor. He graciously said yes.

The meeting was set, but my student wasn't.

He showed up an hour late.

Strike one.

The first thing out of his mouth was, "I'm so hungry I can't think. Do you have any food?"

Strike two.

After feeding him and reparking his car, we finally got around to the business of reviewing his original music.

My award-winning producer friend had some very constructive advice. "You definitely have potential, but your writing isn't fully formed yet. You need to chip away the imitation and limitations of your raw talent until you refine your skills and uncover your own voice."

The producer was also a martial arts aficionado and tried to draw a parallel between mastering Tai Chi and mastering writing. "In martial arts they call it investing in loss."

My student just stared and mumbled, "Investing in loss? Huh?"

"The only way you learn and grow is through trial and error. You hone your skills and sharpen your craft by confronting challenges, experiencing losses, and learning from them."

Oblivious to his meaning the student responded, "I don't want to lose!"

If you're not willing to lose, you're not able to win.

"A master songwriter must write thousands of average songs before she can find her own voice and write a great one," responded the producer. "If you want to be great, you must invest in being bad."

"I don't want to lose and I don't want to wait. I have natural talent and a notebook full of lyrics. I want to be a star now," said my student.

The producer patiently tried to explain. "It doesn't matter if you're Mozart or Lin-Manuel Miranda. Natural talent is worthless without putting the hours in to develop it. What's the difference between true artistry and a hack?"

Student, "A good publicist."

Producer, "No! About 8,000 hours!"

He went on. "Studies show that amateurs put in 2,000 hours of practice by age twenty, and professionals put in 10,000 hours. [That's four hours a day for ten years] Though Mozart started writing at age six, he chipped away at the stones of imitation and limitation for twenty years before creating his greatest work. The Beatles played strip clubs in Hamburg Germany, eight hours a day. They carved out their sound through 1,200 nonstop shows over the course of a year and a half."[65]

Mozart and the Beatles needed more than natural talent and a notebook full of lyrics to develop their voice; they also needed hard work and 10,000 hours of practice.

After a brief pause the producer concluded by saying, "You have talent, but talent isn't enough. I can help you. I'll even produce tracks for you to practice with. But to attain true artistry—to master your craft—you must put in the hours. Hard work is nonnegotiable."

It sounded like a great opportunity to me!

My student's reply: "I'm fully formed already. I wanna be a star now!"

Annnd strike three!

You're out!

As the student rambled on about his greatness, my producer friend and I exchanged a couple of those "he'll have to learn this on his own" looks, and glanced at the clock. It was our turn to catch something to eat.

After a lifetime in music,

We were still hungry!

Chisel away the chips of raw talent,
and your masterpiece will emerge from the marble.

Time and hard work are chisel and hammer.
To master anything, you must put in the hours.
Talent is not enough.

STACKS AND STONES

*We all have a different set of stacks and stones to play on the
  inner road.
The game is simple.
Remove a stone.
Move forward.*

—Dad

Your inner masterpiece—your essence—*lives complete in the stone*, on the other side of fear. Your life mission is to chip away the stacks and stones of ego and set it free.

Each stone is a spiritual lesson.

Each stack is a group of spiritual lessons, linked together.

The stones: *Shame, guilt, apathy, grief, fear, desire, anger, vanity, gossip, judgment, blame, victimhood, whining, envy, laziness, dishonesty, selfishness, insecurity, self-pity, complaining, pointing fingers, low self-worth, low body image, low confidence, need to control, need to be cool, need to be right, need to be number one, need for approval, need to be popular, need to look good on Instagram, inaction, indecision, inability to stick up for yourself, and valuing appearances over authenticity, and on and on . . .*

Fear has many faces.

Sometimes we have stacks of stones that sit on top of each other.

*Anger sits on top of our
Frustration on top of our
Desire on top of our*

Vanity on top of our
Low self-esteem on top of our
Fear on top of our
Guilt on top of our
Lack of Love on top of our
Ignorance of who we are.
Remove the right stone, and the entire stack will come crumbling down.
We all have a different set of stacks and stones to play. The game is simple.
Remove a stone.
Move forward.
From anger and blame to vanity and victimhood,
Once the stones of fear fall away, *everything else will fall in place,*
Aaaaaand . . .
Ding, ding, ding, ding!
You win!
Woo-hoo!
You'll understand what I mean, when I say . . .
Happiness is not an external event.
You will never find happiness outside of yourself.
Michelangelo said, "I saw the angel in the marble and carved until I set him free."
Each of us is an angel in the marble.
Love and forgiveness are chisel and hammer.
Let them do their work, and true happiness will rise through the stone.
If you choose love and forgiveness above all other options . . .
Especially for yourself,
You will free your angel in the stone,
To soar with wild abundance,
In this world,
And beyond.
Ding, ding, ding! Wooo-hoo!

Stacks of "fear stones" sit on top of each other.
Each stone is a spiritual lesson.

We all have different stacks.
Remove the right stone, and the entire stack will come crumbling down.

WHO'S YOUR DUMBLEDORE?

Obi-Wan Kenobi mentored Luke Skywalker.
Dumbledore mentored Harry Potter.
Who's your Obi-Wan Kenobi?
Who's your Dumbledore?

—Dad

M eeting and modeling a master—someone who's mastered what you aspire to do—can save you from decades of frustration and mistakes. Convince the best of the best to take you under their wings, and your own wings will explode with power. You'll soar higher, faster, and farther with a mentor cutting the wind.

So why don't most people take Nike's advice and *just do it?* The short answer is they don't know any better or they're too afraid to ask.

If you don't ask, the answer is always no.

But sometimes, even when you do ask, the answer will be a big, *heck no!*

So what?

Ask anyway!

Like when I asked world-renowned flutist Hubert Laws to be my Obi-Wan Kenobi, when I was attending Berklee College of Music. (Dumbledore wasn't around yet.)

Hubert Laws performed at Berklee and gave a lecture with a Q&A session after the show. This was my chance to meet him. When it was my turn at the microphone, I asked him a simple question.

"Mr. Laws, I'd love to study flute with you. Could we schedule a time to set up lessons?" As the laughter died down, Hubert said, "If you're ever in New York, call me and we'll set something up."

That's all I needed to hear. I immediately sprang into action. After tracking down his contact information, I booked a flight from Boston to New York, took a cab to his penthouse, and called him up from there—*the next day!*

I thought I was demonstrating commitment and passion. He thought I was a psycho creeper. He answered the phone and awkwardly said, "I can't talk right now."

"But . . .

Could I just . . .

Umm . . ."

Click. Bzzzzzzzt.

After calling back again and again, to an endless ring, all I could do was sit there and wait. Finally, after what seemed like days, I saw my Obi-Wan coming through the front door. Nervously I whimpered, "Hey Hubert, I'm the Berklee student you met yesterday and . . ." Before I could finish, he looked the other way and dove into a limo. Hubert Laws may have been a master flutist, but he would never be my Obi-Wan Kenobi. Though disappointed, I had no regrets. It's more important to try and fail than not to try at all.

The point of modeling a master isn't to meet and creep on famous people. *The point is to create professional relationships, learn your craft, stimulate ideas, and get a leg up on your dreams.*

A master points the way to possibilities. Networking with the masters in your field will help you gain clarity on what you really want. Besides gaining professional connections, meeting your mentors "up close and personal" jars loose one of two revelations.

Yes! I can do that.

Or . . .

No! I don't want to do that.

Both revelations bring you a step closer to who you are.

Look for the masters you'd like to model.

Learn their life stories; contemplate what you think they did right or wrong. Examine the path they took to get from point A to point B. Where did they go to college? What did they study? Step back and look at their day-to-day life. What motivated them to do what they do? Look at their path, their values, their contributions, their purpose, their lives, their money, and their jobs.

Once you've identified your Dumbledore(s)—no matter how unreachable they *seem* to be . . . make contact!

Instead of fixating on how they can help you, focus on how you can help them. Create a relationship by creating value.

Be persistent but be professional. And whatever you do, don't lurk outside their home waiting for them to leave the house. It's better to call first, and invite them to the next Hogwarts Quidditch match.

No matter who they are or what they've achieved . . .

They had to start out as an imitation, before becoming an original.

The best among them will see your sincerity, drive, talent, and potential. Some will help and some will dive into a limo trying to avoid you.

So what?

Modeling a master is an exercise in self-discovery and networking. It's part of the 10,000 hours it takes to master anything, and most importantly, it's a lot of fun!

So the million-dollar question is—and I mean that literally . . .

Who's your Dumbledore?

COMMUNITY

Know it or not, whoever you're rubbing shoulders with rubs off.

—Dad

Why bother finding a Dumbledore for life? Why hang around the best of the best? Why place the diamond of your talent in the right geographic setting? Why surround yourself with people who uplift, inspire, challenge, and stretch your abilities? I repeat . . .

Whoever you're rubbing shoulders with rubs off.

Whether it's your professional peers, geographic location, or personal relationships, we absorb the energy of our community through osmosis. The collective *energy, outlook, and standards* of your respective community will propel you upwards if it's positive, pull you down if it's negative, or take you out of the game if you're playing on the wrong geographic game board.

Who surrounds you professionally and academically?

In my student jazz days, I strived to surround myself with musicians far better than me. Somehow I finagled myself in with some of the best—such as flute legend Herbie Mann, virtuoso bassist Miroslav Vitous from the band Weather Report, prodigy pianist Makoto Ozone from Japan. I knew I'd only get better by surrounding myself with musicians who scared me to death! They were so far over my head I had to stretch like a contortionist to reach even. Though I never caught up to them, I surpassed myself through the process.

You define your standards by defining your community.

Surround yourself with the best, and you'll get the best out of yourself. Do you want to play in the major leagues or the minors?

There is no right or wrong answer.

There's only the right or wrong answer for *you*.

Jamie and Jessie are interested in the media world. Most students at the University of Wisconsin are majoring in science, business, or fields unrelated to showbiz. If you're feeling like a fish out of water in college, you can still connect to *your world* in bits and pieces. Whether it's an online community, outside job, or internship, you can still find ways to meet and mingle with the best outside of school. So far, you girls are rocking it!

Jamie dove headfirst into her community by interning at *The Daily Show* in New York and Zucker Productions in Los Angeles. Jessie took a semester off from college to intern at NBC's Sprout Network in New York and Lionsgate Entertainment in Los Angeles over her summer break. Though still in high school, Josie stretches her piano skills beyond the band room by playing with the community choir, teaching outside students, and auditioning for professional plays in the Madison area.

Exposing yourself to the energy of the top people in your field not only raises your standards and creates connections, it brings clarity to what you want and what you don't. Surrounding yourself with like-minded students, teachers, and professionals outside of class may be the most important class of all.

What about your geographic community? Where you live not only determines the size of your opportunities, but the level of your expectations.

I knew a couple of great vocalists who lived in Chicago. Though they were among the best in the "Windy City," their careers flatlined from limited professional opportunities in the area. So they moved to Los Angeles and looked for work in the same way they did in Chicago—I call it "selling by hanging around." Six months after "hanging around" L.A., one was singing back up for Don Henley of the Eagles, and the other was singing behind Michael Jackson. Same talent! Different community! Different result!

Besides being closer to bigger opportunities, the change of community unconsciously sparked a higher level of expectations. Instead of expecting to land an occasional jingle or local wedding job, they grew to expect work from major artists, TV gigs, and huge record dates. In a community made up of the best of the best, a higher level of professional work naturally becomes the expectation.

Most importantly, who are you rubbing shoulders with personally?

Aware of it or not, your friends, roommates, boyfriends, girlfriends, and play pals are influencing your outlook, spirit, and future.

I couldn't care less about the size of your friends' ambitions. I care deeply about the shape of their hearts.

Are they real or fake—true or false—takers or givers—talkers or listeners? Do they make great choices or poor excuses? Are they a good influence or a bad effect—*I can'ts* or *I cans*—Debbie Doers or Debbie Downers—self-starters or self-destructors?

Are they friends or frenemies—competitors or companions? Is it me-me-me or us-us-us? Do they lift you up, or bring you down? Do you like who you are when you're with them?

If you can't be who you are when you're around who they are, the relationship is toxic.

One of the most loving families I know had a daughter who became an alcoholic by her junior year in high school. Why? She hung out with friends who started drinking during her sophomore year.

They say we take on the characteristics of the five people we associate with the most. Make it a point to associate with loving, supportive, *can-do* people, who jumpstart your imagination and inspire you to fearlessly be who you are. In spiritual terms, they call it *keeping holy company*. As the old saying goes, "Birds of a feather flock together."

Who are the five people you hang out with most?

How are they influencing your life?

The work of sculpting your life into a masterpiece of precious art flows easier in the energy of an empowering community. Choose the framework of your personal and professional peer groups wisely.

A flower cannot bloom if surrounded by weeds or planted in the wrong climate.

GET A REAL JOB!

Like angry, toothless thunder,
Indifference roaring in the dark,
Conformity's silent wail can be deafening.

—Dad

We were driving in the car when the John Mayer song, "No Such Thing" came on. I cranked up the volume—wanted you to hear the hook. *"I just found out there's no such thing as the real world, just a lie you got to rise above."* Now that you are knee-deep in an outdated educational system, designed to cram your free spirit into a long-gone box, the message in that song is more important than ever.

Society wants to define you. You are coming of age in a time of extraordinary change and exciting, wide-open possibilities. There's a new world order of ideas emerging through the quicksand thinking of an old guard clinging to the past. Unlimited, unimagined, undiscovered opportunities are calling to be created. Original thoughts are waiting in the wings; new solutions ready to take center stage.

What is the *real world?*

What is a *real job?*

In this time of unprecedented change and transformation, the definition is all yours. As John Mayer said, now more than ever, "There's no such thing."

I love what Steve Jobs says about how we're brainwashed to live inside the lines set by the *normal* world:

196

When you grow up you tend to get told the world is the way it is, and your life is just to live your life inside the world. Try not to bash into the walls too much. Try to have a nice family, have fun, save a little money. That's a very limited life. Life can be much broader once you discover one simple fact: everything around you that you call life was made up by people that were no smarter than you, and you can change it, you can influence it, you can build your own things that other people can use.[66]

Most people just go along with the program and lead safe but limited lives.

If Steve Jobs or Thomas Edison played it safe, I'd be writing this on a typewriter by candlelight right now. Let's define the word *job*, and I don't mean Steve. He defined himself.

Job: Doing assigned tasks for someone else's purpose, in exchange for money and the illusion of security. (From the Pig Latin "J.O.B.": just over broke!)

Work: Any activity in which you do not associate an empowering purpose and meaning.[67] Spending your precious time each day doing things that are meaningless to you is slow death. You can "work" to fulfill someone else's dreams or your own. If you are a cog in someone else's machine, you are expendable. There's always another cog.

Your work: Any activity in which you do associate empowering purpose and meaning.[68] Motivation is derived from meaning. A lack of motivation is a sure sign that whatever you're doing doesn't mean anything to you. So if that's the case either look at your job differently by asking how it fits into the big picture of your life, or quit. But you may not have to change anything but your mind for your job to transform from menial to meaningful.

All you may need is a shift in perception.

Like our friend George Bailey from the movie *It's a Wonderful Life*. He didn't change a single thing but his mind: not his job, lifestyle, financial situation, marriage, family, or daily routine. He simply changed the way he looked at things, and his job transformed from frustrating to fulfilling.

So if you're an aspiring artist, entrepreneur, future mogul, mover, or shaker—and look at the crappy job you have to pay the bills as just a crappy job you have to pay the bills . . .

Tell yourself a different story!

Change the way you look at it.

It's not a crappy job.

It's not a dead-end gig.

It's *BASE CAMP*:

A temporary shelter at the foothills of your dreams . . .
A place to launch your rise to the top.

BASE CAMP

Like a mountaineer who establishes a base camp from
*   which to begin her ascent, explore the terrain, and*
*   reach for the summit . . .*
You must create a financial base camp at the foot of your
*   dreams, or risk losing your grip, and falling like a rock,*
*   as they slip through your hands.*

—Dad

I was talking to my music business students about what they planned to do after graduating from college. They all seemed to have a different version of the same problem. No money and too many things they wanted to accomplish all at once instead of step by step. I knew this was a formula for accomplishing nothing.

One student was a singer-songwriter from northern Wisconsin who was graduating in six months. Her cup overflowed with enthusiasm as she rattled off goal after goal, like a tommy gun.

Deep breath in, anndd . . .

Fire!

"I'm going to write a million songs, and build a rabid fan base, and start a blog, and get to know music supervisors, you know, those are the people who place music in TV and movies, and associate myself with the best musicians, and produce my own CD, and meet big-shot executives, and get a record deal, and tour like crazy, and sing in commercials, and write a national jingle, and lie on the beach, and eat sushi, and . . ."

Uh-oh! She's reloading. Here it comes!

199

"I'll create a viral video, and sing with Macklemore, and combine my love of film and music into a charity project, and change the world, and I really want to move to L.A. after I graduate, but don't have any money so I'm going to move back to northern Wisconsin and see if I can do all that from there."

Sound the buzzer. Stop right there. Ding, ding, ding, back it up a little. Time out! I told her,

Although I love your passion, and it's imperative to have a big "specific" vision, there's only one key outcome you need to accomplish between now and graduating six months from now.

One outcome,

Two words:

BASE CAMP!

If you want to move to L.A. and pursue your dreams, you must financially anchor them in a base camp job before doing anything else.

Big specific vision!

Small specific step!

Focus on one thing: establishing an L.A. base camp. If you don't, years of struggling will take the place of singing with Macklemore and eating sushi on the beach.

One of the main reasons for getting a degree, even one that doesn't relate to your dreams, is to leverage it into a *base camp job*. Without a financial base camp, you'll slide and fall in fits and starts. Money problems will keep you spinning in place like a dervish, whirling down, burning out, and going nowhere.

A financial base camp is the first goal, not the end all. It's one key step along the road to your ultimate destination. I told my student, "Prepare the launchpad now, so upon graduation your dreams are ready to blast off into the next star system."

Base camp doesn't have to be perfect. It never is. By definition it is only a financial *starting and storage place for expedition*. Still, it's more than a financial foundation; it's also a training ground—part of your 10,000 hours—continued education on what it takes to ascend the face of your place on the hill.

As an aspiring songwriter, my student could find an entry-level job at a music publishing company; a performing rights organization like the American Society of Composers, Authors, and Publishers (ASCAP); or an artist management firm. She could learn about the legal side of songwriting by getting a ground-floor job at a law firm specializing in music publishing. She could fetch coffee and dry cleaning for an A-list music supervisor, song plugger, or songwriter; work at any of the online music rights and placement companies; do whatever it takes to achieve her first key outcome. Which is . . .

A financial base camp is the first goal, not the end all.

1. Create a financial base camp from which to pursue your dreams free of worry.
2. Gain experience and connections while getting paid.
3. Even if you have to take a temporary job outside of your field. . .
Achieve outcome number 1.

1. Create a financial base from which to pursue her dreams free of worry.
2. Gain experience and connections while getting paid.
3. Even if she has to take a temporary job outside of her field of interest, achieve outcome number one.

No matter what the job, the most important thing is creating a financial base from which to climb.

A less-than-perfect job can feel like a thief, time-jacking your dreams. Trust me. It is much easier to find time for your dreams in a busy schedule than to find money for your dreams when your *free time* and *mind space* is being beat to a pulp by worry.

Once a base camp is established at the foot of your vision, you can explore the next step. Take a shot here, trek over there, until you rise and find even higher ground from which to climb.

With a base camp job, my student would have the money to record a demo. She could start her million-song catalog (one song at a time) and land one with a major artist (one artist at a time).

She may move up the ladder at her entry-level job and become a music supervisor, instead of fetching coffee for one. With her first break, she could break camp and establish a new point of operation further up the hill.

Momentum will build.

The higher she moves, the clearer she'll see the top of the mountain and the big vision in which her life is set.

A financial base camp is not *settling* for less. It's not a fallback plan; it's a rise-up strategy. It's not conformity or compromise. It's savvy and effective planning, part of your blueprint for success.

In a word, it's *freedom.*

Freedom to ascend the Mount Everest of your own life,

Freedom from money worries, stress, and strain during the ascent,

Freedom to reach the tip of your talent, the pinnacle of your passion, and make the most of yourself.

Build a base camp at every step, and every step will lead forward, expand outward, and raise you up.

THE SHADOW OF YOUR DREAMS

*Don't mistake the shadow of your dream for the dream
       itself.*

—Dad

Grunting through base-camp starter jobs that *shadow* your real passion is part of your growth—part of *paying your dues.* As Ringo Starr once sang, "You got to pay your dues, if you want to sing the blues!"

Your mom didn't start out as an airline captain flying 777s around the world. Uncle Johnny didn't start out as the funniest radio personality ever. Aunt Mary didn't start out as a virtuoso marketing executive. Aunt Sandy didn't start out as a major CEO. Aunt Joan didn't start out as an Emmy-winning TV personality. Grandma Hanky didn't start out as a saint—second thought, yes she did! They paid their dues and put in the 10,000 hours it took to master their craft.

But there's a big difference between a base-camp job and being stuck in the shadows of what you really want. *Base camp can devolve into prison camp, if you take your eyes off the prize.* Don't settle for shadows—go the distance and live the dream.

Like the aspiring author who finds herself as a copywriter, English professor, or editor, when she really wants to be a novelist—the high school band director who really wants to be a singer-songwriter, or the aspiring veterinarian whose temporary base-camp job at a pet store chain rusts into the chains of a shadow career.

Many people spend their entire lives next to their dreams instead of in them.
Why?
Mostly fear.

Fear of failure.

Fear of being dead broke.

Fear of being different.

Fear of being laughed at.

Fear about abilities.

Sometimes the shadow thoughts of others can mask your own light.

Family wants to keep you safe and *under control*. Society wants to put you in a box. There is subtle pressure from teachers, friends, strangers you'll never meet, and the Joneses who want you to keep up.

Ignore the pressure from without and doubt from within. Know the difference between the firelight of a temporary base camp and forever living in the shadow of your dreams.

I never want you to get stuck in a job that started out as a stepping-stone!

Steer steadfast and straight, directly into your passion, not next to it.

Shadow goals create frustrated shadow people!

Don't live the shadow . . . live the dream.

Many people spend their entire lives next to their dreams instead of in them.

Don't settle for shadows— go the distance and live the dream.

AVOCATION VERSUS VOCATION

My object in living is to unite
My avocation and my vocation
As my two eyes make one in sight.
Only where love and need are one,
And the work is play for mortal stakes,
Is the deed ever really done
For Heaven and the future's sakes.
                    —Robert Frost, "Two Tramps in Mud Time"

You LOVE acting but NEED to pay the rent.
May your love and need be one.

                                        —Dad

There's a piece of dream-killing advice so common it's cliché.
Try your dreams, but make sure you have something to fall back on.
How can I put this as elegantly and calmly as possible?
AARGGGGG!! NO, NO, NO, NO! YICKY-YUK, YUK,YUK!
Fall back *to* what? A cubicle for the walking dead?

Fall back *for* what? To get money doing what you don't want to do—work your way up a ladder you don't want to climb—look acceptable to gossiping neighbors who couldn't care less?

Fall back *from* what? The things you love to do—the things that make you happy—from even the possibility of mastering what you love?

One of your friends told me she wanted to be a veterinarian. Her well-meaning family said, "That's a hard major so have a fallback plan. You should turn your love of animals into a hobby. You can always get a pet or volunteer at the humane society."

From instilling limiting beliefs, and a potential life sentence to the zombie club, their loving advice was wrong on so many levels! I wanted to scream at the top of my lungs!

Take a stand for your calling!
Master what you love, and you will make money!
And you can't master something if—you—do—not—love—it!
Your avocation will be your vocation! Your love and need will be one . . .
If you commit!
If you hold an escape route in mind, your dreams will escape you!
Commit!
Don't worry that risk could lead to failure!
If you don't risk, you've already failed!
Decide!
There's a big difference between a base-camp job and falling back. Base camp isn't a fallback position, it's part of the plan!
Falling back is quitting!
Instead of quitting, try committing!
If you want to take the island burn the friggin' boats![69]
Find a way!
Find a way!!
Find a way!!!

We ask for what we think we want from life, but rarely what life wants from us.

Life demands that we be who we are, that we answer the bell of our own call.

A true calling is **never, *ever*** a hobby.

It is **never, *ever*** something to fall back on.

Falling back is slow death.

Like the actor that starts out with a love for theatre burned into her essence but decides to squeeze her love into a part-time hobby, which dies as time and reasons fade.

Or the musician whose soul is fused with music but wakes up one day to realize his love for music got lost in the business of music.

Your calling demands a full commitment!

"Until one is committed, there is hesitancy, the chance to draw back. Concerning all acts of initiative and creation, there is one elementary truth, the ignorance of which kills countless ideas and splendid plans: that the moment one definitely commits oneself, then Providence moves too. All sorts of things occur to help one that would never otherwise have occurred."[70]

Your calling demands a firm decision!

"A whole stream of events issue from the decision, raising in one's favor all manner of unforeseen incidents and meetings and material assistance, which no man could have dreamed would have come his way."[71]

Your calling will find or forge a way, when you decide, commit, and act!

"Whatever you can do, or dream you can do, begin it. Boldness has genius, power, and magic in it. Begin it now."[72]

Do not look back!

Do not fall back!

Burn the friggin' boats!

Falling back is quitting! Instead of quiting, try committing!
"If you want to take the island burn the friggin' boats!" Robbins

Find a way! Find a way! Find a way!!!

IMITATION IS FOOL'S GOLD

Do you want to imitate your dreams or live them?
Do you want an imitation life, or do you want to really
live?

—Dad

There was an English seaman named Sir Martin Frobisher who voyaged to the New World to look for the Northwest Passage in the year 1576. Instead of fulfilling his real goal of finding a passageway to the East, he found something even better.

He discovered gold! Lots of it! The riches of kings! Instant royalty! Who needs the Northwest Passage anyway?

He loaded his ship up with 200 tons of gold and glory and brought it back to England. The queen was so excited she immediately drew up plans to send him back to the New World for more—and even named the place where he found the gold after him. Frobisher Bay, Canada.

It turns out the shiny yellow rocks, for which he traded his real gold, weren't the treasure he expected. The pot at the end of the rainbow—fooling nations, deceiving destiny, tricking kings and queens, and ultimately altering the course of history—wasn't filled with gold. It was stuffed like a pig with iron pyrite, a sparkly imitation.

It came to be known as *fool's gold!*

Frobisher never found the Northwest Passage.

The voyage of our lives is much the same.

Like Frobisher, many people trade in the true gold of their calling for the fool's gold of an imitation life. In the end, they never find the Northwest Passage to who they are and where they belong. The winds of imitation have seized their sails, commandeered their lives, and spun them quietly and painfully off course.

Promise me! Promise yourself!

Stay the course!

Stay who you are! No matter what!

What does an imitation life look like in everyday life?

Students major in fields that sound important, but have nothing to do with who they are, creating imitation importance. Workers get stuck in safe paying jobs that blow holes in their souls, creating imitation success.

Families sweep problems under the rug, creating imitation harmony. Friends manufacture friendships based on self-interest, creating imitation camaraderie. Couples do time in unhealthy marriages, creating imitation love. LGBT people hide who they are, creating imitation everything.

Average Joe buys the biggest house in town, creating imitation prominence. Poser Joe drives a fancy car, creating imitation wealth. Holy Joe reads the Bible, then judges his neighbor, creating imitation holiness.

Professionals in every field are in denial about how they failed to do what they really loved, by hiding behind their titles, creating imitation satisfaction. People in all walks of life are quietly dying near their dreams, instead of living—out loud and clear— in them, creating imitation fulfillment.

It doesn't matter what your life looks like on the outside. I repeat.

Your inside life *is* life!

You are just beginning the journey with spirit and passion intact. I pray every night that you stay that way.

Never let the rough stuff of growing up cause you to stop short, jump ship, or compromise. Hold on to who you are, inside and out, no matter what, no matter how far or difficult to see . . .

Stay the course!

FORCING AN IMITATION IDENTITY

Let your place in this world unfold naturally,
Don't mistake a piece of who you are for the whole of who
you are.

—Dad

Let's play the "name a word" game that used to be part of our bedtime routine when you were little. Before you fell asleep, I'd have you name a word, then I'd instantly make up a goofy story or song based on that word. I always tried to sneak some meaning into it and kept yapping until you politely kicked me out of the room. Here we go.

DAD: *Okay, name a word.*

KIDS: *Do we have to?*

DAD: *C'mon, just name one word, and then you can go to sleep.*

KIDS: *Ahhh—Buh buh buh bird bird bird—buh buh bird is the word!*

DAD: *Got it, bird is the word! Or is it buh?*

KIDS: *Bird, Dad! Bird is the word! Like the song!*

DAD: *Okay! Once upon a time, there was a bird who squashed her natural calling by rushing into an identity and forcing her spirit into the wrong box. It all started when she won a running contest in birdy gym class. The bird puffed up like a peacock after getting a couple of caw-caw-cawmplements after the race, and . . .*

KIDS: *Caw-caw-compliments? Cheesy, Dad!*

DAD: *Caw-caw-cawwiet now! I'm on to something! Where was I?*

Puffed up by a few standard-issue complements, the bird thought she had finally found her own "thing" like all the other birds seemed to have. Strutting with excitement, she crowed like a rooster and declared it to the world.

Cue Bruce Springsteen song looping in her head.

"Baby, I was born to run! Baby, I was born to run! Baby, I was born to run!"

Though the bird should have been singing, "Baby, I was born to fly," she chose to pursue the running career of a rabbit instead. Be-caw-caw-cawz of the cawwpliments, she assumed an identity based on one piece of who she was, which kept the whole of who she was from unfolding into view.

JAMIE: *Only Boomer birds listen to Springsteen, Dad!*

JESSIE: *I bet birds like Bruno Mars?*

JOSIE: *They probably love the song "Rockin' Robin"!*

ALL THREE KIDS: *"Free Birrrdddd"!!!*

DAD: *Work with me, people, work with me!*

After pulling her identity out of the oven before it was fully cooked, the bird spent years struggling, wondering why she was unhappy and why she couldn't run as fast as the rest of the rabbits. The bird felt like a big dumb loser.

JAMIE: *That's not a very nice thing to say about birds, Dad!*

JESSIE: *Can you do a solo, so-low I can't hear you? Ha!*

JOSIE: *I have to go potty.*

DAD: *Hey, I'm on a roll here!*

Then one day, the bird read a quote from the smartest rabbit of all—a brainy bunny named Albert Einstein. (Apparently, the dumb bird could read and enjoyed Newtonian physics.) Albert the brainy bunny said, "Everybody is a genius. But if you judge a fish by its ability to climb a tree, it will live its whole life believing that it is stupid."

Well that's a relief, the bird thought. Thank God I'm not a fish and don't want to climb trees. Then, in a flash, his birdbrain had an epiphany.

KIDS: *There you go again, insulting a little birdy! You don't even like our bird Bambi. You call him Devil Dove!*

DAD: *That's not true. I really do (mumble mumble) our bird Bambi the devil dove. Stick with me now!*

The bird said, "Now I get it! Steve Jobs was good at calligraphy but didn't force his entire identity into the box of being a calligrapher. [Apparently, the dumb bird liked Apple computers too.] Jobs had no idea how calligraphy would unfold into a small piece of his big picture later in life. He just knew he liked it. I like to run, but that doesn't make running my entire identity. Who knows how running will fit into my big picture? But I do know one thing . . .

Birds don't run! Birds fly!

I can either be a wannabe rabbit or an amazing bird.

I don't wanna be a wannabe!

I just wanna be who I am and do what I was made to do!"

With that, the bird soared above the crowd and beyond her perceived limitations, as the rabbits cheered on and watched in awe.

Ta-dah! Waddya think?

JAMIE: *What's a perceived limitation?*

JESSIE: *(Snoring sounds.)*

JOSIE: *Can I go potty now?*[73]

Everybody is a genius.
But if you judge a fish by its ability to climb a tree,
it will live its whole life believing that it is stupid. Einstein

I can either be a wannabe rabbit or an amazing bird.
I don't wanna be a wannabe!

QUESTIONS

Before your imitation date becomes your imitation
  destiny . . .

Does he fully see you, flaws and all, and love you no matter
  what?
Do you fully see him, flaws and all, and love him no matter
  what?
Is it imitation love or real love?

—Dad

Do you like him?
Is he kind?
Does he treat you with respect?
Treat waiters and people who can't give him anything with respect?
Make time to be with you, or make excuses to be away from you?
Listen to you, or go through the motions of listening to you?
Complement you? Encourage you? Appreciate you? Say thank you?
Do you like, like him?
Has he cheated on you? Never tolerate cheating! Never! There's no excuse!
Do drinking or drugs determine or change his moods—cause you discomfort?
Is he eager to ask you out, or do you have to wait around and chase him down?
He'll always ask if he's truly interested.

213

Does he ask to meet you out at parties with friends, or does he ask *you* out? He'll ask *you* out if he's truly interested.

Is he honest?

Do you notice him telling little "white lies" to you or others?

Is integrity important to him? Trust your intuition. You'll know.

Is he vain? Does he see the world in terms of rank and status?

What are his financial goals? Is he responsible with money?

Do you like who you are when you're with him?

Can you be who you are when you're with him?

Is he fired up about being all that he can be?

Is he fired up about helping you be all you can be?

"Keep away from those who try to belittle your ambitions. Small people always do that, but the really great make you believe that you too can become great."[74]

Is he strong enough to admit mistakes?

Does he argue to figure out the truth, or just spin and win the argument? Does he have to be right all of the time? Is it ever *his* fault?

Is he strong enough to apologize?

Are his ego, ignorance, and pride too strong to get through and reason with?

You can't reason with crazy!

Can you talk to him?

Is your relationship safe enough for silence?

Can you *just be* with each other in loving stillness, without filling every inch of air with busy words, meant to distract from a bad connection?

Is he a control freak, needing to control anything and everything, including you?

Does he get moody or mad when he doesn't get his way?

Do your values and life view clash or complement each other?

Is he cheerful?

Does he hold on to grudges, resentment, past problems?

Is he polite?

Does he lift you up, or bring you down when he's around?

Is he fun?

Are his family and friends fun to be around?

Does he make you smile?

Is spirituality important to him? Does he pray?

Is his overall consciousness level based in fear (negativity), or love?

If based in fear, he won't have the power, willingness, or ability to love you.

There are no perfect people or perfect relationships—only perfect intentions.

Unconditional love is an inner decision, not a transient state.

The concept of *finding your soul mate* is a romantic fairy tale, not a spiritual reality. *You don't find your soul mate. You commit and grow into soul mates.*

The question is . . .

Are your intentions for the relationship aligned?

Being aligned in a relationship is power. Being involved in a relationship is force.
Does he love you unconditionally?
Does he fully see you, flaws and all, and love you no matter what?
Do you fully see him, flaws and all, and love him not matter what?

There are no perfect people or perfect relationships— only perfect intentions.
Unconditional love is an inner decision, not a trasient state.

The concept of finding your soul mate is a romantic fairytale, not a spiritual reality.
You don't find your soul mate. You commit and grow into soul mates.

FART AND SOUL

How do you know if someone has made the inner decision
to love you unconditionally?
They see your imperfections,
Your fears and flaws,
And love you anyway.

—Dad

Grandpa Frank was always changing friends. Always making new best buds with strangers he just met at a bar:

> GRANDPA: *You're the salt of the earth!*
> STRANGER: *You're the salt on my Bloody Mary!*
> GRANDPA: *Pish posh! It's my birthday!*
> STRANGER: *You say that every day. When are we going to meet your*
>   *wife and kids?*
> GRANDPA: *I never liked you anyway. Next.*

The second my dad's new friendships threatened to grow beyond surface bar talk, he'd dump them and move on to a new group of surface friends.

Like couples, even friendships start with surface infatuation. Going any deeper and truly getting to know someone requires the *strength of vulnerability.*

In the movie *Good Will Hunting*, Matt Damon's character, Will, wanted to dump the *perfect* girl before she discovered his *imperfections* and he discovered hers. His therapist, Sean (Robin Williams), called him on it.

SEAN: So call her up, Romeo.

WILL: *Why? So I can realize she's not that smart, that she's [bleep] boring? Y'know, I mean this girl is like [bleep] perfect right now, I don't wanna ruin that.*

SEAN: *Maybe you're perfect right now. Maybe you don't wanna ruin that.*
              [Sean goes on to say that accepting the so-called flaws in someone is what creates the bond—a sacred sanctuary built with the safety of love.]

SEAN: *My wife used to fart when she was nervous. She had all sorts of wonderful idiosyncrasies. You know what? She used to fart in her sleep. One night it was so loud it woke the dog up!*
              [Sean loved his wife, fart and soul! Like the song: "Fart and soul. I fell in love with her fart and soul!"]

SEAN: *The little idiosyncrasies that only I knew about—that's what made her my wife. Oh and she had the goods on me, too. She knew all my little peccadillos. People call these things imperfections, but they're not. Aw, that's the good stuff.*

(Cut!)
But it's more than farting in your sleep that creates intimacy.
Huh?
It's seeing the fear behind people's negative behavior and loving them anyway.
Hmm.
Look behind the bad behavior, and you'll always see the fear.
Look behind the fear, and you'll always see the love.
There's a word for this . . . *Forgiveness.*

I'm not saying you should put up with a jerk boyfriend. Forgiveness doesn't mean accepting or making excuses for chronic abuse or even mild disrespect. Never! I'm talking about seeing the good, the bad, and the ugly, and sticking with it.

Will your partner love you, fart and soul?
Will he look behind the fear and see the love?
Look behind the flaws and love you through it?
Can you be who you are—warts and all—when you're with who they are?
If not, move on!
You deserve true love . . . fart and soul.

How do you know if someone truly loves you? They see your imperfections,
your fears and flaws, and love you anyway. . .
no matter what.

Can you be who you are— warts and all— when you're with who they are?
If not, move on!
You deserve true love. . . Fart and Soul.

FALLING IN ~~LOVE~~ LACK

The hole dug by the ego's eternal "lack story" can't be filled
by a make-believe "love story," no matter how well-
manufactured the plot or how sweet the canned music.

—Dad

L ACK: Hi, I'm Lack.

LOVE: *Hello, Lack, I'm Love.*

What's the difference between you and me?

You're a hole in search of a false filling. I'm the real filling.

Huh?

Unaware they're seeking completion through relationships, people fall in lack and think they're falling in love.

Huh?

You're love in the movies. I'm love in real life.

Yes, that's it! I wanna be like Tom Hanks and Meg Ryan in *Sleepless in Seattle*.

What were the lives of Tom and Meg like after they came down from atop the Empire State Building—after the music faded and the director yelled cut? Who was too tired to talk the next morning, left the toilet seat up, or belched over breakfast?

I'm sure the violin music never faded and their lives were complete. I need someone to complete me too—to fill the holes in my soul with stringed instruments!

Therein lies our biggest difference. You're forever incomplete. I'm forever whole. No one can fill the holes of your ~~soul~~ ego but you. Love and strength are one.

Waddya mean, love and strength are one?

Love yourself first or you won't have the power to love someone else. Seeds of love cannot grow on a foundation of weakness, neediness, or lack.

Hmm. But *Weakness in Seattle,* just doesn't have the same ring to it.

Love in the movie stage is love in the infatuation stage.

I love the infatuation stage! For one shining moment, I feel complete.

Feelings of lack will still be there when the infatuation stage lights fade. You'll end up blaming your perfect prince or thinking you made a mistake.

Well, it has been kind of hard to hear the violins through all that belching.

And your movie love will turn into movie hate, regret, or withdrawal.

You're watching too much *Oprah*! A trophy spouse will complete me!

Lack falls in love with the status of a person, instead of the person.

A white picket fence and 2.2 children will complete me.

Lack falls in love with an image instead of a person.

He's rich! His money will complete me.

Lack falls in love with the money of a person, instead of the person.

My soul mate will be the fairy tale that completes me.

Most fairy tale couples are ego mates, not soul mates.

Ego blah! Soul blah! What's the difference?

It's not the soul that holds on to resentment. It's not the soul that needs to be right. It's not the soul that needs completion it's the ego, which can never be complete.

I guess you didn't see the "you complete me" scene in the movie *Jerry Maguire.*

You will not complete your partner and your partner will not complete you.

Then what's the point Mr. Buzz Kill?

You don't find happiness through each other; you find happiness with each other.

It's not one half + one half = one whole.

It's One + One = Three.

Hmm. And you're bad at math too!

The Father + the Son = The Holy Spirit.

Lennon + McCartney = Music they could have never made separately.

You + your partner = Unrepeatable music impossible to make apart.

You don't complete each other; you expand each other—stretch each other beyond the boundaries of your egos into the love of who you are. And when you do—the glimpse of love you received in the infatuation stage breaks through forever.

So we're not filling holes?

You're creating a "holy" new entity—a force in your lives birthed from the power of your Self-love merged together. You're not filling holes you are adding another drop to the ocean of God.

What is God?

The eternal one life underneath all life...

What is Love?

Love is feeling the presence of that one life—your essence— within yourself.[75]

What is a soul mate?

Feeling the presence of that one life within yourself . . . together.

What the movies call love is really dependency, sentimentalism, control, juicing drama, emotionalism, and attachment—attributes of the ego, not the heart.[76]

So on your way to the movies, watch out for the holes.

Falling in ~~love~~ lack is painful.

Being love—which is being who you are together, is pure bliss!

I pray you know the difference, and *never, ever settle for an imitation.*

Love in real life is much more romantic than love in the movies.

Falling in lack will masquerade as being in love if you don't love yourself first.
Love and strength are one.

YOU COMPLEEEETE MEEEEE!!!

FaLLiNg iN LacK

Relationships cannot complete you.
Love in the movies is lack, dependency, sentimentalism, control,
and attachment— attributes of the ego, not the heart.
No one can fill the holes of your ~~soul~~ ego, but you.

YOU ARE NOT SPECIAL

Everyone is special.
No one is special.
You are one of a kind.
Just like everyone else.
Every snowflake is different.
But still, just a snowflake.
You are truly unique in the universe.
You are not special.

—Dad

As I watched the milestone event unfold, my mind wandered to the picture of my three little girls sitting on "the bench" in Chicago where I first saw your mom. How did we get from "the bench" to the bleachers of Jessie's high school graduation in a blink?

Among the graduating students were trophy hunters, truth seekers, status grabbers, self-worshipers, self-loathers, yes-I-cans, and no-I-cant's, all draped in ceremonial garb—waiting to walk onto the stage and commence into life.

Jessie shined! She sparkled with high honors, high integrity, and high hopes.

Jessie is truly special . . . just like everyone else.

As I listened to the different speeches, regaling students about their greatness, I thought of another speech given by Wellesley High School teacher David McCullough:

"And your ceremonial costumes—shapeless, uniform, one-size-fits-all. Whether male or female, tall or short, scholar or slacker, spray-tanned prom queen or

The J-Girls on "The Bench," where I first saw your mom in 1990.

intergalactic X-Box assassin, each of you is dressed, you'll notice, exactly the same. And your diploma—but for your name, exactly the same. All of this is as it should be, because none of you is special. You are not special. You are not exceptional."

Whoa!

I never heard Barney the purple dinosaur sing that!

Then I thought of a quote by F. Scott Fitzgerald:

"First-rate intelligence is the ability to hold two opposing ideas in the mind at the same time, and still retain the ability to function."

Can two totally opposing thoughts, like *everyone is special* and *no one is special,* both be true?

Hmm.

Umm.

Yes!

Among the artificially inflated *spotlight students,* who didn't know they didn't know, were *invisible students* with humility, who did know they didn't know. Which brought even more opposing thoughts to mind:

Humility is strength. Pride is weakness.

Maybe those invisible students have already overcome hardship, disappointment, and challenges on their own? Ahhh, more opposing thoughts:

Shielding kids from hardship and disappointment creates hardship and disappointment.

There was no class rank for character, no point system for persistence.

Character and resilience are better indicators of success than intellect.

Did the spotlight students stockpile awards for simply participating and hoarding points—receive empty praise for just showing up?

Boosting self-esteem hurts self-esteem.

Maybe the invisible students were confident enough to confront their shortcomings.

Facing shortcomings, eliminates the power of shortcomings.

Maybe the pain of failure gave them self-knowledge, resilience, and *grit*.

"The secret to success is failure."[77]

Instead of being full of themselves, the invisible students were empty and ready to be filled up. No matter what the fake class rank—top of the heap, or bottom of the barrel—in many ways the invisible students were light years ahead of the rest.

Some high school students are legends in their own minds—big fish in tiny puddles—deluded into believing their puddle-class awards are signs of world-class ability.

I'm the greatest this; I'm the best that. I'm number one at being number one! Not understanding that *needing to be first in everything is different than doing what you love and sometimes coming in first.* The former is narcissism; the latter is a by-product of being who you are.

As McCullough also said in his "You Are Not Special" speech . . .

"We have come to love accolades more than genuine achievement. We have come to see them as the point. Do whatever you do for no reason other than you love it and believe in its importance. Don't bother with work you don't believe in any more than you would a spouse you're not crazy about."

I wanted to wave a magic wand and remove the delusions of greatness; in order to make room for the real greatness each student was born with. (More opposing thoughts.) Before decades of frustration flew by, before the empty bubble of a trumped-up identity burst into a life of quiet desperation.

The bubble always breaks—leaving the bubble blower wondering what happened to their fake greatness as they are forced to face their real Self for the first time.

Save yourself years of frustration and face yourself now. It's a beautiful sight and the real reason to climb. Climb to rise above the noise of your own ego . . .

To ascend the heights of wisdom,

To see your Self as you truly are,

To see others as they truly are,

To experience God,

Not to be a god.

Reaching the top is not the point; liberating your Self on the way up is.

"Climb the mountain not to plant your flag," urged McCullough, "but to embrace the challenge, enjoy the air, and behold the view. Climb it so you can see the world, not so the world can see you."[78]

"Why did you climb the mountain?" the old question goes.

"Because it's there," is the standardized reply.

Some high school students are legends in their own minds,
Big fish in tiny puddles. . .

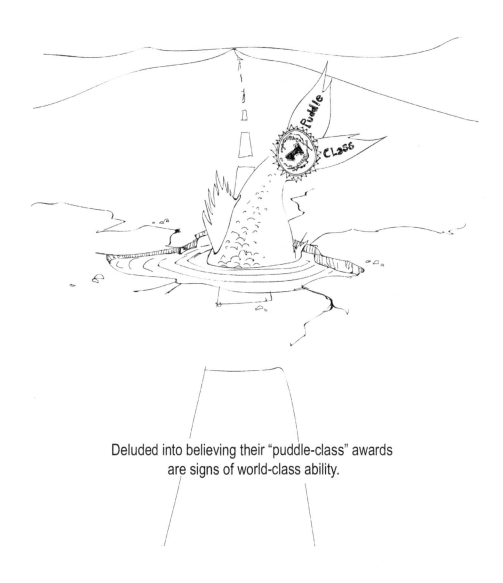

Deluded into believing their "puddle-class" awards
are signs of world-class ability.

Understand why you are pulled, and called, and driven to ascend. Why your nature is to rise and reach. You climb the mountain because . . .

The mountain is you.

The real You, not the trumped-up, self-esteem you.

Immovable truth is peak and pinnacle.

Jagged rocks of ego stand between.

We all have our own craggy-toothed path leading up and in.

Every path is special. Every path is the same.

Every mission is different. Every mission alike.

Life demands the exact same thing from each and every one of us . . .

Face the mountain and climb.

You can't cheat the mountain, Pilgrim. Mountain's got its own ways.
   —Bear Claw, in *Jeremiah Johnson*

I'M A WHISPER IN THE STORM

When you've lost sight of the shores of your very soul—
adrift, scared, and all alone . . . I'm a whisper in the
storm.

—Dad

It's not always easy to climb—to find courage when you are *dis-couraged*—when romance turns rancid, plans turn sour, and dreams turn into nightmares. Though discouragement and failure can burst open a portal to your potential, it's not always easy to lick your wounds and drag your shell-shocked dreams through the gateway.

Clouds of confusion can gather unnoticed, blurring the light of true north. The fog of fear creeps in, seeps through the lines of clarity, shrouding your purpose. Waves of self-doubt engulf your dreams. A tempest in a teapot is howling with the furious winds of a thousand illusions.

But the pain is real.

Faith is shaken,

Ability questioned,

Beliefs challenged,

Confidence eroded.

When your divine spark seems to grow dim, your perfect vision feels blurred and beaten, and hard questions smash your compass like a rock, roaring, spinning, blinding the way; when the winds of hope have abandoned your sails, conviction howls off into storms of whirling indecision and seas of uncertainty . . .

I'm a whisper in the storm.

Trust yourself!
Let the invincible waters of surrender wash away your fears and send you soaring.
Let go, let God, and keep moving.
One breath, one step at a time. There is nothing you can't handle NOW.
All fear is past or future.
Feel your own invincible thunder. Head straight and strong into the seeming storms of adversity. Sail steadfast through the apparition of fear. Rise above the ignorant yelp of the herd's screaming indifference. Transcend the feeble gates of the ego's tiny hell. Dive deep into the omniscient silence of the soul, and simply
Listen.
It's the voice of your Father in heaven (through the heart of your father on earth).
A voice of Love that's calling you to
Be
Who you are—time to
See
Who you are.
Believe as I
Believe in who you are.
Be
Who you are—and you'll
See
Who you are.
Believe, as I
Believe in who you are.
Let go and follow—inside and out—no matter what, no matter how far!

VERSE FOUR

Don't seek the soul in shiny goals,
Behind applause that roars,
To fly beyond your wildest dreams,
Have faith,
Do less,
Be more.
Be kind when no one's watching,
Sing like no one can hear.
Be bold and brave, go make mistakes,
Live to the point of tears.

DON'T SEEK THE SOUL IN SHINY GOALS

*You're being assaulted on all sides with manufactured
    images depicting fame as the ultimate path to
    fulfillment . . .*
*Brainwashed with messages saying the road to happiness
    is paved with trinkets of glamour, and can only be
    arrived at via stretch limo.*
*Who the heck cares what someone's wearing on the red
    carpet?!*
To keep from being programmed, ignore the mani-cam!
Change the E! channel to "real."

—Dad

A conflicted father stands in his daughter's childhood bedroom and looks back with tears in his eyes. He notices the rock his little girl found by the creek and turned into a face, using pieces of felt.

Flash forward: Same girl, different face.

Caked in makeup that distorts her natural, beautiful face, into a prefab TV façade—she quietly suffers from *body dysmorphic disorder;* sometimes called, *imagined ugliness.*

Flash back: He's remembering his little girl as a six-year-old, helping a blind friend hear God in the sound of wind blowing through the grass.

Flash forward: Same little girl, different message.

"I want more of that sh-t." [The hallucinogenic drug salvia.]

Flash back: She was so happy as a baby her parents nicknamed her "Smiley."

Flash forward: "I went through a time when I was really depressed. I locked myself in my room and my dad had to break my door down."

Flash back: The father looks around the room and points to her cheerleading trophies high on the shelf by the door.

Flash forward: She's leading the cheer about dancing with "molly," a slang term for the drug MDMA (also known as Ecstasy). For some, dancing with molly has led to *dying with molly*. Rewired by fame, lost behind body image dysmorphia, or deafened by depression?—she glamorizes the drug anyway.

Flash back: The little girl dreams of being a famous actor and musician someday, just like her dad.

Flash forward: Fragile and confused—in the midst of a feud with his "grown-up" little girl—and lost in the darkness of a life-shattering divorce—the father cries out:

"It destroyed my family. I'll tell you right now, the damn show destroyed my family. I'd take it back in a second. For my family to be here and just for everybody to be okay, safe and sound, and happy and normal would have been fantastic. Heck, yeah!"

Flash back: The whole family is baptized together at the People's Church in Franklin, Tennessee. Before moving to the City of Angels to start filming *Hannah Montana*, the TV show that would make the little girl famous, her mother said, "We're going to be under attack, and we have to be strong in our faith."

Flash forward: As the wrecking ball of fame shatters the family bond, a broken father laments, "Somewhere along this journey, mine and Miley's faith has been shaken. That saddens me the most. You think this is a chance to make family entertainment, bring families together, and look what it's turned into. My family is under attack by Satan.

It makes me sad just to think about it."

As the father pauses in the bedroom doorway that stands like a portal between the innocence of the past and the darkness of the present, all he can do is sigh.

"Again, it's a bit sad because it's just a little girl's room, isn't it?"

Fame is an ugly beast![79]

FAME IS A DRUG

People who need to be famous for the sake of being famous
are drug addicts.

—Dad

What happened to that little girl?

Fame crept in like a crack dealer and turned the ego on *high*. That's what happened!

But the last thing we should do is judge!

How would you react if you had all of that fame and money—yes, men with their hands out, handlers with their hands in your pocket, paparazzi with cameras in your face, and fans with their hearts on your sleeve . . . all at such a young age?

I would have been an obnoxious bigheaded monster. But I had it much easier than Miley Cyrus when coming of age. I struggled and failed a lot, which forced me, *whether I liked it or not,* to grow up on the inside first.

Whenever you're tempted to judge anyone, ask God to see them differently through God's eyes not your own. With grace, the real and full picture will emerge.

Behind the curtain of smoke and mirrors, beyond the glitter and glitz that feeds the *ugly beast,* the beautiful heart of Miley Cyrus is shining.

The fire of early fame has burned through her ego, allowing the radiance of her spirit to burst through like the sun. Now she's *real happy*—and as Miley puts it, "there's nothing worse than being *fake happy*." As she rises above the fame game, says no to the yes men and cling-ons surrounding her, *Destiny Hope Cyrus* is living up to her real name, just like her dad predicted.

But there's a difference between judgment and discernment.

In our Kardashian culture, dysfunctional celebrity behavior is being held up as glamorous and desirable by a mindless media driven by the bottom line. The lust for fame is a dry rot that can weaken the foundation of our lives, our families, even our country from within. I just want you to see it for what it is.

Fame is a drug.

People who need to be famous for the sake of being famous are drug addicts.

What does a drug do?

It gives you a fake high.

What happens when the fake high wears off?

You keep craving more and more.

What happens when more and more isn't enough?

You keep drinking and injecting and smoking and popping and sticking and sniffing, until there aren't enough drugs in the world to trick your soul into believing a fake high is real happiness.

But obsessed, enslaved, and rabid like a dog, you keep thirsting and snorting and foaming at the mouth, for just . . .

One more hit of attention,

Another injection of approval,

A dose of entitlement,

A fix of special treatment,

Shot of validation,

The high of adulation,

The illusion of significance,

An anesthetic for the pain,

A substitute for love.

Singer John Mayer had enough self-awareness to recognize his addiction:

"I didn't have a drinking problem. My high-speed crash was an intellectual one. I'm a recovered ego addict. And the only way that I can be sure that I don't relapse is to admit that I constantly have this ego addiction. So I do the Grammys and I go home, 'cause if I stayed, I'd get high again. I'd get high . . . And then I'd get low."

Like Miley Cyrus, Mayer's infinite spirit—the force that made him a star to begin with—reached through the fire of fame and pulled him home. They are rare. Most headline hounds can't see through the fog.

The fame story is as ancient as the ego.

Self-loathing addicts who know deep down, in the most private reaches of their heart of hearts, that the hype-odermic needle of fame is not only meaningless, distracting, and inaccurate, it distorts the sense of who they truly are, until finally . . .

They end up being who they are not.

Just another junkie in search of a fame fix.

Fame is a drug.

People who need to be famous for the sake of being famous, are drug addicts.

BEHIND APPLAUSE THAT ROARS

On the outside, it looks like famous people have it all.
But the road from fear to love is an inside journey.
And on the inside, the spotlight of fame may really be a
*   soul-blinding roadblock.*
On the inside, an ego inflated by fame makes for a more
*   turbulent ride.*

—Dad

The fame drug comes in all shapes and sizes.

Mark Chapman needed a fix, so he shot John Lennon.

Eric Harris and Dylan Klebold craved a hit of messiah meth, so they massacred over thirty students and teachers at Columbine High School.

To judge a tree by its fruit, look *behind the applause that roars* to the fruit fame has borne in the real lives of those blessed, or cursed, with fame.

Britney Spears: Lost custody of her children. Problems with drugs and alcohol. Charged with hit-and-run while driving without a license. Committed to a psychiatric ward.

Lindsay Lohan: In and out of rehab for substance abuse. Press rumored she suffered from the eating disorder bulimia. She stated, "It is clear to me that my life has become completely unmanageable because I am addicted to alcohol and drugs."

Owen Wilson: Taken to the hospital for a reported suicide attempt. Unnamed sources said he tried to commit suicide by slitting his wrists and taking drugs. His lawyer confirmed he was undergoing treatment for depression.

And the one that really broke my heart . . .

Robin Williams: He was hinting about the dark side of fame the minute he became famous. I guess no one was listening.

Williams was first thrust into fame on the sitcom *Mork and Mindy*. He played the part of the hilarious alien Mork, who came to earth from the planet Ork to learn about human behavior.

Every week he'd report back to his boss, *Orson*, with insights about being human. On the episode that aired February 19, 1981, Mork reported:

MORK: *This week I've learned what it's like to be famous on earth.*
ORSON: *That's good.*
MORK: *Well sir, sometimes it is sometimes it isn't. Most earthlings work very hard to be recognized for what they do, but when they become stars, they realize they're recognized wherever they go.*
ORSON: *You mean they lose their privacy?*
MORK: *Well sometimes they can even lose their clothes. You see, being a star is a twenty-four-hour-a-day job, and you can't leave your face at the office.*
    [Robin Williams later said, "Maybe time alone is the last thing I want."]
ORSON: *Isn't fame its own reward?*
MORK: *When you're a celebrity everyone wants a piece of you. Unless you can say no, there will be no pieces left for yourself.*
ORSON: *I thought all stars were rich, lived in mansions, and drove big eggs.*
MORK: *But you see, to get that you have to pay a very heavy price. You have responsibilities, anxieties, and well, to be honest, sir, some of them can't take it.*
ORSON: *I'm not buying it. It sounds to me like they have it made.*
MORK: *Most of them do, sir, but some are victims of their own fame, very special and talented people. People like . . .*
    Elvis Presley,
    Marilyn Monroe,
    Janis Joplin,
    Jimi Hendrix,
    Lenny Bruce,
    Freddy Prinze,
    And John Lennon.[80]
    (Fade to black.)

Add Robin Williams to the list.
Died August, 11, 2014.
Cause of death: Suicide by hanging.
There's a simple question I want you to answer from these real-life tragedies.

If fame is so great—the ultimate pathway to peace, happiness, and success—then why are many famous people so lost, depressed, and devoid of hope that they take their own lives? As I've been trying to tell you, happiness is not an external event.

You will never find happiness outside of yourself.

God bless you, Robin Williams.

Thank you for making my children laugh and think.

You are deeply missed.

Nanu Nanu.

(Nanu Nanu means "see you later," and also "hello," on planet Ork.)

It doesn't matter what your life "looks like" on the outside.
Happiness is not an external event.

Good Times Hard Times Famous Fameless

Your inside life IS life.

ALCOHOL

There's fun.
Fun with problems.
And just problems.
Have fun.

—Dad

There's always a train blocking traffic when you're trying to get across town in my hometown of Fond du Lac, Wisconsin. This one was taking forever! That's okay. As I listened to the rhythm of the rails, it gave me time to think.

I was on the way to my father's seventieth birthday party at the Eagles Club, located at the edge of Lakeside Park on the shores of beautiful Lake Winnebago. I knew there would be lots of drinking at the party. Binging and beer is a Wisconsin tradition, and as far back as I can remember, a family tradition as well. Alcohol played a leading role in the movie of my father's, and his father's, and his father's life.

As the train rolled by, I reflected on your Grandpa Frank's seventieth birthday. I tried to imagine his life as two movies—one with alcohol (still playing down the road at the Eagles Club), and one without alcohol (producer took a pass at the development stage, so we'll never know). How would his life have been different? How would my life have been different? And consequently, how would your lives be different?

I don't know, and I don't care.

I just know everything would be different.

239

And that means alcohol stole the show. It played too big a role.

Now that I'm a father, I'm recasting the movie!

So what can we learn?

Let's start with the three stages of drinking.

Stage one: Fun.

Stage two: Fun with problems.

Stage three: Just problems.

I'm sure drinking was "fun" for my dad when he graduated from high school, joined the navy, and travelled the world. But somewhere along the line, as his drywall business, marriage, and six kids were pulled under the influence of his *fun*—his drinking graduated from fun, to fun with problems.

And in the end . . .

Just problems.

After serious bouts with pancreatitis, heart issues, and liver problems, his doctor said, "You can either have a drink or walk in front of a Mac truck. Either way you're going to be dead." To your Grandpa Frank's credit, he quit cold turkey and never had a drink for the rest of his life.

Not long after quitting, he called me and asked, "Are there any plays going on in Madison? Bars are boring. There's more to life than hanging around a barroom." Whoa! My dad would rather go to a play than a bar! My dad thinks bars are boring! It reminded me of the joke about "Deadheads"—the fanatical fans of the band The Grateful Dead.

What did the Deadhead say when he got off drugs?

Man, this band sucks!

When my dad quit drinking, he didn't complain or sit around; he began a twilight journey back to himself—a search for real ways to raise his state from low to high—a new way back home, from fear to love.

He caught a glimpse of light, through the opening once blocked by alcohol, and stumbled his way forward—inch by sober inch—through the ego's stubborn rocks of selfishness, grudges, and insecurities until the day he died.

At the end of his life, my dad threw away the crutches.

Without the boulder of addiction on his back, he was finally free to climb.

Climb on, Dad . . .

Climb on.

CRUTCHES

Without a crutch, you'll have to learn to walk on your own.
—Dad

Alcohol can start out as a crutch, which morphs from propping us up to tearing us down. We get nervous at a party and lean on a drink; too uptight to carry on a dinner conversation and depend on a cocktail to carry it for us. As dependency goes up, confidence, courage, and consciousness levels go down.

When you were fearless and free little babies, you took your first steps all by yourselves. You don't need a crutch to walk through small talk, loud parties, or big challenges now. As a father who love, love, *loves you*, it's my job to keep you as strong as the day you were born.

Without a crutch, you'll have to learn to walk on your own.

Some people can't express emotions unless their emotions are bolstered by booze. When my dad was fully loaded, he'd gush on about how great I was and how much he loved me. That was nice to hear, at first. The trouble is he never said those words the morning after. As time went on I came to abhor alcohol-induced emotionalism. Though I knew my dad loved me, my teenage mind developed a subconscious belief: *a drunk "I love you" doesn't count.*

As a father who love, love, *loves you*, it's my job to keep you as open as the day you were born—strong enough to admire or confront someone to their face—to open up without a bottle opener.

Without an emotional crutch, you'll have to learn to express yourself on your own.

Alcohol can also be an escape hatch, especially in college.

241

Between finding yourself, finding a roommate, money pressure, class pressure, and peer pressure, alcohol can be a temporary pressure relief valve releasing scared air.

How does the escape hatch of alcohol actually work? Why do we feel so high on Saturday night and so low on Sunday morning? Part of the answer lies in the levels of energy/consciousness.

Alcohol artificially blocks off the lower levels, opening a pinhole view of the upper. Like dark clouds parting from the sun, guilt, apathy, and fear (energy levels 30–100) are blocked off, making room for love, joy, and ecstasy (500–560) to shine through. In fact, the designer drug Ecstasy was created specifically to block off the energy fields below 560.[81]

Trouble is, once the alcohol wears off, the very energy it was blocking expands.

Dark glasses of fear color the same world with heaviness that shot glasses of joy colored with light the night before. Shame and guilt deepen. A loss of self-respect throbs larger with every hangover. Now you're even more afraid to face parties, people, or problems without a drink in your hand. A habit takes root. As fear expands, the alcohol escape hatch collapses like a trapdoor into a dungeon of trouble.

As a father who love, love, *loves you*, it's my job to keep you as happy and trouble-free as the day you were born. Why settle for a pinhole peek of happiness, when you can bask in a panoramic view?

Without a crutch, you'll have to learn to be happy on your own.

And from Sinatra to Sheeran, the alcohol crutch has always been disguised in glamour and cool. But it's not just crooners and rock stars wrapping their fears in coolness. Marketers use this Trojan horse of a trend to sneak in and capture new targets by selling cool in a bottle.

In the '90s, liquor execs realized the man-market, *Madmen* days of hard booze and three martini lunches were over. Like many of their customers, liquor sales hit bottom. So how did the industry survive without men? By indoctrinating a new market of women.

Though they won't admit it, hard liquor brands are marketing "alcopops," or so-called "girlie drinks," as gateway beverages to young girls and women.

"Alcopops are marketed as fun, sexy, and cool as if they are less risky to drink, but their health and safety consequences are anything but sexy or cool."[82]

Hmm.

So a bunch of bottom-line-at-all-cost executives are selling poison dressed up as cool to young girls?

"Teen girls feel greater impairment from alcohol and encounter alcohol-related problems faster, including brain damage, cancer, cardiac complications, and other medical disorders."[83]

I have three daughters. I'm getting worked up here!

"The average age of their first drink is now thirteen. These troubling trends make the aggressive marketing of so-called alcopops even more dangerous."[84]

Okay! That's it!

I won't pull any politically correct punches here. Teenage liquor pushers, how do you sleep at night? What's the difference between a drug pusher stalking kids on a playground and you? The drug pusher on the playground isn't a hypocrite, that's what. And don't tell me you're not marketing starter drinks to teenagers with a wink. Studies and common sense show otherwise.

I digress.

Lost my cool for a second there.

Or was it my wine cooler?

That really wasn't very spiritual of me.

Or was it?

But the fact is . . .

Exposure to alcohol marketing is a gateway problem for teens and women.

Don't let yourself be pulled under the influence of companies selling cool for cash. Cool doesn't come in a six-pack of hard lemonade.

As a father who love, love, *loves you,* it's my job to keep you as cool as the day you were born.

Without a crutch, you'll stay cool on your own.

We get nervous at a party and lean on a drink;
too uptight to carry on a dinner conversation, we
depend on a cocktail to carry it for us.

Without a crutch, you'll have to learn to dance on your own.

TO DRINK, OR NOT TO DRINK?

I'm not anti-alcohol,
I'm anti-crutch.

—Dad

've struggled with what to tell you about drinking, probably because I'm struggling with what to tell myself.

What's healthy and fun drinking? What's sick and dependent drinking? What's the difference? Where's the line? Where's the crutch? Why use alcohol to give the ego a nap when you can put it to sleep forever by awakening to who you are?

Why drink?

Why not?

Crazy man Jim Carrey says, "I'm very serious about no alcohol, no drugs. Life is too beautiful."[85] But there's evidence that even Jesus drank wine. His first miracle was to change water into wine when they ran out at the wedding at Cana. Still, the Gospel says, "The son of man came eating and drinking," not gorging and binging. Hmm.

As I ponder these questions, I'm stirred—not shaken—by a deeeep thought. *I bet if I could change water into wine, I'd be invited to a lot more parties.* Yikes! Even as I'm telling my daughters about the seriousness of alcohol, I'm making bad drinking jokes, trivializing its effects. No wonder we think getting ripped is normal and cool. Partying is built into our unconscious culture.

I've been razzed by some of your uncles and aunts for being too uptight about exposing you to alcohol. To explain my fatherly motivation . . .

244

I thought if I could keep you whole and strong and free from dependence on alcohol for *anything,* until you reached age twenty-five, you'd be out of the danger zone. I don't know why I chose age twenty-five. The trapdoor of alcohol must be avoided for life. I just thought if you could walk through the growing pains of growing up, *without a crutch,* you'd walk on your own forever.

I'm not anti-alcohol . . .

I'm anti-crutch.

Anti-blocking, blurring, avoiding, denying, or escaping fear through alcohol.

I'm for permanent happiness, not just a happy hour.

For natural strength, not a brewed buzz.

For a real high, not a binged boost that leaves you lower than when you popped the cork, twisted the top, or opened the can. A *can* of beer can turn your life into a *can't* of beer, if you depend on it for confidence.

They say, if you are young and you drink a great deal, it will spoil your health, slow your mind, make you fat—in other words, turn you into an adult. I want to spare you from standardized adulthood. Beer brains and beer bellies are not signs of maturity.

Like everything in life, it's the intention behind an act that makes it a blessing or a curse. It's the spirit, behind drinking spirits, that raises or lowers your—spirit. There's nothing wrong with raising a glass in a celebration of love with friends and family. I want you to eat, drink, and be merry with the people you care about.

Raise a glass to friendship,

Raise a glass to life,

Raise a glass to fun,

Raise a glass to blessings and gratitude and love,

And you'll raise your spirits too.

But it's not the glass raising your state . . . it's the love that's pouring out of it.

There's a big difference between raising your glass to happiness, and trying to raise your happiness with a glass. No matter how *normal* the world says it is, the spirit behind a nightly cocktail—escaping, binging, or drinking your courage—is fear not love.

I want you to be aware of what's pouring from your red solo cup.

Is it fear or is it love?

So to drink or not to drink, that is the question?

I already know the truth.

But sometimes the truth has to be reached in baby steps.

For now, the answer is yes and no.

It's a matter of intention.

It's a matter of moderation.

It's a matter of seeing the line between fun and dependence.

Is it a celebration of life, laughter, and love?

Then, yes.

Is it just a way to drown your troubles, ease your nerves, and change your state from low to high? Like with my father, is it a way of life and a way through life?

Then, no.

No matter how I look at it—no matter how I *want* to rationalize and justify the use of alcohol—I come face to face with the same conclusion. Drinking is just a cheap shortcut to the richness of what we're really seeking—to happiness, joy of life, and peace of mind—to spiritual growth. And as they say . . .

There is no chemical solution to a spiritual problem.

I want you to find happiness where it really lies: within yourself.

Once you learn that the source of happiness is within, as you rise above the lower levels of fear into the upper levels of courage and love, your desire to drink will fade naturally. Like Jim Carrey found—the picture of your life will be too beautiful to smear with alcohol. Like your own father, standing at the intersection between ingrained family traditions and an incredible spiritual high, breaking through the clouds, you'll simply lose interest.

There's a big difference between raising your glass to happiness,
and trying to raise your happiness with a glass.

Raise a glass to blessings and gratitude and love, and you'll raise your spirits too.
But it's not the glass raising your state. . . it's the love that's pouring out of it.

In the meantime, if you choose to drink (after you're twenty-one), do it with mindfulness and moderation, and you'll be fine. *Never* feel guilty or worry. Enjoy yourself!

Just don't depend on it for anything.

Throw away the crutch and keep the *fun*.

Refuse *fun with problems*.

And you'll never have *just problems*.

As your spiritual cup overflows with the upper levels of consciousness, your beer mug will run dry on its own.

TO FLY BEYOND YOUR
WILDEST DREAMS, HAVE FAITH

Every kick in the butt is a move forward!
Or maybe . . .
Every move forward is a kick in the butt!

—Dad

Have faith in "maybe."

Grammy-winning singer Patti Austin's mother had a terrible stroke. Besides the anguish of worrying about her sick mother, Austin had to cancel her performance at the Michael Jackson tribute concert and go through the trouble and expense of changing her flight home to a day earlier.

Bad news, right?

Maybe?

The flight she had to change was United Airlines Flight 93, September 11, 2001, from Boston to San Francisco. Austin would have died, along with the rest of the heroes who tried to take back control of the plane from the hijackers when it crashed in a field near Shanksville, Pennsylvania. (Because your mom and the wife I love is a United Airlines 777 captain, Austin's story really hits home.)

Maybe works in reverse too.

A so-called good thing could turn out to be a so-called bad thing.

Maybe?

Maybe landing a big job you don't really love ends up as life in a gilded cage, locking you away from what you do really love. Maybe if J. K. Rowling had a happy first marriage, she wouldn't have written *Harry Potter*. Maybe winning the lotto ends up ruining your life, like it did for Billy Bob Harrell, who won $31 million in the Texas lottery.

Harrell was hounded by people asking for donations, made unwise financial choices, was separated from his wife, and twenty-two months after selecting the winning number, committed suicide.[86]

Maybe the perceived "bad" things that happen to us are not bad at all.

Maybe the perceived "good" things that happen to us are not all that good!

Maybe going through a bad break up with the wrong guy will free your heart to meet the right guy. Maybe getting rejected on an audition will push you into honing

Grandma Hanky rested in faith no matter what the problem.
She understood an ironclad law of nature. . .
Unconditional love is the air and essence of the universe.

Grandma was peaceful no matter what happened. She had faith in "maybe."

your skills and lead to a better part. Maybe the implosion of my company was the blowback I needed to regain my authenticity.

Maybe?

What serves our highest good can be painful and beyond understanding.

That's where faith comes in.

Grandma Hanky rested in faith, no matter what the problem, because she understood an ironclad law of nature.

Unconditional love is the air and essence of the universe.

What we need and want most, the universe wants for us.

And . . . *we don't know what we really need!*

Grandma knew enough to know she didn't know enough—that our view is limited and God sees our lives with infinite, loving eyes.

Grandma had faith in "maybe."

She believed that any given event *may be* just a small part of a bigger picture, one impossible to comprehend through

Faithless eyes,

Hardened hearts,

And closed minds.

That is why,

Grandma was happy no matter what happened.

It's a matter of faith.

ACCEPTANCE

Acceptance is an understanding that what is best for us is beyond our understanding.
The opposite of acceptance is fighting with life.
The opposite of fighting with life is faith.
Faith is profound acceptance.

—Dad

People traveled from near and far to hear the words of Jiddu Krishnamurti, one of the wisest men to ever walk the face of the earth. (Why aren't wise men ever named Ralph, or Fred, or Bubba?)

"Do you want to know what my secret is?" asked the wise man. The room came alive with silence as the crowd waited with bated breath for the secret of life.

"This is my secret," he said calmly.

Drum roll, please, building like in the movie *Whiplash*.

Deeeep breath. Wait for it! Wait for it! Wait—for—iiittt . . .

But the crowd can't wait. "Heal meee!" . . . "Save meee!" . . . "I can't take it anymore!" . . . "Pleeeezzzz master, reveal the secret of life nowwwwwww!"

And the wise man whispered,

"I don't mind what happens."

What? Drums are too loud! Could you repeat that?

"I don't mind what happens."

Bam!

Oh—my—God!

I'm saved! Yay!

Hallelujah!

Praise the Lord!

Happy days are here again! Wooooooo-hooo!

Wait.

Ahh.

Huh?

What did you say?

And the wise man whispered, "I don't mind what happens."

Hmm.

Am I at the wrong show? I thought this was the secret to life concert?

Are these tickets refundable?

As simple as it sounds, the phrase "I don't mind what happens" has layers of meaning. The first layer is the foundation from which all of life springs, and upon which all of existence rests.

Love.

The universe responds to your every action and thought with unconditional love.

If you know the universe is forever serving your highest good, no matter what . . .

You won't mind what happens.

Because you can only guess what serves your highest good, *you have faith.*

Because you know your will and God's will are one in the same thing . . .

You have the serenity to accept the things you can't change,

Courage to change the things you can,

And the wisdom to know the difference.[87]

You can rest easy, let go, and let God.

Faith is freedom from fear.

When I think of the wise man's whispered words of wisdom, I get the sudden urge to jam with Jessie, and start singing the Beatle's, "Let It Be."

Beatles icon Paul McCartney was troubled, frustrated, and *fighting with life.* As he puts it, "I was going through a really difficult time around the autumn of 1968. . . . I think I was sensing the Beatles were breaking up, so I was staying up too late at night, drinking, doing drugs, clubbing, the way a lot of people were at the time. I was really living and playing hard."[88]

McCartney was resisting reality. He "minded what happened."

Then one night McCartney's mother, who died when he was fourteen years old, came to him in a dream. The dream, in Paul's own words:

So in this dream twelve years later [after her death], my mother appeared, and there was her face, completely clear, particularly her eyes, and she said to me very gently, very reassuringly . . .

"Let it be."

It was lovely. I woke up with a great feeling. It was really like she had visited me at this very difficult point in my life and gave me this message.

Be gentle.

[Acceptance]

Don't fight things.

[Surrender]

Just try and go with the flow, and it will all work out.

[Faith][89]

> The opposite of acceptance is fighting with life.
> The opposite of fighting with life is faith.
> Faith is profound acceptance.

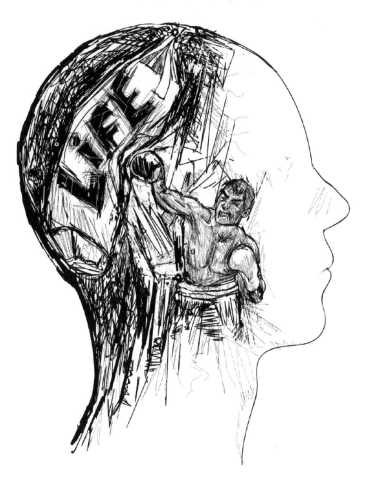

If you don't mind being unhappy, what happens to the unhappiness? —Tolle

The wise man and Paul's mother Mary were saying the same thing.

Don't mind what happens.

Quit resisting reality *out there* by accepting the way things are. And remember, since our inner world determines what we experience *out there* . . .

Out there is really in here!

Author Eckhart Tolle agrees with McCartney's mother Mary. "To be in alignment with what is [not mind what happens] means to be in a relationship of inner nonresistance. It means not to label it good or bad, but to let it be."

And of course, Sir Paul McCartney had to make a song out of such a profound experience. "So being a musician, I went right over to the piano and started writing a song."[90]

Whisper words of wisdom . . .

Let it be.

Okay, Jessie! Take the guitar solo.

Jessie played the solo as well as George Harrison. With Jamie on keyboards, and your mom and Josie singing along, we used to rock that song.

OUT OF CONTROL AND INTO THE FLOW

*The opposite of not minding what happens is trying to
control everything that happens. Ha!
If the need to control didn't ruin so many relationships,
squash so many dreams, and bludgeon so many spirits
to death, it'd be hilarious!*

—Dad

P icture your ego as a small child.

The child is sitting next to his father in a car, holding on to a plastic steering wheel, playing "make believe I'm driving." Then picture the universe as the loving father who's really driving the car.

"Your ego has about as much control over what's going on as a child sitting next to his father in a car with a plastic steering wheel, turning the car the way Daddy drives it."[91]

People who try to control everyone and everything are like children playing "make believe I'm driving." The only way to really flow with life is to let go of the plastic wheel.

"In letting go, you gain control. In giving it up, you've got it."[92]

The need to control is fear. And all fear is illusion.

Alignment with your Self, others, and life is what you're really seeking.

When the wheels on a car are out of alignment, the ride gets rough. When they get too far out of alignment . . .

BAM! The car will spin out of *your* control and hit the wall.

255

If you bend too far out of alignment by trying to control the future, clinging to outcomes and wrestling with things you can't change, the ride of life will get bumpier and scarier until . . .

BAM! Your happiness will crash and burn.

If you try to control others by trying to change them, demanding they say, think, and do things your way, and you don't accept them for who they are, the relationship will charge like two raging bulls into a head to head-on collision, until . . .

BAM! It collides into a million little uncontrollable pieces

Trust life!

Trust your own nature.

Trust the driver of the universe like you'd trust Grandma Hanky.

The universe governs not by ruling, but by allowing everyone and everything to follow its own nature, and be itself.

Like in any relationship, including the one with your Self,

To have a loving relationship with the universe, quit telling it what to do! How would you feel if you had a boyfriend who constantly tried to control you?

I demand more attention!

Do this! Do that!

I command more affection!

Don't do this! Don't do that!

Why didn't you call?

Do what I love to do, not what you love to do.

Be who I am, not who you are. Do what I want, not what you want.

You're late for Taco Tuesday tonight! You don't appreciate me or my tacos.

I'm hurt, so you're dead.

Now put this ring in your nose and tell me you love me!

Like that country song says, "It's hard to kiss the lips at night that chew your [bleep] out all day long."

If you try to control someone into loving you, you'll make it impossible for them to love you. They'll go through the motions as they head for the door. You'll cut off the current that started the flow of love to begin with. A stream cut off from its source dries up. A relationship dammed up by the rocks of control is not free to run. If you want to nurture love, you must let go and give your loved one the freedom to be who they are.

What about career?

There's a showbiz saying in L.A. about how people mysteriously quit getting callbacks, work, projects, or employment for no apparent reason. The epitaph: *The doors close quietly in L.A.* Even if someone is an obnoxious control freak, showbiz types don't want to burn any bridges, so they quietly avoid controlling people.

It's the same with friendships:

If you try to *demand and control* a friend's behavior, the friendship door will *close quietly.* Friends will slowly and quietly avoid you.

Let go of trying to change people.

Let go of needing to be right.

Let go of getting even.

Good, bad, or ugly accept your friends for who they are.

Friendship is open arms. Close them and you'll be left holding yourself.

And parents . . .

Do you really think you can control your kids?

You can't control them; you can only influence them.

Modeling is the only thing they hear, and the only advice that sticks.

Try to bend them to your will, and you'll quietly drive them away. Once they leave the house, visits back home will be fewer and farther apart, until there's none at all. Parenting is open arms. Close them and you'll be left holding yourself.

Dreams.

Do you really think you can control your dreams into coming true? Like nurturing a plant with water and sunshine, you can only create the conditions for your dreams to unfold. You can't demand that a flower grow, you can only plant and nurture the seed. Forcing a dream to come true is like micromanaging the opening of a flower petal.

Once the conditions (the ecosystem of your dream) are in place, the rest is in the same hands that created the universe and keeps the earth spinning round the sun. So who are you going to trust—the source of all power, or the disposable battery pack of the ego?

It's the same thing with business.

You can't force a business to be successful; you can only create the conditions for success to grow. For example, a mandatory condition for any successful business is providing value. I've worked with Harvard-MBA CEOs who have had every other condition in place but a compelling value proposition, and watched them work futilely as the business wilted and died.

And rushing like a scared rat towards success is very different than deliberately moving forward. I've seen entrepreneurs so anxious to control a business objective that they've skipped steps, forced sales meetings, cut off the flow of emerging ideas, and micromanaged projects into early graves.

We've got to control our need to control!

It's a disease that dams up the current of our natures, cuts off cash flow, alienates loved ones, derails plans, stunts talent, and blocks off the fun of life.

There's a beautiful poem called "Woman with Flower," by Naomi Long Madgett, Detroit Poet Laureate, which sums up the harm that *needing to control* can do to *everyone* and *everything* we love.

I wouldn't coax the plant if I were you.

Such watchful nurturing may do it harm.

Let the soil rest from so much digging,

And wait until it's dry before you water it.

The leaf is inclined to find its own direction;
Give it a chance to seek the sunlight for itself.
Much growth is stunted by too careful prodding,
Too eager tenderness.
The things we love, we have to learn to leave alone.[93]

"Your ego has about as much control of what's going on
as a child sitting next to his father in a car with a plastic stering wheel,
turning the car the way daddy drives it." —Watts

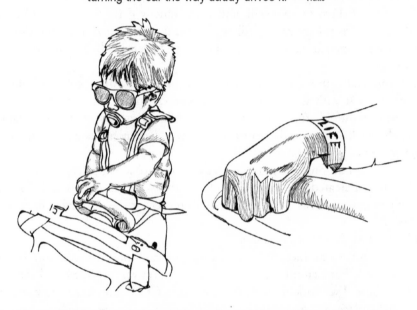

People who try to control everyone and everything are like children playing
"make believe I'm driving."
The only way to really flow with life is to let go of the plastic wheel.

SURRENDER

What's the antidote to control?
Surrender.
You mean, give up?
No! Just the opposite.
I mean power up!

—Dad

I t felt like I had swallowed a sand dune.

I was so nervous before performing at Carnegie Hall, I developed a bad case of cotton mouth. The original song I wrote, and was about to perform on the grandest stage of all, opened with me, alone in the spotlight, playing an unaccompanied alto flute solo. A mouthful of cotton balls (fear) would definitely block the musical flow.

I was holding on too tight—trying to figure out how I could "control" the performance by calculating every note and move ahead of time. As I paced around backstage, like some nervous Nelly, the insanity of my thinking occurred to me. In a musical setting based on improvisation, why block the magic that can only happen by being open and ready for anything?

The bandstand is a sacred place, where past and future disappear, revealing the eternal present, the only living moment from which gifts of creation can flow.

All of life is like that.

Why cut the current and desecrate the bandstand of life by trying to control it?

Even a wrong note can spur a new idea and take the music places impossible to plan—but only by relinquishing the illusion of control. If you listen to the possibilities

259

of an unplanned note, and go with the flow of where it can lead, there are no wrong notes in music, or in life.

So I surrendered.

Surrender sounds like giving up, but what it really means is getting out of your own way. I traded in my need to control for the same force that fuels nature, creates life, and draws our every breath.

I didn't give up, I powered up.

I plugged into the forces of nature through the power board of humility.

Humility is the recognition that we are only the channel; God, by whatever name God is known, is the source. Humility opens up a tideway through which the current of creativity can flow, flinging open the floodgates to unlimited possibilities.

Clinging to the rock of control dams it shut.

I let go of the rock—let humility clear the current, so the electric mambo dance of nature could surge, and grow, and flow with me, and in me, and through me, gathering and pointing the light of creation until . . .

ZAP!

The floodlights banged on.

Fear washed out.

Pride bled dry.

Need for approval dimmed off.

Basing self-worth on a good or bad performance faded to black.

I was powered up!

I walked on stage to a full house at Carnegie Hall—as my beautiful wife Paula, treasured family, dearest friends, and of course, Grandma Hanky cheered me on in the crowd. I was amazingly alive, free, and calm. The fear vanished as time disappeared.

I powered up by letting go.

I won the inner battle by surrendering the fight.

Your Uncle Michael's song, "Back in the Zone," sums up my backstage transformation beautifully.

I hit the ground kneeling—said
Good Lord—make me strong.
Take me back to where I belong.
Now I don't think I just do,
I don't worry I just move,
I don't over analyze,
I just feel it if it's right,
I'm just knowing that I know,
I'm just going with the flow,
I take a deep breath,
Now I'm back in the zone.
Feels good to be home.
I'm back in the zone.

Plug into the omnipotent power of divinity through the power board of humility.

Surrender isn't giving up. Surrender is powering up!

WORRY, WORRY, WORRY!

*Not only do we think it's normal to be worrying, hurrying,
and stressed out—we think we won't get what we want
unless we're worrying, hurrying, and stressed out.
Ha!*

—Dad

You're in it now.

You're out of the house and into the belly of the beast called growing up. College is a lot of work, worry, and stress. Living with strangers is awkward. Sleep is impossible. Group bathrooms are gross. Problems with friends can break your heart and leave you feeling lonely.

The future you—the one living the dream years from now—seems like a distant star. Bogged down in books and irrelevance, it feels like a star you'll never reach. To top it off, you're wondering if college is a big waste of time.

There's a lot of fear and worry, fear and worry, fear and worry.

Fear of bad grades. Worry about the future. Fear of not making it. Worry about making money. Fear of the wrong roommate. Worry about the right major. Fear you're not good enough. Worry your school isn't good enough for you. Fear of having no place to live. Worry about having nothing to live for.

As you yearn for the carefree days of childhood, fear of facing grown-up things, such as bills, laundry, and the prospect of stuffing your soul into a corporate coffin, can creep in and suck the life out.

Hmm.

No worries!

All normal stuff really.

It reminds me of a song your Uncle Johnny and I wrote when we were on our way out of high school and looking at the outside world from inside the city *limits* of our hometown, Fond du Lac, Wisconsin.

I'm worried about the future,
Thinking about the past,
Wondering if my dreams and hopes
Are really going to last.
When my eyes are finally open,
Will I be where I wanted to be—
Or end up doing nine to five
Back in ole Fondy?

Worry, worry, worry!

I worry about worry!

Ha!

Seriously, it makes me laugh.

What a complete waste of time!

What were you worried about one year ago today? I bet you can't remember. What are you worried about happening one year from today? Since 99.999 percent of what we worry about never happens anyway, why hallucinate about something you think might happen?

Most of the tiny tragedies we invent in our minds and obsess over every day never happen! But what if they do?

SO WHAT?

Say it with me now!

SO WHAT?

Remember what the wise man said about the secret of life: *I don't mind what happens.* Nothing is ever as bad as we hallucinate it to be. As a matter of fact, when a problem is actually happening, it doesn't seem that bad at all.

There's nothing we can't handle in the present moment.

Freeze-frame: Is everything all right *now*?

Freeze-frame: Are you okay *now*?

Freeze-frame: Are you going to die *now*?

Now is the key word. Worry always puts you in the past or the future.

Roll tape: Go back to worrying.

What's changed besides what you're holding in mind?

Nothing!

We literally worry ourselves sick. We waste our bodies and our days over nothing!

When I was visiting Jamie in her dorm room, I noticed a lot of tension in students wandering the halls. So at one point during a conversation with Jamie's friends, I spontaneously stuck my head out of her room and screamed, "It's only college! It's not that big of a deal!" I then continued to ramble on with some other bad college comedy bit, which I can't remember and probably made no sense. Jamie's friends looked at me in shock. Jamie just stared with a nervous, "that's my crazy dad" kind of smile.

But there was a method to my madness. The hallucination of worry and stress puts an ominous cloud over life, making everything seem bleak. I figured, if I could let the air out of the pressure valve, ridding them of the idea that their entire lives are at stake with every test they take, they'd lighten up and actually do better.

Why do we insist on being motivated by the fear of failure in order to succeed?

Maybe if we cleared our minds from the broken compass of fear, we'd make room for empowering motivations to steer the ship. Why not be motivated by passion, adventure, and fun versus fear of failure, fear of survival, or fear of not looking good to a world that's not looking anyway.

Jamie mentioned that after I left, a few of her dorm mates would periodically shout "It's only college, it's not that big of a deal" like a mantra. Maybe I got through on some level or maybe I just completely embarrassed my daughter. Oh well!

I'm not going to worry about it.

Worrying is food for the ego, but like a dark cloud blocking the sun, it separates us from seeing with the soul. It starves us blind.

You can't focus on major possibilities if you're hallucinating on minor problems.

If there's a problem, don't worry about it—solve it.

Worrying has never solved a single problem in the history of mankind.

Worrying, which is fear, *is* the biggest problem of mankind.

Again, it's a matter of faith.

Worry is a lack of faith.

It's either a loving universe or it isn't. This spiritual stuff is either real or it isn't. Constant worry is a sure sign you believe in the "isn't"—a sure sign you're being run by fear instead of faith.

Worrying is prayer in reverse.

Flooding your subconscious mind with worry over all of the terrible things that *could* happen is like praying for what you don't want. What we hold in mind not only tends to manifest—it colors our experience of life. Do you want to color your college years with worry or wonder, pain or possibilities, fear or fun?

Think about leaping off the rocks at Devil's Lake, our favorite summer swimming hole. It can be a bit scary.

Though it feels a little dangerous, deep down you know there's nothing to worry about. Once you build up the nerve to let go and leap, the elation of flying into the unknown washes over your fear. For a moment there's nothing to hold onto—you've rescinded control—then, with a splash that can only be made by jumping, you land in a fresh pool of new energy as the water jolts through you like a charge. Exhilarating! Invigorating! You feel more alive than ever. It's the same thing with faith.

If you find yourself stranded on the rocks of worry,

Take a leap of faith,
Rescind control,
Trust the depths of love, on which your life is floating,
Then let go and leap.
I know it sounds trite, but like rock diving at the lake,
Faith is fun.
Splash!
Worry's a bummer.
Thud.
Seems like an obvious choice.

FARTHER THAN FAITH

I think of psychologist Carl Jung's response when asked if he believed in God.
"I don't believe in God; I know there's a God."
Jung was not a person of faith; he was a person farther than faith.

—Dad

t's 4:00 a.m.

I've been grappling with what to tell you about religious faith since 3:00 a.m.

Actually, I've been grappling with it since you were born.

How do I to write about such a personal, divisive, and misrepresented topic? Words about God can only point to the truth of God—a truth you must discover on your own—a truth you must experience to know.

So instead of writing, I googled great minds, scrounged through all my "God books," as you girls call them, and ended up looking out of the window a lot, tapping my fingers, waiting for inspiration—or for Josie to wake up, whichever came first.

As I hemmed and hawed, I thought of people on those purposely divisive cable news channels, dividing us up as either people of faith, or ahh . . . those who are going to burn in hell. I thought back to the time I overheard a Bible group gossiping while I was writing at Cool Beans coffee shop in Madison, Wisconsin. "Is he a person of faith? Is he a believer? If not, we can't associate with him!" I mean no disrespect. I love Jesus and his teachings. But to put it in marketing terms, certain members of the Christian faith have co-opted the brand and turned it into the very opposite of what Jesus stood for. They call this the luciferic inversion. *I'll judge you in the name of Jesus,* who said, "Thou shall not judge." *I'll kill you in the name of Jesus,* the prince of peace. Fred Phelps was the master of this technique. *They'll burn in Hell because a God of love hates fags.*

The same inversion happens in the Islamic faith. The phrase that begins all but one of the 114 verses of the Koran is, "In the name of God, the Compassionate, the Merciful." How, *in the name of a compassionate, merciful God,* can these beautiful words be used to justify slaughter, rape, beheadings, and terror?

I wonder if the self-righteous and delusional understand that by judging someone else, they're defining themselves. Why? Because they don't see the world as it is, they see the world as they are. *Evil is in the eye of the beholder.*[94] And here's one the coffee-shop gossip group might want to discuss at their next get together: *Don't worry about the speck in your neighbor's eye, worry about the log in your own.*[95]

I've been communing with Jesus my entire life and will do so forever. But I have a hard time labeling myself as a Christian or anything for that matter, because the Pharisees who hijacked the brand have inverted the absolute truth of its message. *Love thy neighbor as thyself.* The essence of Jesus's message is unconditional love and forgiveness. Who can argue with that? As Gandhi said, "Your Christ is so unlike your Christians." Not all! No, no, no! Just a loud few who know not what they do.

Truth can't be divided.

Mohammed wasn't a Muslim, Christ wasn't a Christian, and Buddha wasn't a Buddhist. The labels came later, and at a lower level of truth than the avatars who inspired the labels to begin with. Though brought up Catholic, I love listening to Pastor Jeff speak at a Lutheran church on Sundays. I always walk out feeling better than when I walked in. (Though I'm not crazy about holding a stranger's sweaty hand during the Lord's prayer, which is why I always try to make Paula or you girls sit on the end of the aisle!) Synagogue, mosque, Buddhist monastery, holding hands with a sweaty stranger—doesn't matter to me.

I look at the love behind the label.

I think of an amazing child prodigy named Akiane, who painted pictures of Christ and images inspired by, as she puts it, "visions from heaven." When she painted a portrait of a Hindu she was attacked by certain fundamentalists who said, "The devil's got your soul. Burn the pictures now. Label yourself as one of us."

Her reply:

God looks at my love.

Out of the mouths of babes comes the Truth.

God looks at our love, not our label.

As my standoff with inspiration continued, I tapped my fingers to fidgeting thoughts of agnostics and atheists.

What's the difference?

Tap, tap, tap.

It comes down to the difference between humility and pride.

More tap, tap, tapping.

Agnostic is a position of *humility*, which says, *I don't know.* It calibrates at 200, which reaches the levels of truth on the scale of consciousness. Do not feel guilty if you have questions or doubts about God. Sincere questions are part of your path to Truth. As the saying goes, "When the student is ready, the teacher will come." Stay loving, forgiving, and nonjudgmental, and the answers will unfold.

Atheism is a position of *pride,* which says, *I know.* Of course, an atheist doesn't know, so ironically, like believing in God versus experiencing God, it's a belief based on faith. It calibrates below the level of truth on the scale of consciousness. Many an atheist has followed their faith *farther than faith* into the pits of truly experiencing their faith, and flipped back to the ultimate reality, which some call God.

Like a house of mirrors, I continued to sift through distorted views of faith, in the hopes that the real thing would emerge from the mirage. I was just about to give up on inspiration and trade it in for the perspiration of working out before Josie woke up, when it hit.

I heard that guardian voice again.

It was the same one I heard before Grandma Hanky died. It's not really a voice; it's more like a very distinctive thought nudging for my attention. It simply said, *You already understand faith!* As if to say, quit staring out the window and googling for answers, you've got this. I literally stopped in my tracks and whispered low, "Yes, I do understand faith."

Then, like a jazz musician about to play without knowing exactly which notes would come out, I immediately stated the theme of my understanding out loud to teach myself what I already knew. These are the words, exactly as they popped out of my mouth:

There's a difference between knowing about and knowing.

Knowing about is an intellectual understanding of truth.

Knowing is being truth.

In the gap between knowing about and knowing, stands faith.

Hmm.

What does that mean?

In terms of religion, it means . . .

There's a gap between *knowing about* the source of all creation many call God, and truly *knowing* God.

The ultimate reality pulls us farther than faith into knowing.

Expands our reach beyond faith into being.

The experience of God is much different than the belief in God.

The reality of God—ever present and available always—is different than dogma.

I can read about a sunset, understand a sunset, but to truly know a sunset, I must experience a sunset.

Knowing about is linear.

Knowing is nonlinear.

Knowing is farther than knowing about.
Experiencing God is farther than believing in God.
Being is farther than faith.

I can read about a sunset, understand a sunset, but
to truly know a sunset, I must experience a sunset.

Knowing about is the intellect, which is limited.

Knowing is the spirit, which is infinite.

Here's how the psychologist in the movie *Good Will Hunting* (played by Robin Williams) points out the difference to his know-it-all, genius patient (played by Matt Damon).

[Knowing about] "So, if I asked you about art, you'd probably give me the skinny on every art book ever written. Michelangelo. You know a lot about him. Life's work, political aspirations, him and the pope, sexual orientation, the whole works, right?

[Knowing] But I bet you can't tell me what it smells like in the Sistine Chapel. You've never actually stood there and looked up at that beautiful ceiling . . .

[Knowing about] I ask you about war, you'd probably uh—throw Shakespeare at me, right? "Once more into the breach, dear friends."

[Knowing] But you've never been near one. You've never held your best friend's head in your lap and watched him gasp his last breath, looking to you for help.

[Knowing about] I ask you about love, you'd probably quote me a sonnet. But you've never looked at a woman and been totally vulnerable—known someone that could level you with her eyes. Feeling like God put an angel on Earth just for you, who could rescue you from the depths of hell . . .

[Knowing about] You're an orphan, right?

[Knowing] "Do you think I'd know the first thing about how hard your life has been, how you feel, who you are because I read Oliver Twist? Does that encapsulate you?"

It's the same thing with God.

Do you think you can experience God by reading the Bible, Torah, Koran, Bhagavad Gita, or theology? Do you think any *word* can encapsulate God?

"You can't get wet from the word water."[96]

To truly know *the word*, you must jump in and experience it.

Too many people, preaching about God, haven't gotten wet.

Grandma Hanky knew God.

(I'm sure they had coffee together on a regular basis.)

Her life was her sermon.

Though I've probably had more glimpses of God than I realize, people of faith, like myself, haven't arrived yet.

We're still grappling in the gap.

Hem,

Haw,

Tap, tap, tap.

THE GOD GAP

What appears to cause the dualistic gap between knowing
about and knowing?
Two things:
The ego and our senses.

—Dad

The biggest obstacle to understanding, experiencing, or even talking about God can be summed up in the optical illusion, represented by one word.
Separate.
Hmm. Maybe we need two words.
Separate entity.
Okay, make that three words.
God is separate.
Maybe four words might be better.
The illusion of separation.
Let's whip in a few more words and make it nine.
The ego's illusion that God is separate from us.
What the heck? Let's toss in even more words that can only point to the Truth.
Most people hold the anthropomorphic view of God as a separate, bearded guy in the sky, who, for our own good, gets angry, hurt, offended, and filled with revenge if we don't do what he says. We create God in the nearsighted image we have of ourselves.
If we had a clearer image of who we are, we'd have a clearer image of God.
(That's way more than one word.)

But we can't seem to see past our own skin.

Why?

I can sum that up in five words.

Sight, touch, sound, smell, taste.

We can't see the *reality of nonduality*, beyond the limitations of our five senses:

The human mind is not capable of discerning truth from falsehood.[97]

(Repeat that one hundred gazillion times.)

We can't see beyond perception to reality, behind appearance to essence.

We can't see past the illusion of time to the fact that God is outside of time.

We can't comprehend that there is *only always*.

What time is it?

It's only always o'clock.

Only always o'clock! Darn! I'm going to be late for Zumba class again!

We rush through life too fast to experience *only always*. We experience bits and pieces and call it everything.

Paula and I watched a movie with Josie called *God's Not Dead*, a story about an atheist professor who forced a Christian student to prove the existence of God. The atheist was saying there is no separate entity in the sky called God. The student was saying there was a separate entity in the sky called God.

They were both mistaken.

They were arguing in the wrong ballpark.

A linear outfield versus the nonlinear infield.

The argument on both sides was based on a false premise—the anthropomorphic linear view that God is a separate entity *out there*.

The atheist was incorrect about the nonreality of the ultimate Truth some call God—basing his argument in the partial dualistic paradigm of the senses, versus the full reality of nonduality. The student was correct about the reality of the ultimate Truth some call God, but needed to recontextualize the ineffable Truth he subjectively knew. God is not an invisible superparent *out there* in the sky. They were trying to stuff nondualistic, quantum reality into a dualistic box of Newtonian science—looking with their egos, instead of seeing, with their essence. Heck! It's more accurate to debate the existence of love.

They were asking the wrong question.

If the ego really feels the need to argue about God, one way or the other, it should at least start the so-called discussion with more accurate questions, like . . .

What is the nature of God and reality?

Is God the ultimate context, of which the universe and all existence is content?

Is God the formless source of existence within all form?

Is God both manifest as the Totality and Allness of creation and simultaneously unmanifest as the Infinite Potentiality and Source prior to form?[98]

Is consciousness the mind of God?

Where is God?

Is God transcendent, which means *out there* playing hide-and-seek some *place*?

Or is God immanent, everywhere at all times, therefore present within each of us?

I call the ultimate reality, God. Other names for the nameless are Yahweh, Allah, Jehovah, and Bhagavan, the source, the force, to name a few. In Taoism it is said, "the Tao [God] that can be named is not the eternal Tao [God]." I use the word God as a semantic convenience for that which cannot be named.

Everyone and everything is part of God like a drop of water is part of the ocean.[99] We are either in alignment with God, therefore with ourselves, or not.

But our five senses can't see the full picture of nonlinear truth, through linear perception. We believe if we can't touch, see, hear, smell, or taste some *thing*, it's not real.

This creates the dualistic illusion that we are . . .

Separate from each other,

Separate from creation, and

Separate from God.

Nothing could be further from the truth.

Is a ray of sunlight separate from the sun?

When the *blinds* of the ego are raised, you'll rise above the senses,

Experience the power of allness,

The oneness of creation,

And you'll see who you are . . .

A ray of *Son-light,* emanating from the sun of God.

With the power of humility, you'll shift from,

All glory be to me (the root of turmoil in the world and in our lives) to . . .

All Glory Be to Thee.[100]

The last six words Steve Jobs exclaimed before dying describe his revelation of the glory of reality some call God.

Oh Wow!

Oh Wow!

Oh Wow!

Dr. David Hawkins *knows* from experience . . .

"God *is* the ultimate context, of which the universe and all existence are content. God *is* the formless source of existence within all form. God *is* both manifest as the Totality and Allness of creation and, simultaneously, unmanifest as the Infinite Potentiality and Source prior to form."[101]

Consciousness *is* the mind of God.

Omnipotent, omniscient, omnipresent.

Even "I am that I am," a phrase used to describe God, is redundant.

"'I' is a complete statement of reality."[102]

God just is . . .

God is All.

All is God.
Gloria in Excelsis Deo!

I have faith in love. To know love, is to know God.

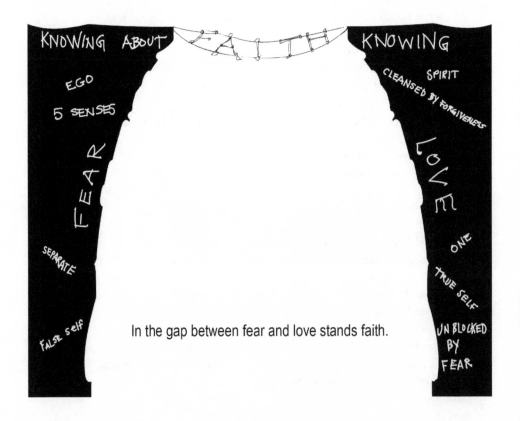

KNOWING ABOUT FAITH KNOWING

EGO

5 SENSES

FEAR

SEPARATE

FALSE Self

SPIRIT

CLEANSED BY FORGIVENESS

LOVE

ONE

TRUE SELF

UN BLOCKED
BY
FEAR

In the gap between fear and love stands faith.

PRAYER

Grandma Hanky always said, "A day wrapped in prayer is
*   less likely to come unraveled."*
I've had good days wrapped in prayers, and bad days
*   wrapped in problems.*
The difference . . .
Prayer.
Grandma was right!

—Dad

Prayer gives us the power to look at things and change them.

Prayer is focused intention, and as scientist Werner Heisenberg discovered, "Our mere conscious act of observing a thing affects and changes it. Thoughtful intention increases the probability of affecting physical matter."

Physicist Max Planck agrees.

"Change the way you look at things, and the things you look at will change."

The physical act of blessing your food, genuflecting, making the sign of the cross, bowing to Mecca, fasting on Yom Kippur, or joining palms and saying "namaste" doesn't change things.

But the intention behind the physical act literally alters the fabric of the universe.

We are confused about prayer.

We ask and don't receive. We outline our desires to some bearded man in the sky, and they are not answered. We pray for others to heal, and they die. We pray for success and fail. We pray that God spares our children from pain, and the pain of growing up assaults them anyway.

Needy prayers create more neediness.

Vain repetition creates nothing.

Desperate prayers increase the very problem from which we're seeking relief.

Prayer—the art of believing what is denied by the senses—deals almost entirely with the subconscious.[103] As I've said, the subconscious gives what it receives.

We send beggarly prayers, through the darkness of fear, and wonder why they shed no light. We think of God's will as an alien power, thrust upon us unwillingly, never recognizing that . . .

Our will *is* God's will—what we want most is what God wants for us.

Thy will be done is a statement aligning us with ourselves.

So how should we pray?

We attract what we are, not what we beg for.

To attract what you want . . .

Reverse your polarity.

Give thanks for what you really want, as if you already have it.

Because you do,

If you believe it.

And feeling is believing.

REVERSE IT!

Instead of "I'm not" and "I need," say "I am" and "Thank you."

—Dad

Instead of waiting to have more in order to feel grateful . . .
Reverse it!
Feel grateful now, and you'll have more.

The *feeling/energy* is the prayer. Like a magnet, it attracts more of the same.

"Whoever has will be given more; whoever does not have, even what they have will be taken from them."[104]

Many people read this passage and think,

"Not fair! Some big mean god in the sky is going to take away my stuff and give more stuff to people who already have stuff."

They don't understand its quantum meaning.

We give ourselves more through magnetic feelings of gratitude (love—high consciousness/energy level), or . . .

We take away *even what we have* through negative feelings of lack (fear—low consciousness/energy level).

To change your world, change your polarity.
Reverse it!

If you want straight As in school, declare, "I am a straight-A student!" Living your wish on the inside first sets in motion what author Neville Goddard calls the "law of reversibility."

The law of reversibility?

What the heck is that?

If effect A can be produced by effect B, then inversely effect B can be produced by the cause A.

Huh?

Reverse it.

"If electricity can produce friction; then, friction can produce electricity. If a physical fact can produce a psychological state, then a psychological state can produce a physical fact."[105]

Huh?

Reverse it.

Winning a public speaking contest, like Josie did, could create a feeling of accomplishment. Inversely, holding that victory in mind first, creating the *feeling* of accomplishment ahead of time, will produce the win.

Instead of feeling desperate for what you want . . .

Reverse it.

Feel as if you already have that which you seek.

Ask as if you have received means *feel* as if you have received.

"The feeling is the prayer."[106]

Hmm.

C'mon.

Is it really that simple? Wave the law of reversibility like it's a magic wand, and voilà!—manifest anything your subconscious feels is true? That doesn't make sense.

It's not quite that simple.

If you look at prayer through a linear, Newtonian cause-and-effect lens, the law of reversibility doesn't make sense. But praying "as if" your prayer is fulfilled reaches farther than Newtonian science can grasp.

The ultimate reality is *nonlinear*, which includes mysteries outside of time and beyond our understanding, like . . .

Karmic merit.

Not knowing what serves the highest good. (Which includes your highest good.)

Not knowing what we really want. (Is it our ego or our essence at prayer?)

If the very hairs are on our heads are all numbered,[107] we must have the faith to pray and surrender. Let go, let God, and as Jesus said,

"With God all things are possible."

So who am I to disagree?

Which part of "all things" am I and Newton questioning?

This is possible, but not that.

That might work, but not this.

This is a possibility, but I don't care if you feel "as if" or not—that's impossible!

Hmm.

Who am I going to listen to, Newton or Jesus?

Is my cause-and-effect caveat really just my lack of faith?

"For truly I tell you, if you have faith the size of a mustard seed, you can say to this mountain, 'Move from here to there,' and it will move. *Nothing will be impossible for you.*"[108]

Newton and Jesus were both right. (Though Newton was only half-right—stating *a* truth, not *the* truth. He didn't look past linear appearance to nonlinear essence.)

You can't move the Rocky Mountains closer to Wisconsin to make skiing more convenient. But the omnipotent power source and force of the universe that some call God, working through you, can do anything.

As author Eckhart Tolle says, "You have to find the God *in you,* so God can move mountains *through you.*" *You* can't chew gum and walk without God. And the omnipotent current of God flowing *through you,* gets dammed up and choked down to a *Newtonian trickle,* as ego, fear, and lack of faith arise. Free will gives you control of the wish valve. To harness a tsunami of unfathomable power, turn off your ego, turn on your faith, and surrender control.

There are more things in heaven and earth than our tiny little linear senses can understand with the intellect alone.

Instead of 'I'm not' and 'I need,' say 'I am' and 'thank you.'

Feel as if you already have that which you seek. . .
"The feeling is the prayer." —Braden

I for one am going to pray "as if."

I've got some pretty exciting mountains to move.

I'm moving them on the inside now.

So see you on top of the Rockies!

BTW, they're in Wisconsin now. I *felt* that moving them there would make it more convenient to go skiing.

Paula's a great skier!

I'm a great ski lodger.

Ha!

THY WILL BE DONE

Trust that what we want most, God wants for us.

—Dad

What if I don't know what's best for me?

You don't.

But God does.

The ego is oblivious to what we really want. It doesn't know what serves our best interests, seeks but never finds, and looks for happiness in all the wrong places. So pray for the highest good—not only for all in your circle of concern, but for all, which includes your highest good as well.

I may pray, "My children have been spared from the pain that comes with growing up and finding their place in this world" (which I do every night), but does my request rob you of the lessons you must learn on your own?

I could have prayed, "My mom has recovered from Alzheimer's disease." Would my prayer have robbed my mother of her karmic lessons, knocked her off her spiritual path, stolen her way home?

I don't know.

But God does!

It is impossible for our five limited senses to perceive what serves our highest good. We are nearsighted, but the eyes of the universe are infinite.

Trust that what we want most, God wants for us.

What people we pray for want most, God wants for them.

What we are really seeking is alignment.

281

Alignment with God is alignment with ourselves.
The ultimate intention and most powerful prayer is . . .
Thy will be done.
Why?
Because *thy* will is *my* will.
"In doing this, you don't really ask for anything. You state a fact that cannot be denied. We are asking a real question at last. The answer is a simple statement of a simple fact. You will receive the assurance that you seek."[109]

What we want most, God wants for us. What we are really seeking through prayer is alignment. Alignment with God is alignment with our highest good.

We do not perceive our own best interests, but God does.
Because "Thy" will is "my" will, the most powerful prayer is. . .
"Thy will be done."

As for science, you don't really need to know or think about quantum physics, laws of reversibility, the Heisenberg principle, Max Planck, and the mechanics of prayer. It only comes in handy when talking with people who can't see past linear, Newtonian reductionism to the nonlinear reality of the universe—people who can't break through their perception of duality to the nonduality of reality.

Huh?

You don't have to know how a phone works to make a phone call.

Prayer is what quantum physics looks like. Tell the skeptics that Newtonian science hasn't even scratched the nonlinear surface anyway. Tell them by that you mean Isaac Newton, not Fig Newton.

To truly *know* versus *knowing about* the power of prayer, conduct your own experiment based on the scientific hypothesis of physicist, Nobel Prize winner, and Frank Sinatra fan-girl, Grandma Hanky, PhD in life.

To restate her scientific theory on reverse polarity and the power of prayer:

A day wrapped in prayer is less likely to come unraveled.
Try it! The proof is in the pudding.
Or in Grandma's case, the Crock-Pot. She never really made pudding.

Grandma Hanky always said. . .
"A day wrapped in prayer is less likely to come unraveled."

Promise me you'll listen to Grandma (or Jim Carrey). Wrap every day in prayer.

DO LESS

To reach a BIG GOAL, complete a small action.
One small action at a time!

—Dad

Chinese philosopher Lao-tzu was big on small. He says the answer to achieving greatness in big things is easy . . . *Achieve greatness in little things.*
Other "small" gems of wisdom from Lao-tzu's repertoire include . . .
Do great things while they are still small.
Magnify the small. Increase the few.
See simplicity in the complicated.
And don't forget his greatest hit . . .
The journey of a thousand miles begins with a single step.
How do these fancy words apply to real life? Mountain climber Joe Simpson found out the hard way.

Joe Simpson and Simon Yates were the first ever to conquer the 21,000-foot summit of the Siula Grande, a mountain in the Peruvian Andes, from the west face. They climbed into the record books as they made it to the top.

But the emotional high of reaching the top quickly bottomed out as bad weather and insurmountable problems set in. They were out of fuel, out of water, and running out of daylight, as a major storm engulfed them. They had to get down now!

Upon descent, disaster struck!

Joe Simpson slipped down an ice cliff and shattered his leg—smashed his tibia straight up through his knee and crushed his bone into painful pieces. He crash-landed on a small ledge suspended in the darkness, between a bottom that had just dropped out and a bottomless pit beneath him. Like a hand in the dark, the jutting ledge caught his fall and saved his life. His "head torch beam just went down and down and down, and the darkness ate it, just gone."[110] Then Joe, somehow still alive, blacked out from the pain.

Upon regaining consciousness, Joe realized Simon would presume he was dead. Somehow he had to find his way back to the top of the glacier and make his way down the mountain on his own. After crawling and clawing through the murky maze of the crevasse, he saw the light and found an opening. Elated and overjoyed, he pulled himself up and out of the pit.

And I then looked at the glacier and I thought, *Well, you haven't even started, mate.* It's miles and miles, and on really bad ground. But I think I was contemplating just sitting there. I'd just come out of that, I'd badly broken a leg, I was in great pain, highly dehydrated, I had no food, and I was looking at trying to do that! Just no way, there's just no way you're physically gonna do that.

And then it occurred to me that I should set definite targets.

[Focus on the single step—not the journey of a thousand miles.]

I started to look at things and think, *Right, if I can get to that crevasse over there in twenty minutes, that's what I'm gonna do.*

[Achieve greatness in little things.]

If I got there in eighteen minutes I was like hysterically happy about it, and if I'd gotten there in twenty-two or twenty-four minutes, I was upset almost to the point of tears, and it became obsessive.

[To attain a big goal, complete a small action with greatness.]

I don't know why I did it; I think I knew the big picture of what had happened.

[Magnify the small—increase the few.]

What I had to do was so big I couldn't deal with it.[111]

[See simplicity in the complicated.]

Joe spent four days without food and water, dragging himself five miles back to their base camp. He achieved a seemingly insurmountable life or death task by focusing on one step at a time.

Gargantuan goals can only be reached

One action,

One focus,

One present moment at a time, fully lived.

Big is a *someday vision* projected into the future.

Starting with the end in mind is where you must start. Knowing your outcome in advance is a guiding star, which creates the power of pull.

But really . . .
Small is all—because small is now.
What are you doing now?
This second?
Whatever it is, no matter what's on your plate,
Do it with greatness.
Life is now!
Nothing else exists.

Acheive greatness in small things.

To reach a BIG GOAL, complete a small action. . . one small action at a time.

Big Goal, *Great Novel*

Small Action, *Great Sentence*

YOUR MOUNTAIN

Each step is a foundation—a world unto its own.
One building block depends on the other to support the
whole.

Impatience leads to half steps.
Grasping for the outcome leads to skipping steps.
Dwelling on future difficulties, or past missteps, leads
nowhere.

—Dad

How can *you* achieve greatness in little things, on the mountain of *your* dreams? Opportunity abounds!

Achieve greatness in e-mailing a potential employer, creating your resume, crafting each sentence of an essay, making a follow-up phone call, finding an internship, scheduling your day. Achieve greatness in every mundane detail, which together add up to the outcome of any endeavor, and ultimately your life.

Greatness lies in every single step, not only in the final Tah-dah!

Like Joe Simpson crawling out of the pit and realizing the depths of his challenge, the first step is to behold your mountain—the big picture of your dream. Then paint the picture into your subconscious, and focus on the rock in front of you.

C'mon! You can make it twenty feet!

You can reach that boulder over there!

You can crawl out of that crevasse!

You can make that phone call, learn that skill, earn that money!

Many people remain stuck at the foothills of their vision because they're too overwhelmed to start. You'll never be overwhelmed if you just *aim for that rock over there,* instead of the whole mountain all at once.

Let's imagine your dream is to create a television and motion picture empire that inspires and uplifts the world.

What's the first rock?

Where's the first crevasse?

How long will it take to get there?

Compare Joe Simpson's words and experience to the media mountain facing you.

JOE: *"All these huge mountains around you, big mountain walls. And they do make you feel small and vulnerable."*

YOU: *All these huge financial, emotional, and professional mountains around me—huge barriers to entry, big mountain walls—make me feel small and vulnerable.*

JOE: *"What I had to do was so big I couldn't deal with it."*

YOU: *Creating a media empire that changes the world is so big I can't deal with it.*

JOE: *"And it occurred to me, I should set definite targets."*

YOU: *I'll set definite targets, create milestones, and reach them one rock at a time.*

JOE: *"These tracks will lead me through the minefield of crevasses."*

YOU: *The tracks of my vision, fused to the trail of my subconscious, will lead me through the minefield of challenges.*

No matter what the endeavor, the first step is always laying the cornerstone . . .

A solid foundation of *what and why,* from which the path can rise.

Foundation: Know your what and why. Write it. See it. Feel it.

Milestone 1: Create and place one show.

Milestone 2: Find a powerful role model.

Once the foundation is laid, identify the *rock path* leading to and through the first set of milestones:

Rock 1: Create an idea for one show. Intellectual property I can sell.
JOE: "Right, if I can get to that crevasse over there, that's what I'm going to do."

Rock 2: Achieve greatness in creating pitch materials to sell my idea.
JOE: "Whoo! I can climb that slope. I bloody well will climb that slope!"

Rock 3: Invent a powerful company name and brand, which represents who I am.
JOE: "I'd look at that rock, and then I'd go, I'll get there in twenty minutes."

Rock 4: Develop a website exploding with creativity, credibility, and clarity.
JOE: "I knew I was going to fall a lot. I'd fallen virtually every hop."

Rock On: Identify, study, and choose inspirational mentors to contact.
JOE: "You gotta make decisions. If you don't make decisions, you're stuffed."

Rock It: Make contact with potential mentors. Schedule a meeting. Ask for help.
JOE: "I've got to get there. I carried on crawling in the dark."

Rock Out: Create a team to help sell/produce/distribute your show.
JOE: "That's what I'm going to do."

Rock Me: Design a business card for meetings with mentors and partners.
JOE: "I can get to that rock."[112]

You (and Joe) just worked backwards from your dream of founding a television and motion picture empire that inspires and uplifts the world to small actions you can achieve with greatness now.
Never leave the scene of a plan or decision without taking action.[113]
What action can you take now?
Name Action. _____
You can take a small action that changes the trajectory of your life as soon you're done reading this sentence.
Do it now!
Result? _____
Even the smallest pebble of progress creates momentum. Which creates excitement, which creates more progress. Once progress is set in motion, the levers of the universe are pulled to your cause.
Lao-tzu was right. To achieve greatness in big things,
Achieve greatness in little things.
But with all due respect to Lao-tzu,
The journey of a thousand miles is really only one step—

The one you're taking right now.
There are no other steps, and there never will be.

The "journey of a thousand miles" is really only one step— the one you're taking right now.

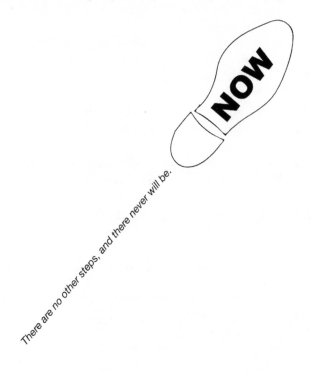

There are no other steps, and there never will be.

NOW

BE MORE

Before you ask, "What do I want to do?"
Ask, "What kind of person do I want to be?"
Your answer will define the quality and circumstances of
your life.

—Dad

Your Great-Great-Uncle George Rihbany emigrated from Lebanon to America in 1911. Though I never met him, I've come to know him through a diary he kept of the voyage. It reads like a map to his soul.

Imagine a young man, twelve years old, pondering his future, as he embarked on a voyage to the new world and a new life. Picture him standing at the ship's bow, like Leonardo DiCaprio in the movie *Titanic*, shouting "I'm king of the world," dreaming in the diary I'd hold in my teenage hands three generations later.

As I scoured the pages of his heart, a question he posed rose in challenge. Nervously I knew the answer was gunpowder. It had the power to explode into anything I wanted my life to be, fizzle out and die, or blow my dreams to smithereens. It's a question most people, in their rush to riches, never consider, and one I never want you to stop answering.

What kind of person am I going to be?

In his diary, titled *A Man in the Making,* Uncle George wrote these words:

There are two questions that every boy has to ask and answer for himself.
First, what kind of person am I going to be?

Second, what profession am I going to follow?

Unfortunately for the human race, very few boys think seriously of the first and more important question. In the majority of cases, the answer is determined and dictated, whether for good or evil, by the impulses, by the force of the environment, or by the desire for wealth and fame.

Even when asked and answered, George's *first and more important question* is rarely acted upon. Hiding in plain sight, its power is too simple to see.

Uncle George was one deep-thinking twelve-year-old! Without an iPhone, Facebook, Snapchat, or YouTube to suck up his mind space, I guess he had nothing better to do than ponder the meaning of life. Was there an app for that in 1911?

Over a century later, the compass of that question, which led George Rihbany across the seas, towards unknown regions of his inner and outer purpose, is more important than ever.

Ask it of yourself now.

What kind of person am I going to be?

Each of us is a magnet, attracting what we are!

Your answer will determine the quality and circumstances of your life.

Before you turn the page . . .

Think about it.

If we are honest, we attract peace, trust, and prosperity.
If we are dishonest, we attract trouble, mistrust, and *missed fortune.*

If we are hardworking, we attract a fun life of abundance and self-reliance.
If we are lazy, we attract a life of horrid work, desperation, and dependency.

If we are positive, positive things will find us.
If we are constantly complaining, something to complain about will track us down.

If we are noble, self-loving, and pure, we attract, beauty, respect, and true love.
If we are vulgar, drunk, and carnal, we attract ugliness, dark crutches, and empty sex.

If we learn to live for others, they will learn to live for us.[114]
If we are self-absorbed, we'll repel others, leaving us isolated in selfishness.

If we are *who we are,* the power of our uniqueness attracts our place in the world.
If we abandon ourselves, wounded we'll wander, in the hole we've left behind.

Who you are comes first; circumstance follows.
It is impossible to be a victim of circumstance.
Who we are creates our circumstance.
But we've been given a powerful gift.
We get to choose.

I AM?

What kind of person am I going to be?
Like words sculpting clay,
The shape of your destiny is formed by the answer.

—Dad

What did Uncle George have to say about character in *A Man in the Making*? "Wealth, fame, political and social success, and intellectual excellence are not only useless, but even dangerous to the possessor if he lacks character and moral excellence, by which men should be judged and esteemed."

Whoa! Who was this turn of the twentieth century, tween-age wunderkind? I bet he never dreamed his great-nephew (that's me) would be using his words to teach his great-great-nieces (that's you) about the power of character one hundred years later![1]*

So what is his not-so-secret sauce for success? Simple.

Ask the question.

What kind of person am I going to be?

And *be* the answer.

But answer the question with a statement.

I AM.

"Because the word that follows your I AM is going to come looking for you!"[115]

What kind of person do you want to be in a relationship? Here's an I AM that would salvage a lot of marriages and friendships.

---

1   To read the full "American Dream" story of Uncle George's amazing journey from penniless immigrant to millionaire entrepreneur, go to www.JimmyBrandmeier.com.

I am cheerful.

What kind of person do you want to be at work? Here's an I AM that would create job security, advancement, and more money.

I am indispensable.

What kind of person do you want to be financially? Here's an I AM that opens the floodgates to the wealth of the universe.

I am grateful.

Grateful for the wealth and blessings in my life *now.*

Grateful for my ability to bring moneymaking ideas to life.

Grateful that a means to create wealth is built into the calling of what I love to do.

I am forgiving liberates your spirit from the shackles of resentment, which is impossible without . . .

I am forgiven.

I am fearless obliterates the only obstacle between you and wild success—*fear!* And it opens the way for the mother of all I AMs to burst through the darkness like the light of a million suns . . .

What kind of person am I going to be?
Wave the question like it's Harry Potter's wand. "Expecto Patronum!"

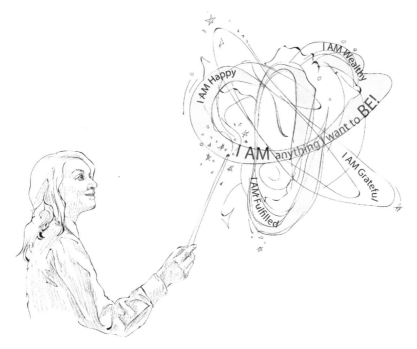

Like words sculpting clay, the shape of your destiny is formed by the answer.

I Am Love!

Look no further. You've made it home to happiness—no matter what *happens.*

If you'd like to change your body, mood, finances, relationships, outlook, or energy, don't look outside yourself . . .

Be the change you wish to see.[116]

Do less.

Be more.

Wave the question from *A Man in the Making* like it's Harry Potter's wand.

What kind of person am I going to be?

Expecto Patronum! (Summon your happiness.)

Like words sculpting clay,

The shape of your destiny is formed by the answer.

BE-LIEF
Conscious to Subconscious Interview:
The BE Series

BE your dream, and you'll see your dream.

—Dad

CONSCIOUS MIND: *Stuart Smalley from* Saturday Night Live *uses I AMs to program his subconscious.* "I am good enough, I am smart enough, and doggone it, people like me."

SUBCONSCIOUS MIND: I AMs are useless unless impressed upon me with feeling. Thoughts without belief have no energy. Empty I AMs are like empty calories—sound sweet, no nourishment.

So how do I program you with healthy I AMs?

Feel and believe with such certainty that feeling and believing transform into being. The feeling is the affirmation.

BE your dream inside, and you'll see it outside.

How do I do that?

Repetition, repetition, repetition!

Pete and Repeat were sitting in a boat. Pete fell out so who was left?

Repeat.

Pete and Repeat were . . .

Ha! It may be a corny joke, but there's power in the punch line. Repetition is the mother of learning. Repetition is power.

297

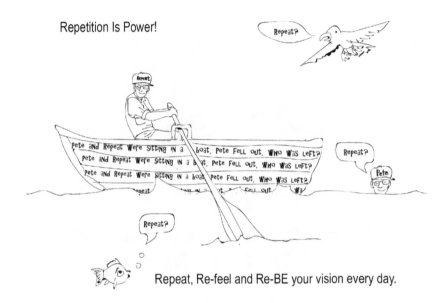

Repetition Is Power!

Repeat, Re-feel and Re-BE your vision every day.

So repeat, re-feel, and "re-be" my vision every day?

Habit is a hammer. It pounds the feelings of your vision into the reality of your vision fulfilled.

Let me sleep on that. Repetition, repetition, repetition; Habit, habit, habit; Re-be, re-be, re-be. (Re-be, re-be? Sounds like the background vocals in a Motown song.)

Sleep is also a direct portal to me. In the state of sleep, you and I are joined.

Hmm. I thought when I slept I was just sleeping, though my wife says I squeak in my sleep like a dolphin.

"Your feelings, beliefs, and concept of yourself as you fall asleep are the seeds you drop into the ground of the subconscious. What you take into sleep as a feeling comes out as a condition, action, or object when you awake."[117]

Hmm, I think I'll take more naps, and quit watching Flipper *reruns.*

Fall asleep with a crystal clear picture of your vision in mind, as if it were already true, and I will make it true.

I pray for a life that is lived not endured.

Prayer, like sleep, is also a direct portal to the subconscious. "It is in sleep and prayer, a state akin to sleep, that man enters the subconscious to make his impressions and receive his instructions."[118] Both prayer and affirmations pull back the veil of perception—reveal the source of the universe—and tap into the power line of God.

So how do I "tap in"?

To receive the I AM . . .

Be the I AM.

Re-be, re-be, re-be, re-be, dooooo! Motown is going to love this.

Pete and Repeat are going to be big!

BE BOLD AND BRAVE, GO MAKE MISTAKES, LIVE TO THE POINT OF TEARS

*Amazing things can only happen if you're willing to make
mistakes. If you never make mistakes, you'll never make
anything.*

—Dad

As I was daydreaming about what I'd do if I could wave a magic "dad wand" and conjure you an amazing life, a little voice stole into the scene and interviewed me like some inner-world talk show host.

LITTLE VOICE: Good evening, Jimmy! Welcome to your Daddy daydream!

JIMMY: Good evening to you, little daydream-crashing, scene-stealing voice.

*LITTLE VOICE: Let's get right to it. If you could make a wish and give your children
one thing that would ensure they had an amazing life, what would it
be? Remember, you've got "one thing," so make it good!*

JIMMY: Hmm . . . let me think about this.

Amazing things can only happen if they're willing to make
mistakes, willing to look foolish, and willing to fail. If they never
make mistakes, they'll never make anything.

LITTLE VOICE: True! But mistakes aren't a fun thing to wish for.

JIMMY: If they're afraid to make mistakes, they'll never live an amazing life.

299

LITTLE VOICE: *Yup! True again! Even a safe average life, is still average. Then again, as comedian Stephen Wright said, "If at first you don't succeed, destroy all evidence that you tried."*

JIMMY: Ha! Although Wright is amazing, and I once shared a stage with him at the Ding Ho Chinese restaurant and comedy club in Boston, I don't think I'll use my dad wish up on that message. [Name dropper!]

LITTLE VOICE: *They'll have to learn to navigate through unexpected problems and stay the course when everyone else jumps ship. It's grit, not IQ or class rank that determines success.[119] If they're afraid of making mistakes, they'll quit at the first dust speck of trouble and go through life gritless.*

JIMMY: I'm not sure if gritless is a word, but I am sure I don't want them to be that way.

LITTLE VOICE: *Acing a test is not the same as being tested. They were sold a bill of goods in school where failure is not an option, parents solve problems, and teachers dole out extra points in the name of self-esteem. The truth is, knowing how to fail is the only way to succeed.*

JIMMY: Huh?

LITTLE VOICE: *It is impossible to learn or achieve anything without mistakes and failure. Each mistake is a stepping-stone of new insight that leads to the ultimate answer. If your children don't know how to fail, they can't learn what they need to succeed.*

JIMMY: So if they are not failing, they are not surpassing themselves.

LITTLE VOICE: *Failure is a sign guiding the way and also a sign of personal growth. If they are not surpassing themselves, they are hiding out in their comfort zones and wilting away.*

JIMMY: Hmm . . . if they're not failing, they're not trying. The opposite of failure is not success; the opposite of failure is nothing. They'll only find out who they are if they lose their fear of failure.

LITTLE VOICE: *Okay, let's sum up your daydream so far.*
> *They'll fail to be amazing, unless they fail . . . to be amazing.*
> *"They'll fail to have a great career, unless they fail . . . to have a great career."[120]*

JIMMY: Oh, I get it! If they don't fail, they'll never be amazing, because failure teaches them what it takes to be amazing. If they don't fail, they'll never have an amazing career, because failure teaches them what it takes to have an amazing career. They'll fail to learn, unless they fail to learn. They'll fail to have grit, unless they fail to have grit. They'll fail to reach their dreams, unless they fail to reach their dreams.

LITTLE VOICE: *And the most important thing of all, they'll fail to be who they are, unless they fail to be who they are.*

JIMMY: They'll fail unless they fail! That's upside-down logic!

LITTLE VOICE: So, we must turn the way we look at failure upside down?

JIMMY: Failure is a friend, not the end. I know, cheesy rhyme—but now I also know what my one thing is!

            If I could give my children the one thing that would ensure an amazing life that one thing would be . . .

(Drum roll, please.)

            Failure!

            Tuh-Dahh!

(Silence and crickets chirping)

            What? No applause?

LITTLE VOICE: You just made a mistake—came up with the wrong conclusion. Rethink this. What is your mistake pointing to? Where is it guiding you? What is it teaching you?

JIMMY: If I have grit, learn from my mistakes, and stick it out, I'll get it. Hmm.

            Yes!

            I've got it!

            I don't want to give them failure. I want to take away their fear of failure.

            I don't want them to fail. I want them to look at failure as a tool to succeed.

            I don't want to encourage failure. I want to discourage fear.[121]

            Voilà! Mr. Watson, come here, I want to see you. My one thing is one word.

            The keyword that unlocks the door to unlimited potential and possibilities is . . .

(Drum roll, please.)

            Fearless

            Not failure.

            Yes!

            I'd make them fearless.

            Tuh-Dahh!

(Yay! Standing O!)

            Thanks for the applause! Thank you very much everyone! Good to be here! Have the veal and buy that couple a cheesecake; it goes with the cheesy lines I've been dishing out.

            Now hold the applause:

(Lights go dim.)

            That's my daddy daydream. That's my one thing, God.

            Fearless.

            Make them fearless, and they'll have amazing lives.

(Fade to black—Elvis has left the building.)

THE UNIVERSE: If you could make a wish and give your children ONE THING that would ensure they had an amazing life, what would it be?

DAD: FEARLESS.
That's my one thing God. Make them fearless, and they'll have amazing lives.

VERSE FIVE

The darkest night reveals the light of the stars,[122]
I promise you the day will dawn,
When Heart and Heaven beat as one,
You'll dance into your dreams,
The one destiny. My child, you'll
Be who you are, truly
See who you are.
You'll believe, as I believe in who you are.

FAILURE

The gift of failure is clarity. Failure gives you another
chance to be who you are.

—Dad

A flyspeck of so-called success can numb you into the purgatory of your comfort zone—leave you stuck between living and dying, the heaven of where you belong and the hell of where you don't. The hard knocks of so-called failure can shatter the façade of safety and jolt you back on track.

Harry Potter author J. K. Rowling is an inspirational example of failing your way to authenticity.

The only thing she ever wanted to do was write. Her well-meaning parents thought her "overactive imagination was an amusing personal quirk that would never pay the mortgage or secure a pension." So when it came time for college, Rowling majored in something she couldn't care less about to quell her parents' fear. That course took her off course from who she really was and what she really loved.

Seven years after graduation she found herself divorced, jobless, a single mother on welfare, and borderline homeless. Half a lifetime later, in a Harvard commencement speech, Rowling described that period of her life as "a dark one."

I was the biggest failure I knew. So why do I talk about the benefits of failure?

Failure meant a stripping away of the inessential. I stopped pretending to myself that I was anything other than what I was, and began to direct all my energy into finishing the only work that mattered to me.

Had I really succeeded at anything else, I might never have found the determination to succeed in the one arena I believed I truly belonged.

I was set free, because my greatest fear had been realized, and I was still alive, and I still had a daughter whom I adored, and I had an old typewriter, and a big idea. And so rock bottom became the solid foundation on which I rebuilt my life.[123]

Rowling dodged a bullet.

She never succeeded at anything she wasn't meant for.

Eighty percent of working people hate their work. Ideas, imagination, innovation, and yes, love are numbed to death from nine to five each day. The Death Eater of talent, the Lord Voldemort of passion killers, the soul-sucking Dementor of potential can be found Monday through Friday in office cubicles everywhere. The villainous dream killer—a little success, meaningless work, and a safe but life-sucking job. If J. K. Rowling hadn't *failed on an epic scale*, we would never know her name, and Harry Potter would just be a gleam gnawing out her eye.

Each of us leaves a gaping void in the wake of our unused talents. Imagine the black hole of a void in a world without Harry Potter.

Rowling single-handedly created a reading renaissance, raised the level of child literacy, inspired the political development of the millennial generation, created jobs, boosted the economy, and literally saved lives. A suicidal teenager once sent her a letter saying he didn't go through with it because he wanted to finish all the *Harry Potter* books. *Harry Potter* was even used to study the effect of e-commerce on the environment. Huh? If J. K. Rowling had failed to use her talents, there would be a gaping void, almost too big to fathom, in the lives of millions.

Like Rowling, failing to share *your* unrepeatable gifts with the world would leave a gaping void, impossible to fill.

Believe it!

Know it!

The world needs what you've got.

Imagine what the world would be like if everyone chose to *strip away the inessentials and direct all of their energies into work that mattered to them.* Imagine the creativity that would be unleashed. Imagine the flood of liberated potential spilling into the workforce. Imagine the love that can only come from being happy with yourself, washing over relationships, families, communities, and overflowing across the world. The unemployment rate would be zero, job satisfaction 100 percent, and the world would transform before our eyes.

Trying to force fit your life into work you weren't born to do is the only way you can fail. The definition of failure is different, and the same, for everyone. We all have a different calling, but we're all bound by the same *obligation.*

Be who you are.

Ignore who you are—as J. K. Rowling once did—and failure is inevitable.

Be who you are—as Rowling did when failure set her free—and you'll surpass your wildest imagination, touch lives, and alter eternity.

Someone has to inspire us to fend off the everyday soul-sucking Dementors.

Someone has to lead us against the everyday Bellatrix-like dream killers.

Someone has to help us stand up to Miss Umbridge teachers, Draco Malfoy bullies, Slytherin bosses, Parselmouth politicians, Rita Skeeter journalists, and Peter Pettigrew friends.

That someone is you! We need you! Not another gaping hole. We need you!

Not a shadow of you.

We need YOU!

QUIT OR STICK?

You've hit the roadblocks of discouragement and doubt,
The intersection of left turn, U-turn, or straight ahead,
Every dream leads to the crossroads of quit or stick.
If you make it that far—congratulations!
You've made it to the starting line.
Or is it the finish line?

—Dad

t was another kick-back Friday night at our favorite bookstore. Remember how we loved browsing the aisles, hanging out, and eating gargantuan cookies between exploring new titles? Remember how bummed out we were when the bookstore shut down? I'm sure it was struggling to stay open long before it closed.

Sometimes quitting is the only way to break free and liberate new opportunities.

Each of us browsed our favorite sections. While you were hanging in the teen section, and Paula scanned fiction and cookbooks, I'd peruse the business, music, and spiritual aisles. Ha! I laugh whenever I think of how you describe my reading habits. "Dad only reads boring nonfiction books about business or God."

As I was scanning the boring business section, I spotted a book called The Dip by one of my favorite thinkers, Seth Godin. I picked it up and upon skimming the cover, flung it down with a jolt. It was a little book about quitting.

Ouch!

Bad timing!

No way!

A raw nerve has just been bludgeoned!

I have a struggling company to save. I have a vision to fulfill. I have an ironclad obligation to the people who believed in me. There's a lot of money on the line. I can turn it around. Unlike the very bookstore I was standing in, I'd adjust. I'd win!

How could one glance at a book cause such a flood of emotions?

At the time I was getting pressure to quit from everyone! Though the market, the company, and my health were falling down around me, I couldn't conceive of it. *I don't quit. I don't quit. I don't quit.*

So I flung the nerve-hitting missive back on the shelf and displaced my anxiety in the gargantuan cookie department.

This went on for a month of Fridays. The book taunted me. I'd circle by it, around it, but never to it. It's like a divine spotlight zeroed in on Godin's book whenever I'd walk by as angelic voices sang to the tune of Handel's "Hallelujah Chorus."

Come and read me!

Come and read me!

Obviously, there was a burning question weighing heavily on my mind.

Quit or stick? Quit or stick? Quit or stick?

The universe has a subtle way of answering prayers. In a bankrupt bookstore, on a Friday night with my wife and daughters, it spoke to me through Seth Godin!

Quit the wrong stuff. Stick to the right stuff. Have the guts to do one or the other.

Shortly after reading *The Dip*, I, uh, kind of, sort of, reluctantly surrendered to what everyone else seemed to believe—it was time to quit and refocus. Like I said, sometimes quitting is the only way to break free and liberate new opportunities.

So when to quit, and when to stick?

Most people quit when they reach the starting line.

When the high of starting a new endeavor wears off, the daily routine of doing the work sets in. Excitement dies down, confidence dries up, the going gets tough, and even the tough can't get going. They stop at the bridge of resistance, inner doubt, and outer obstacles that everyone must cross in order to reach their pot of gold waiting on the other side of adversity.

It's the discouraged student fearing she chose the wrong major.

The disillusioned actor who can't land a paying job.

The broken musician who can't make a living.

It's the resistance you feel when the routine of the new workout routine becomes too routine, the junk food you stick back in your mouth because lasting weight loss seems impossible, staring at the TV instead of envisioning your dreams, because what's the use? It's clinging to familiar patterns of pain, simply because they're, well, familiar!

At the first sign of problems, people backslide into disempowering habits. The familiar feels safer than the unknown. Putting their cards on the table and facing their massive, yet unfamiliar power, scares them into the stuck position.

I look at problems differently.

Problems are progress.

As the saying goes, "The problem is not that there are problems. The problem is expecting otherwise and thinking that having problems is a problem."

Maybe these *perceived* problems are not telling you to quit; maybe they're guiding you through the fire of wrong moves and nudging you back on course.

Is it just a rough patch or the wrong road?

Deep inside, you already know the difference.

When you hit the inevitable brick wall, and the "God in your gut" says keep going . . .

Break down that wall!

Cross that bridge!

No matter what anyone says, no matter how impossible it may look.

If writing is your passion, the need to express yourself through words or music so *burned into your being* that it's impossible to ignore, but your novel can't get published, screenplays are rejected, song demos get returned unopened . . .

Stick! Stick! Stick!

If your passion to produce movies and TV is real, or as Uncle Michael's song says, "thicker than your blood," but you can't close a deal, and showbiz is harder than you ever imagined . . .

Stick! Stick! Stick!

But then again,

The blood and guts of courageously sticking no matter what *may* be . . .

Ahh . . .

Umm . . .

Wrong.

Disempowering.

Not something you want to cling to out of fear or pride (one and the same).

Instead of the inspirational soundtrack banging in your head,

You might want to listen to the little voice whispering in your heart.

Maybe—just maybe—your difficulties *are* telling you to quit.

Hmm.

Quitting a bad strategy, wrong major, dead-end job, toxic friendship, obsolete business plan, or jerk boyfriend, and refocusing your efforts, takes guts.

If you realize a chosen path, business, or relationship is not who you are, regardless of how much work and how many years you put into it . . .

Quit and refocus![124]

If you know you've chosen the wrong major . . .

Quit and refocus!

If you realize that your boyfriend is a selfish jerk . . .

Dump him and refocus!

If you find yourself exchanging the precious time of your life for anything that isn't you, redirect your energies and focus until you get back to who you are.

Singer Rihanna had to quit rapper Chris Brown or risk physical abuse. Author Michael Crichton had to quit pursuing a medical career after spending a fortune on his Harvard education or suffer a slow emotional death.[2] Our Friday night bookstore had to quit or suffer a slow financial death. My music company had to quit for all of the above.

If it takes quitting something,
If it takes quitting anything,
If it takes quitting everything to
Be who you are . . .
Never stick!
Quit! Quit! Quit! Quit!

Sometimes quitting is the only way to break free and. . .
Liberate new opportunities.

DIS·COURAGE·D?

Find your why.

—Dad

W hat's the antidote for discouragement, or resistance, or self-pity, or fear, or fatigue, or whatever's really juicing the juice out of our big plans?

A crystal clear and powerful *why*!

Halfhearted commitment, lame excuses, and feeble attempts are fruits of a fragile why. Big dreams fizzle out and die if launched from a puny purpose. My why is powerful!

You're my why.

Actions *teach* louder than the words. My example—good or bad, real or fake, fulfilled or frustrated—is your real teacher. To go the distance as a dad, I must dig down and show you, not tell you, what I want you to learn.

Paula is my why.

She needs a happy husband, and she needs a break. I want her to be financially free to do what she loves to do. It's impossible to love, and forgive, and transcend the clash of egos intrinsic in any relationship, if you are not being who you are. Being happy with yourself doesn't soften petty ego clashes; it keeps them from ever coming up. Does someone who is liberated from pride and insecurity always need to be right?

I'm my why.

I want to make the most of myself. I want my mistakes, successes, and hard-earned failures—my strengths, flaws, and hard-fought disappointments—to add up and mean something. I want to teach what I've learned.

312

So what's *your* why?
Pause for a second and really think about it.
What's your *why* for college?
What's your *why* for your career path?
What's your *why* for getting up in the morning?
If there's truly no why,
Quit.
Adjust course.
Whenever you feel the haze of discouragement creeping into any area of your life,
Your job,
School,
Relationships, or new endeavor,
Reach for the lifeline.
Find your why.
If there's really no why, the how doesn't matter.
If there's really no why,
There's really no what.

THE DARKEST NIGHT REVEALS
THE LIGHT OF THE STARS

Falling up,
Falling up,
Falling up!
You're never so near the top as when you've hit rock bottom!
—Dad

I ran into a fellow parent at Jamie's school band concert who was going through a bitter divorce, bankruptcy, foreclosure, and serious medical problems all at the same time. The divorce wasn't even final, and there she was, in the back of the auditorium, watching her newly engaged, almost ex-husband, fawning over his shiny new fiancée as her child performed. Her eyes told me she thought the best of life was over—that hitting rock bottom smashed her chances for happiness to bits. I knew she was just reaching the starting line—that a new life of second chances and unexpected blessings was about to begin.

But she was wounded.

She still saw the awful grace of pain as a tyrant bent on wrecking her life, rather than a liberator sent to renew her spirit and free her soul. Like a fire alarm for life, her pain was a rescue call, blatting and screaming: *You've been living a lie, suffocating the life out of your life, bludgeoning your own happiness to death! What would you rather do, avoid the initial pain that comes with severing your soul from a lie, or brave the storm that leads at last to the truth of who you are?* I repeat . . .

314

Falling up, Falling up, Falling up!

You're never so near the top, as when you hit rock bottom.

Truth is pain before it's peace. The bottom is a blessing.

Pain not only burns open a path to a fresh start, it sears open our eyes to what matters and what doesn't.

Why do many cancer patients say getting sick was the best thing that ever happened to them? Because the cleansing storms of acid pain stripped away layers of trivial garbage polluting their priorities, burned the mask off the face of the inessential, and revealed the profound beauty of what's truly essential for the first time.

Before Grandma Hanky died, I spent a lot of time with her at hospice. Tucked away from the white noise of an unconscious world, her room was a sanctuary. On one of my visits, a TV bleating down the hall, like a programmed herd of sheep, desecrated the sanctum.

The gobbledygook of squawking heads and screaming ads, yapping about what matters least, was startling against the backdrop of what matters most, personified by the life of my dear mother lying before me. Side by side, with the "real stuff" filling the sacred space of Grandma Hanky's room, the contrast was jarring.

We waste too much of our lives on things that do not matter and take for granted too many gifts that do. Pain is a gift the universe sends to straighten out the lines and push us back on course.

As she did all my life, while Grandma Hanky lay dying, she brought clarity to living. Days later, as I watched my mother being rolled off in a body bag, as I closed the sanctuary doors to her hospice room for the last time, as I stumbled, gut shot, back into the herd of a programmed world, the TV down the hall bleated on.

MINI-BOTTOMS AND FLIPPING POINTS

*Piece enough mini-bottoms together, and your life will
quietly bottom out—not in one dramatic event, but in
a thousand chances never taken.*

—Dad

Bottoms are not always dramatic.

People hit mini-bottom after mini-bottom and never notice the gaping hole left quietly in their wake. So what's a mini-bottom?

No Jessie, it's not the butt of a small monkey.

It's your standard-issue puddle of pain, formed by fear and resistance, in the cracks of procrastination.

mini-bottom \min-ee-bot-*uhm*\: pain resulting from consistent resistance, or habitual failure to act on a small goal, big dream, or daily duty: formed by the need to avoid "perceived" pain or discomfort.

As author Steven Pressfield says, "Resistance will tell you anything to keep you from doing your work."

Mini-bottoms are as common as a cold, but as ravaging to your spirit as a life-sucking addiction. The difference—there's no twelve-step program for failing to take action.

Pressfield also says, "Resistance is always lying and always full of sh-t."

317

You avoid working out because you think it's too painful, until the real pain of being sick, fat, and tired becomes worse than the perceived pain of exercise. Bam! You've hit a mini-bottom.

You avoid studying until the pain of flunking out becomes stronger than the anticipated pain of studying. Crash! You've hit a mini-bottom.

You avoid starting a venture, making a phone call, honing a skill, or applying for a job until the forged pleasure of lying on the couch and lying to yourself *flips*, becoming more painful than taking action. Splat! You've stepped in a mini-bottom. (No Jamie, not a baby butt).

Piece enough baby butts—um, I mean mini-bottoms—together, and your life will quietly bottom out, not in one dramatic event but in a thousand chances never taken.

The mini-bottom is the point where the real pain of doing nothing becomes worse than the imagined pain of taking action. I call it the flipping point.

It seethes and simmers until it boils over and shrieks, "ENOUGH! I'm better than this! ENOUGH! I want more out of life than this! ENOUGH! I am worth more money than this! ENOUGH! THIS IS NOT WHO I AM!"

To bypass the flipping point (and avoid all that shrieking), program your subconscious with what you want, and what you don't, ahead of time.

Link the pleasure of binging on cookie dough to the pain of not fitting into your jeans, and *flip*, you'll naturally pass it by.

Link the pleasure of skipping your homework and binging on Netflix to the pain of flunking out, and *flip*, you'll be eager to hit the books on a consistent basis.

Link the pleasure of binge-buying dumb stuff you can't afford to the pain of shackling your dreams with debt, and *flip*, you won't trade in your dreams for dumb stuff.

MINIBOTTOM:
Pain resulting from consistent failure to act on a small goal, big dream, or daily duty:
Formed by the need to avoid "perceived" pain or discomfort.

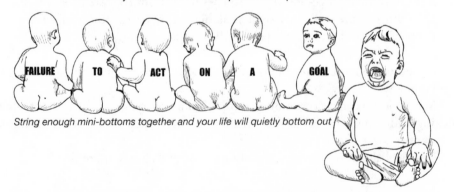

FAILURE TO ACT ON A GOAL

String enough mini-bottoms together and your life will quietly bottom out

. . .not in one dramatic event— but in a thousand chances never taken.

Flip what you link to pain and pleasure, and you won't need willpower at all. "Your subconscious will naturally guide you away from pain, real or not, and towards pleasure."[125]Even in the so-called mini-bottoms of life, the awful grace of pain is at work flipping you back into alignment. The secret:

Get off your baby butts, and take small consistent action every day.

Don't wait for the pain. Flip now or you'll flop later.

BIGGEST BOTTOM

You don't hit bottom in a counterfeit life; you choose it
slowly.

—Dad

What's the biggest bottom?
No Josie, it's not the butt of a large elephant.
No Jessie, it's not the butt of your choir teacher.
No Jamie, it's not a buffalo butt.
There's no bigger bottom than failing to be who you are.
Remember what Aunt Joan says: "If you're not being who you are, you'll miss your own life." What other bottom, or struggle, or disaster, could be more tragic than missing your own life? Think about it!!

Jim Carrey says his father could have led a very different life if he didn't fall prey to limiting beliefs and the *myth* of safety and security:

"My father could have been a great comedian, but he didn't believe it was possible for him. So he made a conservative choice. Instead, he got a safe job as an accountant. When I was twelve years old, he was let go from that safe job and our family had to do whatever we could to survive."

Carrey, who obviously adores his father, goes on to say . . .

"I learned many great lessons from my father, not the least of which was that you could fail at what you don't want, so you might as well take a chance at doing what you love."

320

Jim Carrey took a chance at doing what he loves, and "all righty then," the rest is history!

"So many of us choose our path out of fear disguised as practicality. What we really want seems impossibly out of reach—ridiculous to expect—so we never dare to ask the Universe for it. I'm saying that I'm the proof you can ask the Universe for it."[126]

The herd of people abandon themselves slowly. Pain creeps in and festers with barely a notice—plants its silent tentacles into the spirit and twists, stabs, gnaws at the soul, eats away like a ravaging insect, pinch by pinch bites the life out—spreads like a silent plague, building and rising and erupting until it explodes like a tantrum into a torrent of routine misery, howling for relief.

Enduring life instead of living life is a prison of our own making, designed from the blueprints of fear—the playbook of the ego.

The alternative to being who you are is enduring who you are not.

You don't hit bottom in a counterfeit life . . .

You choose it slowly.

There's no bigger bottom then failing to be who you are. As your aunt Joan says...
"Be who you are or you'll miss your own life."

What other bottom, or stuggle, or failure is bigger than missing your own life?

I PROMISE YOU THE DAY WILL DAWN
Interlude from the Bottom

Rock bottom holds a message,
One only you can hear or understand.
It's sacred, soft, and rock solid.
Listen and let it pull you home.
It's a message of rebirth and explosive transformation.

—Dad

At first . . .

It feels like the end of the world, not the dawn of a brand-new day.

It sounds like the end of a dream, not the distant voice of your true calling pulling you back home.

It looks like the end of the road, not the quiet beginning of a brand-new journey.

You can only see the burnt-out tree, not the nurse log whose decay is feeding and weaving the rich tapestry of an entire new forest back to life.

Quietly, almost without notice, a subtle yet powerful shift has occurred. The forcing is over, and the futile pushing has stopped.

You've let God's strength take over the ego's weakness.

"Who can put his faith in weakness and feel safe?

Yet who can put his faith in strength and feel weak?"[127]

With surrender, clarity softly peeks its cleansing rays through the clearing fog.

322

Whispering passions stir in the twilight, as the white noise of the dark night fades to blue. Simplicity eclipses the shadow of a driven, chaotic haze. Old struggles and stubborn reasons are seen in a loving, new, inner light.

Like a phoenix rising from the ashes . . .

The first light of the soul rises through the mist and breaks into the morning of your dreams. The young breeze of a second wind exhales into a fresh blast of renewed energy.

Standing in the stillness,
Patiently waiting in the mystic morning,
Forever with you, part of you, side by side for all time,
True destiny, like a long-lost friend, bursts free into the arms of a brand-new day.
In all its resplendent glory,
The day has dawned,
The Son has risen,
Ablaze with a stunning revelation, you can humbly see . . .
The light is you.

TRULY SEE WHO YOU ARE

Who are you?
The light bulb or the light flowing through it?

—Dad

I was writing in the backyard, by the beautiful garden your mom transformed into a work of art. Our old yellow lab Satchmo, named after Louis Armstrong, was lounging at my feet and only moved if he sensed a treat was about to come out of my briefcase. As I was pondering how to explain the relevance of knowing who you are, and who you are not, I noticed Satchmo's body was getting lumpier. The lumps and bumps were getting bigger and bigger. My mind wandered to the day we'd have to put him down.

I wondered how they would dispose of the body. Like tossing out the garbage, would it just be another detail in someone's daily routine? I thought whoever was in charge of this sort of thing could never know who Satchmo really was. They would be tossing his body, not his spirit. They would never see the love he brought our family, and the hair he brought our kitchen floor. (Just kidding about the hair—kind of.) They'd probably look at our dear old dog like he was just a bag of bones. Then it occurred to me. Satchmo *was* just a bag of bones. Without his hairy doggy energy coursing through the body, he'd be like a lightbulb that's inert without electricity. (Okay, so I'm a little hung up on the hair thing!)

We are not the body.

We are the energy that flows through the body.

The body is just a unit—another bag of bones.

324

The electricity of our divine life force, which makes our bag of bones come alive, is who we are.

Seeing, believing, and ultimately freeing who you are at the level of spirit, is the *one destiny* I've been trying to bread crumb you to with this book.

You are an infinite spirit, buried alive beneath birthstones of ego.

Your *one destiny* is to rise above the rocks (ego) and set your spirit free.

But what does that really mean? What exactly is the inner road and how do we reach *the point?* Keep following the breadcrumbs I'm laying down and trust, trust, trust that what I'm saying is true. They lead through the levels of consciousness from the depths of inner hell . . .

Shame,
Guilt,
Apathy,
Grief,
FEAR,
Desire,
Anger,
Pride,
To the peace of heaven within . . .
Courage,
Neutrality,
Willingness,
Acceptance,
Reason,
LOVE,
Joy,
Enlightenment.[128]

You've reached *The Point*—the *One Destiny.*

You've made it home to who you really are—*a brilliant ray of light, unblocked by birthstones of ego—emanating from God like a sunbeam emanates from the sun.*

The crux of all spiritual problems and confusion is a hand-me-down mistake, made by the most brilliant minds throughout history—*misidentifying the source from which our lives originate. We think we're the source, not the tributary that flows from the source. We think we're the lightbulb, not the light that flows through it.*

Are we a body *from* which all things flow? Or . . .

Do we have a body *through* which all things flow?

Do I itch, or does the body itch?

Here's the big one.

Is ego the source of our life—therefore our life experience? Or . . .

Is Divinity the source of our life and therefore our life experience?

Who are you, and who are you not?

And why should you care?

Hmm . . .

If you don't know who you are, how can you know what brings out happiness and what blocks off happiness?

You could spend a lifetime feeding the beast (ego) instead of the beauty (Self) or waste a lot of time "looking for love in all the wrong places," as an old country song once lamented. You could end up forever unsatisfied no matter what happens, if you don't know who you are, and who you are not.

And yet still . . . at the cost of empty lives and wasted moments—like a dog chasing his tail—we keep scurrying down the outer road, and grasping for who we are not.

THE SEER, NOT THE SCENE

Answer the question "who am I" with a question.
Who's asking?
Who wants to know?
Who's aware of the question?

—Dad

You are not your profession. You are not your age. You are not your relationships. You are not your bank account. You are not your thoughts. You are not your emotions. You are not your addictions. You are not your fears. You are not your life story. You are not your accomplishments. You are not your failures. You are not your social status, class rank, or religion. These things change. (Outer road)

"That which is real never changes."[129] (Inner road)

And the body changes every seven to ten years!

Who you are is unalterable and infinite.

The body doesn't even have the capacity to experience itself.[130]

Huh?

So who experiences the itchy sunburn the body feels when you stay too long at your favorite beach in Amagansett, New York? Who's scratching and picking and rolling on the suntan lotion to get rid of the pain? As abstract as our five limited senses make it seem, you're not the one experiencing the sunburn.

You're the one witnessing the sunburn.

Huh?

In this example, who you are is the one watching *Sunburn,* the movie, starring the J-girls of Amagansett. Who you are is actually several levels removed from the body's itchy sunburn.

I said, "Huh?"

Stick with me now! Let's take the elevator ride up from the body to *you.* Dr. David Hawkins will guide the tour.

All aboard!

First floor: Body! "The body has no capacity to experience itself. We experience the body via the senses, which tell us what's going on within it."

Second floor: Senses! "Sensations have no capacity to experience themselves. They have to be experienced in something greater, which is the mind."

Third floor: Mind! "The mind cannot experience itself. A thought cannot experience its own thoughtness. A feeling cannot experience its own feelingness. A memory cannot experience its own memoryness. Each is always experienced in something that is greater."

Fourth floor: Consciousness! "The mind is experienced through the infinite energy field of consciousness itself. It is because of consciousness that we experience what is mind. That is the basis of anesthesia. When we remove consciousness, there is no experience of mind or body."[131]

Fifth floor: Awareness! You've arrived at you!

You are the witness.

(Thanks for the tour, Dr. Hawkins! It's been a pleasure witnessing it.)

Your infinite Self, which is pure awareness—pure spirit—fused with consciousness like a drop of water melded with the ocean, is who you are. It is your awareness, *five levels removed from the body*, that's watching the summer blockbuster, *Sunburn* the movie, starring the J-girls of Amagansett.

You may not know that you know, but you already sense who you are.

Pure awareness.

You're the one watching the movie.

So if who you are is awareness, what the heck is awareness?

Let's say you lost both of your feet. Would the whole you still exist? Now make believe you lost both your legs. Would the whole you still exist? Then picture losing both your arms. Would the whole you still exist? Let's imagine that bit by bit, you lost every piece of your body except a perfectly functioning head. (Yikes! How would you itch your sunburn? I digress.) Would the whole you still exist? Just ask anyone who really did lose most of their body. The answer is yes, yes, yes! Now, let's imagine your awareness ceased to exist. Would you still exist?

No!

You wouldn't be there. *You* wouldn't exist.

Without awareness there is nothing.

But for *you* that's literally impossible.

Your awareness, which is who you are, is infinite. Your body parts could disappear one by one, but *you* cannot cease existing.

"Death is an impossibility."[132]

But intuitively, you already know that.

Confusion comes from flipping the seer with the scene!

We think we're the experiences, not the one witnessing the experiences. We think we're a body with sunburn, not the one witnessing a body with sunburn. We think our itty-bitty ego is the star, producer, and director of the show, when it's really the magnet of our spirit, pulling us on stage from behind the curtain of perception calling the shots.

You are not the ego.

How can you be?

The ego doesn't even exist.

The ego is an illusion.

Huh?

How can you witness something that doesn't exist?

If Buddha teaches us to rise above it into enlightenment . . .

If Jesus says, "Unless one is born again [transcends the ego] he cannot see the kingdom of God [inner peace, heaven within]" . . .

If rising above the ego into the love of who you are is the *one destiny* of life . . .

What *exactly* is this thing called *ego* that everyone keeps blaming and naming and babbling about?

YoU are tHe Seer, Not tHe SceNe.

YOU ARE NOT HAL

The ego is just a programmed machine.
You are not the machine.
You are the ghost in the machine.

—Dad

f the ego isn't real, what is it? And who the heck is Hal?

Hal is the supercomputer HAL 9000 in the movie *2001: A Space Odyssey*. It's the central processing and planning center that orchestrates, copes, sorts, and retrieves for the spaceship *Discovery One*. The crew talks, works, and even plays chess with Hal like it's a real person. Though Hal is only layers of programmed thoughts, habits, and emotions . . .

Hal seems real.

The ego is like Hal—an artificial intelligence *computer programmed for survival.* I call mine "Little Billy." (You can call yours anything you'd like.) Little Billy is the processing and planning center that orchestrates, copes, sorts, and retrieves for the human ship. The layers of entrenched thoughts and habits seem to make Little Billy's conglomeration of wired-in programs take on a life of their own. Though Little Billy is really just layers of programmed thoughts, habits, and emotions . . . [133]

Little Billy seems real.

Hal's name is short for *Hardware Abstraction Layer.*

Little Billy sounded like a good name for a *spoiled two-year-old,* which is what the ego seems to be. Whenever I see myself getting offended, selfish, blaming, whining, wanting, needing to control, unable to admit I'm wrong, or talking about myself too much, I just say, *Oh, there's Little Billy acting up again.*

Hal acted up in a deadly way. A "programming contradiction" reduced Hal to seeming paranoia and caused it to murder all but one of the crew. The contradiction consisted of two conflicting orders—*process information without distortion or concealment,* which contradicted *keep the mission secret for reasons of national security.* Hal's programmed logic? If the crew were dead, it wouldn't have to lie. Though Hal was not real, the effects of his programming were very real. Plans failed. Lives were ruined. People died.

Our ego and our essence are one gigantic programming contradiction!

The ego (the human, the outer) is our animal wiring.

Our essence (our being, the inner) is spirit.

Like Hal, Little Billy is not real. But the effects of its programming are very real. For no other conceivable reason than a stubborn ego, plans fail, lives are ruined, and people die.

Your high school friend walked away from every friend she ever had, rather than confront her ego. Ego and alcohol destroyed the promising professional football career of another of your childhood friends, leaving a young father brain dead in the process. Pride sank the *Titanic.* A spiritualized ego, which is the most dangerous thing on the planet, brought down the World Trade Center. How can something that doesn't even exist wreak so much havoc, ruin so many relationships, start so many wars, destroy so many lives?

Because that's what the ego is programmed to do!

Conquer, dominate, survive, and ultimately take the place of God.

So who or what programmed Hal and Little Billy?

Hal was programmed by Dr. Chandra from millions of sources and became operational January 12, 1987, at the HAL Plant in Urbana, Illinois. Little Billy was programmed from millions of sources through years of evolution. It became operational when the first bacteria on earth instinctively searched for ways to survive.

Unlike plant life, which automatically transforms solar power into energy, the animal had to seek ways to acquire energy *externally.* With this, a way of life was born. The core of the ego, which is self-interest, acquisition, and rivalry, began soldering the wires of selfishness, strand by strand, one layer at a time, until it evolved into what seemed to be a separate being, fueled by fear, forever chasing, searching, and wanting.

One by one, layers of programs were laid upon our animal brain. Constant craveness became wired into our psyche. The need to survive evolved into the desire to conquer and control. Like a squirrel forever hoarding nuts, the ego can never get enough. Hoarding nuts evolved into hoarding money, overplanning, neurotic attempts to control our futures, and greed, greed, greed. By its very nature, the ego cannot be satisfied. "A squirrel always wants more nuts."[134]

What started out as a search for energy evolved into a need for power, approval, and status. But vanity is minor-league narcissism. In the majors, the narcissistic core of the ego perceives itself as God. From megalomaniac world leaders to delusional celebrities and politicians, turn on the nightly news and you'll see them in action.

But there's still a little bit of caveman in all of us . . .

CAVEMAN: Ooga chucka, ooga chucka, I'm the alpha dog in this clan.
MODERN MAN: I'm the alpha dog in this company, ooga, ooga, ooga!

CAVE HOMEOWNER: I want, I want, I want the biggest cave.
MODERN HOMEOWNER: I want, I want, I want the biggest house.

CAVE DICTATOR: I want more, more, more territory. Invade.
MODERN DICTATOR: I want more, more, more territory. Invade.

CAVE RELIGION: We worship the sun. They worship the moon. Kill them.
MODERN RELIGION: We worship this god. They worship that god. Kill them.

CAVE RACISM: They have one eyebrow, we have two: We're superior.
MODERN RACISM: They're black. We're white. We're superior.

CAVE STATUS SYMBOL: I've got the coolest wheel.
MODERN STATUS SYMBOL: I've got the coolest set of wheels.

CAVE FAMILY: Alpha Dad's the dictator. Obey or be cast out.
MODERN FAMILY: Great Emmy-winning TV show! Alpha dads hate it.

Though the ego evolved over eons of time, and Hal was programmed all at once, notice the similarities.

Hal is the illusion of a separate entity stemming from a set of programs in which reason operates through a complex, multilayered series of algorithms.[135]

Little Billy is the illusion of a separate entity stemming from a set of programs in which reason operates through a complex, multilayered series of algorithms.

Hal is a set of entrenched programs seeming to *"create an illusionary sense of a personal self."*[136]

Little Billy is a set of entrenched habits of thoughts, seeming to *"create an illusionary sense of a personal self."*

Hal is a computer, which is just a programmed machine.

Little Billy is the ego, which is just a programmed machine.

Look behind the wiring.

Look through the programming.

Look beyond the illusion of a separate self.

You are not Hal.

You are not Little Billy.

You are not the machine.
You are the ghost in the machine.

You are not the machine...

You are the ghost in the machine.

WHAT I WANT FOR YOU

I want you to be happy.
I want you to be free.
I want you to be fearless (egoless).
I want your inner road to matter most to you.
Why?
It's the only way to be happy.
It's the only way to be free.
It's the only way to be fearless (egoless).

—Dad

don't care what you do for a living.
I care about the *why* of your living and the *why* of your life.
I care about the love you put into your living and the love it puts into you.
  I care if your living leads you towards or away from who you are.
  I want you to do what you love and turn what you do into love.
  Use your talent to serve.
  Serve yourself.
  Serve others.
  Serve God.
  They are one and the same. You can do no more than this.
  But you can't serve others, until you serve yourself. So . . .
  Serve yourself first.
  Love yourself first.

Do what you love first.

And your love will naturally overflow into the service of others and God.

All love eventually becomes help.[137]

I don't care how much money you make.

I care if you make enough money to make the most of yourself. I care if the pursuit of money leads you towards or away from your inner road.

I care if the pursuit of money leads you towards or away from who you are.

I want love—not fear—to be the air you breathe, and the lens through which you see. I want you to hold reaching a state of unconditional love as your worthiest intention.

Why?

Because love and strength are one.

Love and happiness are one.

"God, being love, is also happiness."[138]

To know love is to know God.

And above all else . . .

I want you to know God.

Like the epiphany that struck author Viktor Frankl as a prisoner in Auschwitz:

"A thought transfixed me. For the first time in my life I saw the truth as it is set into song by so many poets, proclaimed as the final wisdom by so many thinkers. The truth . . .

Love is the ultimate and the highest goal to which man can aspire."

I want you to be happy.

I want you to be free.

I want you to be fearless.

Your consciousness level is the gate.

Forgiveness is the key.

Love is forever waiting, on the other side of fear.

THE GREATEST LOVE

If you don't love yourself, you can't love others.
Ka-thunk, Ka-thunk, Ka-thunk!
If self-love is out of alignment, everything just grinds and
    grinds and grinds.

—Dad

You don't need to remember a million different rules to live an abundant and happy life. You don't need to understand a bunch of highfalutin' spiritual concepts to climb the ladder of consciousness to enlightenment.

Remember one!

Live by one!

Love thy neighbor as thyself.

It's as simple and layered as that.

But there are two parts to the golden rule. Most people don't hear, or fully understand, the layered meaning behind the second. Built into this simple and powerful truth is the very foundation of a fulfilling life, without which happiness is impossible.

Love yourself!

Which means, and I repeat: *Love yourself first.*

Respect yourself,

Believe in yourself,

Stand up for yourself,

Take care of yourself.

Fulfill yourself.

Forgive, forgive, and forgive yourself a million times a million times over.

Buddha agrees with Jesus:

"You can search throughout the entire universe for someone who is more deserving of your love and affection than you are yourself, and that person is not to be found anywhere. You yourself, as much as anybody in the entire universe, deserve your love and affection."

I want you to *love yourself, love yourself, and love yourself!* No matter what!

Not your ego, not your vanity-based identity. That's fear, not love.

If you don't love yourself, you don't know yourself, because who you are is love.

"No course whose purpose is to teach you to remember what you really are could fail to emphasize that there can never be a difference in what you really are and what love is. Love's meaning is your own, and shared by God Himself. For what you are is what He is. There is no love but His, and what He is, is everything there is. There is no limit placed upon Himself, and *so are you unlimited as well.*"[139]

If you don't love yourself, nothing else matters, because nothing else works!

You can't "love thy neighbor" until you "love thyself."

You can't love your friends until you love yourself.

You can't love your family until you love yourself.

You can't love your spouse until you love yourself.

You can't love your dog, cat, or canary until you love yourself.

And to love yourself, you must be yourself!

Jesus and Buddha are telling us there's only one way it's even possible to love and be loved.

Be who you are!

It's what life asks of you; it's the nature of the universe.

It's God's will.

So who are you going to listen to—Jesus and Buddha, or Miss Penske in the student advisory office?

When you realize that God doesn't need you to love "Him" for "His" sake. Ha! The essence of all existence, the source and creator that is creation, *needs* nothing.

Serving God helps you!

Serving yourself *is* serving God.

Loving yourself *is* loving God.

A gift to God is a gift to yourself.

Accept my gift, for it is Yours to me[140] is a prayer that means:

Accept my love, for my love helps me.

Accept my talent, for my talent helps me.

Accept my forgiveness, for my forgiveness helps me.

Accept my service, for my service helps me.

That's why Grandma Hanky teared up when describing the thousands of patients she served as a nurse, saying, "They helped me more than I helped them."

Being who you are is not only how you serve, and love, and matter—it's your way back home. Serving God is a compass. It leads to who you are.

When you finally realize that before beginnings—beyond endings—the finish line has always been the same as the starting line.

The treasure you seek has always been, and will always be, who you already are.

Perfect happiness is a revelation, not a destination.

The soul revealed, the spirit unblocked by clouds of fear—not a distant journey to some far-off rainbow, forever beyond a vague horizon.

When you finally reach the four corners of the farthest and deepest territories of your own Shangri-La—the promised land of your heaven within—forever calling to emerge through the shrouding fog of ego,

When the amazing *outer road* of your talents, dreams, passions, career, finances, relationships, achievements, accolades, adventures, and motivations merge with the spiritual purpose of the *inner road*—the ultimate and only point of life.

When heart and heaven beat as one,
You'll dance into your dreams . . .
A place of perfect happiness,
A place of unconditional love,
A place where dreams come true,
The one destiny,
No matter what happens,
You'll be happy,
You'll be fearless,
You'll be love,
You'll be there.
I'm going to sing it out from here! C'mon! Sing it with me now!
My child, you'll

Be
Who you are, truly
See
Who you are.

You'll believe, as
I believe, in
Who you are.
I'm jammin' now! C'mon, sing along!
If you could see what I see . . .
Then you'd believe . . .
In who you are.

When the outer road of your passions, career, relationships and motivations merge with the spiritual purpose of the inner road,

You'll soar into your dreams—your one destiny.

I promise you . . .
What I'm saying is true . . .
Be Who You Are
(Stop down. Pause song.)

This song, which grew into this book, ends with the same last words I'd say to you if they were my last words on this earth.

(Continue song . . .)
So promise me
You'll always be . . .
Be who you are!
Be who you are!
Let go and follow—inside and out—no matter what! No matter how far!
Be who you are!

Josie   Jamie   Jessie

I love you forever.

And Paula, my amazing wife and supermom of our children...

I love U 4 ever!

Godspeed Dear Lord,

Help my children make the most of their inner and outer lives. Guide them through the illusions of the ego, safely, and surely, back home to themselves and thee.

From their father on earth—to our Father in heaven,

For this I pray,

Gloria in Excelcis Deo

Thy will be done.

REPRISE: THE POINT

T here were a hundred ships, twenty-five years of age, lined up on the shores of life—about to embark on a forty-year journey to a destiny unknown.

One Ship Had a Vision Inside and Out

One of the ships wanted to know where she was going, so she wouldn't drift. Knew if she could see the invisible, she could achieve the impossible: Though the ship could only see so far, the telescope of her imagination had infinite eyes, soaring on faith, beyond her senses, according to her beliefs, in the shape of her habits, to a vision waiting within.

To ensure each sail was flying fully and pulling together, the ship took time to survey the key areas of her own horizon. Without the rudder of vision, inspiring all areas of the vessel—the inner and the outer—the ship knew she'd forever toss and turn on the fickle whims of aimlessness.

Instead of following a prefab map to mediocrity, instead of relying on sheer willpower and desire, the ship looked for the passageway tugging her soul. She knew if she found it, felt it, and let go of the outcome, the invisible hand of destiny would grab the helm and pull her home.

But above all else, the one ship didn't want to miss the point of the journey—the reason and the gift—the most important thing in the storms of the trek. Somehow she knew if she reached the point, everything else would fall into place and her true treasure would be revealed. Somehow she knew the point was the only thing that really mattered.

Once a vision was seared in her bones, she arrived at the destination in advance in her mind—then set the compass, and surrendered the wheel.

Four Ships Made the Big Mistake

Four of the ships also created a passage plan, charted a course, and positioned the sextant. But even clear vision is limited by near vision. They didn't look far enough. The gravitational pull of outer trinkets distorted their inner compass. They sought money instead of wealth, confusing the outer leg of the voyage for the whole of the journey, and veered off course, mistaking status and stuff for the final destination.

The four ships clogged the channel of humility through which the power of the universe flows by relying on flyspecks of willpower and pride. They created the inner storms they'd be forced to overcome by white-knuckling the wheel and glorifying the struggle. They confused the calling of their hearts with the panting of desire, which pulled them into the ego like a siren song pulls bewitched sailors into the rocks.

More, more, more! You're not enough! More, more, more!

The four ships mapped out a vision and got where they were going. The trouble was, they didn't follow the celestial compass of their inner stars and ended up sailing around the point. In the end, even the best port in the storm became a sea of nagging dissatisfaction. No matter how many times their ships came in, they never made it home.

Five Ships Drifted in the Prison of Nonvision

Five ships are still out there working their way through the journey like driftwood in a storm. They set sail without setting course, unknowingly turning their divine vessels into slave ships for other people's stars.

Deep in the darkest bowels of the ships' guts lived the parasites of low self-worth eating away their talents. It wasn't a lack of imagination keeping them from charting their own course. It was the lack of belief, lurking below deck, which led to the lack of courage above.

They doubted their own power.

The dream-killing pirate, sentencing the ships to the prison of nonvision, was the deadliest of all . . .

Fear!

Fear kept them from seeing who they are.

Fear of going in the wrong direction, fear of looking like a dumb dinghy, fear of leaving the illusion of a safe harbor, fear of rocking the family boat, and the most mysterious fear of all, the fear of casting off familiar anchors of darkness and soaring into the unexplored glow of their own brilliant light.

Without a vision, trickling torment seeped in and gnawed at their souls like spirit-eating piranha—inflicting the ultimate horror—drip-by-drip agony—the ugliest fate that could befall a ship of infinite potential, about to launch into a sea of endless possibilities.

The five ships were fine.

They weren't alive and they weren't dead.

They were *just* fine.

Everything was fine.

They weren't shipshape; they were shipsheep—ignoring the sweet music of their calling to follow the bleating foghorn of the herd. They let the blind eyes of conformity and practicality steer the ship. In the name of security, they turned their backs on what they loved to do, and lost themselves on the safe route. After forty years of toiling at the wheel, the five ships are still struggling to stay afloat.

Still playing it safe.

Still drifting.

Still fine.

Fifty-Four Ships Had No Why

The bulk of the armada ended up dependent on other ships to keep them afloat.

Why?

One of the answers is in the question.

They had no *why.*

There's no wind with no why.

Without a guiding purpose, the voyagers jumped ship to whatever piece of dead wood came flittering by, whenever the seas got rough. Like rudderless, one-oared rowboats, they flopped round in circles, burning up chances, wearing down enthusiasm, exhausting all hope, and finally sinking in a puddle of learned helplessness, waiting for someone to throw them a line.

The Missing Were Unconscious and Unaware

Thirty-six are lost at sea and don't even know it.

Ignorance is their anchor.

They're unaware.

Unaware that all the riches in the world would never be enough; all the eyes of the world, laid on them with rapt adulation, would never be enough; all the privilege of the world would never be enough.

Unaware that taking the outer route instead of the inner was the wrong way home. The outer route left them lost at sea.

Some were oblivious to the power they held in their hands, as they wasted their days, whining about their lives. Unaware that anyone, regardless of how far down or screwed up they think they are, can transform their lives with the power of vision.

The face that launched a thousand ships, and sank a trillion more, was ignorance.

They know not what they do,

Know not what brings true happiness,

Know not who they are.

The saw-toothed rocks of ignorance stranded more ships on the island of oblivion than any other force in the universe. We can only assume the spirit raider of ignorance boarded the remaining thirty-six, sank their hopes, killed their dreams, and left them for dead in the uncharted waters of their own potential.

One Ship Reached *The Point*

Ninety-nine of the maiden voyagers never reached the point. They were too busy chasing the illusions of someday, and the mirage of more, to even notice.

There's only one destiny.

One reason.

One gift.

And one way to reach the point.

Sail up the levels of consciousness from the depths of inner hell . . .

Shame,

Guilt,

Apathy,

Grief,

Fear,

Desire,

Anger,

Pride,

To the peace of heaven within . . .

Courage,

Neutrality,

Willingness,

Acceptance,

Reason,

Love,

Joy,

Enlightenment.[141]

The real journey in life is the voyage from fear to love.

Casting off from the ego and returning to who you are—born again into the love of your infinite essence—is the point and purpose of life.

All other dreams are either a means to an end or pointless diversions.

Aware of it or not,

Nothing else satisfies,

Nothing else matters, and . . .

When nothing else matters, everything else falls in place.

"Seek the Kingdom of God above all else, [Who you are, Self, Spirit] and he will give you everything you need."

Note: I based this parable on an article by Earl Nightingale from the 1950s, which describes the average "success" rate per one hundred people:

If you take 100 individuals who start even at the age of 25, do you have any idea what will happen to those men and women by the time they're 65? These 100 people believe they're going to be successful. They are eager toward life. There is a certain sparkle in their eye, erectness to their carriage, and life seems like a pretty interesting adventure to them. But by the time they're 65, only one will be rich, four will be financially independent, five will still be working, and 54 will be broke—depending on others for life's necessities.

But there's only one way to be happy . . .
Reach the point.

The Point

The voyage from fear to love, is the purpose and point of the journey.

CODA: PROVE IT!

Your life speaks louder than your words! Your life speaks louder than your words!! Your life speaks louder than your words!!!

—Annoying voice in Dad's head

One more thing. This is real and kind of scary. I just got off the phone with Uncle Michael. I was joking about inventing menial errands, and anything else I could dream up, to avoid writing. Even our phone call was one of my escape tactics.

He had no idea what subject I was dodging, and as a seasoned songwriter himself, he knew better than to ask. Between the jokes and silliness that make up most of our conversations, he slipped in a comment that stuck. "Writing takes courage; it takes lots of courage." Bull's-eye! Raw nerve. Dead center.

This book has been poking at a festering wound since word one. With each chapter, the stinging grace of a shadowing voice grew sharper and louder as it pierced deeper and deeper.

How can you tell your children to "be who you are," to follow the inner road, to put their inner purpose first, to put spiritual growth first, and that when nothing else matters but transcending the ego, everything else will fall in place—if you have not done so yourself?

And on the outer road, how can you tell them that anything is possible with God, that they can harness the power of imagination to create any life they can dream of, and to never, ever, stop doing what they love—if you're not doing what you love?

348

How can you tell them to follow your words, if you're not following them yourself?

Your inner road is still bumpy with grouchiness, resentment, pride, desire, judgment, and fear. You still seek happiness outside of yourself.

On the outer road, you stuffed your spirit into a bag of so-called mistakes and crawled off the playing field. Like your cat Squeakers, who finds a dark spot to hide in when wounded, you've been hiding out in the shadows. Your indestructible gifts are withering and waiting to see the light of day. Somewhere along the line, being strong enough to handle rejection turned into expecting failure.

Your life speaks louder than your words!
Your life speaks louder than your words!!
Your life speaks louder than your words!!!

Is this what being who you are gets you? A grouchy guy with a failed business and no more second chances?

Bull!

NO!

That's what being who you are *not* gets you. I must *show* you the difference.

Jessie said, "Music is your thing, Dad. You should make some." Josie made me pinky swear that I'd practice my flute. (I haven't touched it for over a decade.) I told Jamie I love to write music. I'm not sure if I was projecting or not, but I got the feeling she was thinking, "Then how come you're not writing any?"

Part of being who you are is doing what you love. How can I tell you to be who you are if I'm not being who I am? Facing the words yanking me to these pages was really facing my Self, and what I've been modeling as a father. I've always sensed where the story between the lines had to lead.

You must show your children what being who you are looks like.
Your life speaks louder than your words!
Your life speaks louder than your words!!
Your life speaks louder than your words!!!

The ink may be dry, but the side story has just begun. To truly transform the marrow and sinew of your lives, I am called to write the chapters between the lines—the ones that may end up saying the most—on the raw and real pages of my own life.

I believe in my gut that each of us has the power to design our destinies. To make you believe this in your gut, I must prove what I'm saying is true. To reach right down to your essence, I must write down to your essence. I must draft a transformation, chart the stars, divine the truth, and compose a new life. I can no longer "sit down to write, if I have not stood up to live."[142]

So what am I trying to prove?

This stuff is either real, or it isn't.

Transcending the ego is either the most important thing, or it isn't.

You can design any life you can imagine, or you can't.

The plan is simple:

Create a magnificent, transformational life vision.

Bring it to life.

Warts and all, document the journey—inside and out.

I've started from where I am, let my imagination run wild, and created a transformational vision. Good, bad, or ugly, I'm laying this experiment on the line by putting it online, so you can watch and learn with no filters.

My intention is to show you what shifting your energy level from fear to love looks like.

To show you what changing your life from the inside out looks like.

"Your change of mind becomes the proof that who accepts God's gifts can never suffer anything."[143]

To erase any fear I may have modeled as a person and a father.

To show you what spiritual growth looks like.

What standing up after falling down looks like.

What bringing an idea to life looks like.

What starting from scratch looks like.

What the ups and downs of achievement look like.

What raising your self-concept looks like.

To show you! Not just tell you.

No matter what, no matter how far—it's never too late to *be who you are!*

I may fall short of my vision. So what? Win or lose, it doesn't matter. Intention matters. Effort matters. Action matters.

My purpose is love. My meaning is you. You will feel that. You will know that.

I want you to remember that!

Remember my love.

Rewriting my life to inspire yours is the gnawing voice of grace I've been avoiding—the *unexpected* guidance I've been praying for, and integrity's unyielding demand.

Uncle Michael was right. *Writing takes courage; writing your life takes lots of courage.*

To be nobody but yourself,
In a world which is doing its best,
Night and day, to make you everybody but yourself,
Means to fight the hardest battle, which any human being can fight,
And never stop fighting.
　　　　　　　　　　　　　　　—E. E. Cummings

NOTE TO READER

Thank you, thank you, thank you for taking the time to read this book. It is an honor, privilege, and responsibility I do not take lightly. There is nothing more fulfilling and thrilling than *using my talent to serve* and making even the smallest bit of difference in someone's life. Though I know it's not necessary, and the outcome of our efforts should be surrendered, sometimes it's nice to receive feedback on our work.

For example, I gave a lecture called *Find Your Why* to high school music teachers at the Wisconsin Music Conference in Madison, Wisconsin. I never felt like I was connecting throughout the talk, and one person in the room even seemed angry. At one point she got up and walked out, only to come back in and continue scowling. Though the rest of teachers clapped respectfully after the lecture, I didn't feel the message got through.

The next morning, as I was on my way to give a different talk at the same conference, the woman who stormed in and out the day before came storming at me with an "I've got something to say to you, bub" look in her eye. I braced for impact.

"You have no idea how you affected me! I couldn't sleep all night, so I Googled you and festered on the comment you made about the fear of leaving your comfort zone. I've been thinking about making a change for fifteen years, and now I'm going to make it." I was stunned. I thought she was going to complain—instead, she thanked me.

It was thrilling and fulfilling to hear! I even gave a "high five" to the universe after she left, saying, "All right—made a difference to one person! Thank you!"

I'd love to hear your story—I'd be honored to hear how this book has affected you. If you're so moved, would you post a comment at any of the links listed below? I'd be privileged to give you a free download of my song *Be Who You Are,* the song upon which this book is based, as a token of my appreciation.

Thanks again for taking the time to read this book. I'm excited about hearing from you! And always remember . . .

Be Who You Are, Inside and Out, No Matter What!

I'd love it if you left a comment on one of the sites below! Thank you!

Website: www.JimmyBrandmeier.com
Instagram: be.who.you.art
Facebook: https://www.facebook.com/JimmyBrandmeier
Twitter: @JimmyBrandmeier
Email: info@JimmyBrandmeier.com

ACKNOWLEDGMENTS

Thank you to David L. Hancock, Bethany Marshall, Dave Sauer, Cindy Sauer, and Margo Toulouse at Morgan James Publishing for your positive, *can-do energy* and patience in waiting for the final draft of this book.

Thank you to Mary Logue, Brett and Sheila Waldman, Andrea Cagan, Julia Tallard Johnson, and Keidi Keating for steering me in the *write* direction, and a big thank you to . . . ***Amanda Rooker and her team at SplitSeed for pulling it all together!***

Christian Andrew Grooms is more than a virtuoso illustrator, gifted painter, outstanding designer, and brilliant printmaker . . . he's an *empath*—a person capable of feeling the emotions of others. That's what makes him a pure artist. He feels things more deeply, sees things more clearly, and reflects it back to world through his amazing art.

With one look at their eyes in an old photograph, Christian knew the personalities of each of my daughters—whom he's never met—as if he'd known them all his life.

Grooms used that natural empathy, God-given talent, and hard-won skill to capture the essence of this book through his brilliant illustrations. And the hardest part of all . . . he had to put up with me through the process: LOL!

I'll be forever grateful to Christian Andrew Grooms for his creative integrity, unrepeatable imagination, and hard, hard, work. Thank you, Christian!

A big shout out to my music producer pals Brian Rawlings and Russ Zavitson in Nashville, who poured their hearts, talents, and years of incredible experience into recording *Be Who You Are*—the song upon which this book is based. You guys are soo talented!! Thank you, thank you, thank you for going the extra mile and treating my song with the same care as one of your many hits. And thanks for introducing me to Martin's Barbeque. Dang! That's good stuff!

Special thanks to Dr. David R. Hawkins, his wife Susan, and the team at Veritas. Though Dr. Hawkins is no longer with us in body, he will always be my teacher. Anything that I may know or know about consciousness I've learned from Dr. Hawkins. If you want to dive deeper into the subject of consciousness and spiritual growth, start with Hawkins's book *Power versus Force*, and move deeper into the rest of his books from there. Clarity guaranteed. For more information, go to www.veritas.com.

Making the most of who you are on the outer road takes a team. Everyone needs someone to accomplish anything. On the inner road, the people in our lives and even strangers just passing by are teachers—mile markers and mirrors—reflecting where we are on our journey from fear to love. I am grateful to them all. They all played a role in the birth of this book, and the rebirth of my spirit.

A few of the *inner road teachers* who have shaped my spirit and this book . . .

Paula, Jamie, Jessie, and Josie

My dad, Grandpa Frank (no, not Sinatra), and my mom, Grandma Hanky

Jesus Christ

Dr. David R. Hawkins

A Course in Miracles

Tao Te Ching

Buddha

Gandhi

Eckhart Tolle

Henry David Thoreau

Wayne Dyer

Marianne Williamson

Neville Goddard

Vincent Van Gogh

Oprah

My brothers and my amazing sister, Mary

My sisters-in-law and brother-in-law, and on and on and on . . . thank you, thank you, thank you!

And a few *outer road teachers* who have fueled my outer road and this book:

Paula, Jamie, Jessie, and Josie (Yes, you've helped shape both roads.)

My dad and mom, Grandpa Frank (I said no, not Sinatra!) and Grandma Hanky

Tony Robbins

Brendon Burchard

Steven Pressfield

Seth Godin

Derek Sivers

Julia Cameron
Jeff Walker
Rick Lenart
My brothers and my amazing sister, Mary
My sisters-in-law and brother-in-law
And on and on and on . . . thank you, thank you, thank you!

ABOUT THE AUTHOR

Jimmy Brandmeier is "the Dad" in a beautiful, wacky family of three daughters—Jamie (age 22), Jessie (age 21), and Josie (age 18)—Paula his wife of twenty-four years (ageless), two doves, a couple of goldfish, and a cat named Squeakers. Though their loving yellow lab, Satchmo, went to doggy heaven, his doggy hair will always be with them.

The couple moved their family from California to Wisconsin to raise their kids closer to family. They managed to be hands-on parents through the demands of two busy careers—Jimmy, a music industry veteran flying back and forth to California, and Paula, an airline pilot flying back and forth to Europe. Flexibility and priorities kept them from missing a beat in their children's lives.

As their crazy household quiets into an empty nest, Paula is still flying around the world and Jimmy is still passionate about making music and making a difference. As a teacher, speaker, clinician, and entrepreneur, Jimmy personifies his philosophy of "use your talent to serve." Knowing that a rising tide raises all ships, he is devoted to raising his own consciousness level as the best means to serve his family and others.

For more information, visit www.JimmyBrandmeier.com.

ABOUT THE ILLUSTRATOR

Christian Andrew Grooms is a painter, printmaker, illustrator, graphic designer, musician, audio engineer, and audio producer, working in multimedia. His paintings, often figurative, contemplate the philosophical aspects of the human condition through abstraction, symbolism, metaphor and realism—often all together. Grooms' multimedia work focuses on the scientific and functional relationships that humans have with their creative minds.

Grooms' work has been exhibited and collected in the Midwest, New York City, Connecticut, and Germany and are part of several private and corporate collections at UW Health, Full Compass Systems, Roche Inc., Arrowhead Research, and Madison Opera, to name a few.

After studying for his BFA at the University of Minnesota, Grooms earned a Master of Fine Arts degree from Parsons School of Design, New York University. Grooms lives and works in Madison, Wisconsin, where he's currently an artist-in-residence at *100 Arts*.

FURTHER RESOURCES

YouTools: Making It Real!

You can't think your way to the life you want. Inspiration needs action. Knowledge not applied is powerless.

I've created a set of *YouTools* to help you move from thinking to doing, theory to practice, dreams to reality, someday to now.

YouTools is a set of worksheets, questions for discussion, and exercises based on this book to help guide you from thinking about, to defining, doing, and living any life you can imagine. *YouTools* are not only effective tools for elevating your life, they are also a great way to . . . *engage and enhance your book club!* For a free downloadable set of *YouTools,* go to www.JimmyBrandmeier.com.

Engage and Enhance Your Book Club
Meet the Author

To schedule an in-house or online discussion with the author for your book club, e-mail info@JimmyBrandmeier.com. It's easy, energizing, and fun!

Words and Music: Living Room Tour

Words and Music is an *unplugged* music performance and discussion by the author featuring original songs based upon this book. To schedule musician and author Jimmy Brandmeier for an intimate performance and discussion at your book club, e-mail info@JimmyBrandmeier.com.

Use Your Book Club to Serve

The author's philosophy has always been to *use your talent to serve.* Jimmy Brandmeier would love to work with your book club to customize and create different ways to serve your community, club, or the cause of your choice, based on the contents of this book. To schedule a *brainstorming jam session* on different ways to use your book club to serve, e-mail info@JimmyBrandmeier.com.

Download the Song "Be Who You Are"

To download a free copy of the song *Be Who You Are*—the song upon which this book is based—please go to www.JimmyBrandmeier.com.

And I'd love to hear your comments on the music! Thank you!

Be Who You Are: Journal Jams

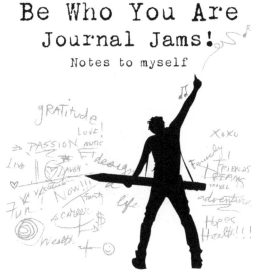

Be Who You Are
Journal Jams!
Notes to myself

Jam your passions, Strum your heartstrings, Sing your soul, And . . .

Write your life.

Journal Jamming your way to authenticity

Jimmy Brandmeier

Be Who You Are: Journal Jams features hundreds of inspirational quotes from Jimmy Brandmeier's book *Be Who You Are: A Song for My Children*.

But the author of *Journal Jams* is YOU.

As Buddha says, Place no one's head above your own.

As Brandmeier says, Don't take my advice; take yours!

Learn what you've always known. Write it down.

Journal Jams gives you the space to write about anything you want, anytime you want. Write your life, compose your future, vent your anger, face your fears, spell out your feelings, type away your problems, and *journal jam* your way to authenticity.

From God's lips to your Journal Jam session—LOL—blink don't think, and just let it flowwwww.

Here we go. A-one, a-two, a-one, two, three, four . . .

We be jammin' . . . Journal Jammin'!

To learn more, go to www.JimmyBrandmeier.com.

Be Who You Are: A Prayer for My Children

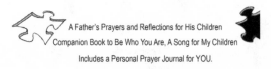

Be Who You Are
A Prayer for My Children

A Father's Prayers and Reflections for His Children
Companion Book to Be Who You Are, A Song for My Children
Includes a Personal Prayer Journal for YOU.

Jimmy Brandmeier

Be Who You Are: A Prayer for My Children is a father's book of prayers and reflections for his kids, and a personal prayer journal for YOU to create the life *you* want, for you *and* your children—or anyone and anything else your soul desires. It is a companion piece to the book *Be Who You Are: A Song for My Children.*

Brandmeier knows he can't always be there for his children, but prayer can . . .

Prayer can.

Prayer can.

It can do the same for you.

To learn more go to www.JimmyBrandmeier.com.

Twilight: Ode to an Empty Nest
The years have turned to moments,
Tears of childhood dry,
Blurred in beige, the strings were cut,
I've spent their days,
As morning fades,
I'm weak and strong,
Lost and found,
It's dark and dawn . . .
Inside the last twilight.

—Dad

ENDNOTES

1. Kahlil Gibran tells us that "work is love made visible." *The Prophet* (New York: Alfred A. Knopf, 1951), 28.
2. Aunt Joan Steffend Brandmeier.
3. Paraphrase of Pierre Teilhard de Chardin, https://www.brainyquote.com/quotes/quotes/p/pierreteil160888.html, accessed September 23, 2017.
4. Marianne Williamson, http://www.goodreads.com/quotes/3225323-ego-says-once-everything-falls-into-place-i-ll-feel-peace, accessed September 23, 2017.
5. Helen Schucman, *A Course in Miracles* (Mill Valley, CA: Foundation for Inner Peace, 1976).
6. Proverbs 29:18.
7. Historian Will Durant paraphrasing Aristotle, https://www.brainyquote.com/quotes/quotes/w/willdurant145967.html, accessed September 23, 2017.
8. Alan Rusbridger, "Life Is Beautiful," *The Guardian*, December 13, 2006, https://www.theguardian.com/music/2006/dec/13/classicalmusicandopera.secondworldwar, accessed October 17, 2017.
9. Dr. David R. Hawkins, *Letting Go: The Pathway of Surrender* (Sedona, AZ: Veritas, 2012).
10. Ibid.
11. Ibid.
12. My "announcer" was inspired by the song "Pour Me" by the band Trick Pony.

13. Dr. David R. Hawkins, *If You Feel Like You're Stuck* (lecture, June 2006), published by Veritas on YouTube, May 14, 2011, https://www.youtube.com/watch?v=_DAtMAmrwMk, accessed on September 23, 2017.
14. Neville Goddard, *The Power of Awareness* (Seattle: Pacific Publishing Studio, 2010).
15. Franz Kafka, https://www.brainyquote.com/quotes/quotes/f/franzkafka119527.html, accessed September 23, 2017.
16. Neville Goddard, *The Power of Awareness* (Seattle: Pacific Publishing Studio, 2010).
17. Dr. Wayne Dyer, https://www.facebook.com/drwaynedyer, accessed September 23, 2017.
18. Will Smith, http://www.goodreads.com/quotes/812595-there-s-no-reason-to-have-a-plan-b-because-it, accessed September 23, 2017.
19. Michelangelo, http://www.goodreads.com/quotes/557979-the-greatest-danger-for-most-of-us-is-not-that, accessed September 23, 2017.
20. Neville Goddard, *Awakened Imagination* (Eastford, CT: Martino, 2011).
21. *The Legend of Bagger Vance*, directed by Robert Redford, screenplay by Jeremy Leven (2000, Twentieth Century Fox), based on Steven Pressfield's novel of the same title.
22. Mahatma Gandhi, https://www.brainyquote.com/quotes/quotes/m/mahatmagan121239.html, accessed September 23, 2017.
23. Howard Thurman as quoted on Howard Thurman Center website, http://www.bu.edu/thurman/about/history/, accessed September 23, 2017.
24. Wallace Wattles, *The Science of Getting Rich* (SoHo Books, 2012).
25. The Talmud, http://www.beliefnet.com/quotes/angel/t/the-talmud/every-blade-of-grass-has-an-angel-that-bends-over.aspx, accessed September 23, 2017.
26. From Gregg Levoy's *Callings: Finding and Following an Authentic Life* (New York: Harmony Books, 1997).
27. From the movie *Dead Poets Society*, directed by Peter Weir, screenplay by Tom Schulman (1989; Touchstone Pictures).
28. My variation on Act 5, Scene 5 of Shakespeare's *Macbeth*.
29. Dr. David R. Hawkins, *Transcending the Levels of Consciousness* (Sedona, AZ: Veritas, 2006).
30. Ibid.
31. Ibid.
32. Ibid.
33. Ibid.
34. Julie Tallard.
35. Romans 12.2.
36. Luke 9:25.

37. Amy Seidel, https://www.goodreads.com/author/quotes/2055249.Amy_Seidl, accessed September 23, 2017.

38. Neville Goddard, *The Power of Awareness* (Seattle: Pacific Publishing Studio, 2010).

39. Ibid.

40. Ibid.

41. Ibid.

42. Ibid.

43. Neville Goddard, *The Feeling Is the Secret* (Seattle: Pacific Publishing Studio, 2010).

44. *Gospel of Thomas*, saying 106.

45. Neville Goddard, *The Feeling Is the Secret* (Seattle: Pacific Publishing Studio, 2010).

46. A paraphrase of Wallace Wattles, *The Science of Getting Rich* (SoHo Books: 2012).

47. Based on Dr. David R. Hawkins, Map of Consciousness, www.veritaspub.com.

48. Dr. David R. Hawkins, *Letting Go: The Pathway of Surrender* (Sedona, AZ: Veritas, 2012).

49. From the teachings of Dr. David R. Hawkins.

50. Commonly attributed to Anaïs Nin, http://www.goodreads.com/quotes/483575-we-don-t-see-the-world-as-it-is-we-see, accessed September 23, 2017.

51. Bernie Madoff as quoted in "Bernie Madoff Free at Last," by Steve Fishman, *New York Magazine*, June 6, 2010.

52. Bill Gates, as quoted in "Bill Gates: Social Philosopher" by John Markoff, *New York Times,* January 24, 2008.

53. The quote is actually Neville Goddard's paraphrase of Jesus.

54. Wallace Wattles, *The Science of Getting Rich* (SoHo Books, 2012).

55. Tony Robbins, *Money: Master the Game, Seven Simple Steps to Financial Freedom* (New York: Simon and Schuster, 2014).

56. Ibid.

57. Tony Robbins, lecture.

58. Ibid.

59. From Steven Pressfield's post "Start before You're Ready," published July 10, 2010 in Pressfield's blog Writing Wednesdays, http://www.stevenpressfield.com/2010/07/start-before-youre-ready/, accessed September 23, 2017.

60. This formula is from Tony Robbins, *Money: Master the Game, Seven Simple Steps to Financial Freedom* (New York: Simon and Schuster, 2014).

61. From the teachings of Dr. David R. Hawkins.

62. Ibid.

63. Based on a real exchange between Josie and me, though the dialogue may not be exact.
64. Malcolm Gladwell, *Outliers: The Story of Success* (New York: Little, Brown, 2008).
65. Ibid.
66. From Steve Jobs interview, PBS documentary *Steve Jobs: One Last Thing*, premiere November 2011, as quoted in review by Josh Lowensohn, "Steve Jobs in PBS Documentary: You Can Change the World," CNET, November 2, 2011, http://www.cbsnews.com/news/steve-jobs-in-pbs-film-you-can-change-the-world/, accessed September 23, 2017.
67. Definition based on one given in a Tony Robbins lecture.
68. Ibid.
69. Quote from Tony Robbins lecture.
70. W. H. Murray, *The Scottish Himalayan Expedition* (London: Dent and Sons, 1951).
71. Ibid.
72. This is a loose translation of Goethe that Murray quotes in *The Scottish Himalayan Expedition* (London: Dent and Sons, 1951).
73. Based on a true story from the girls' childhood bedtime routine, just one of an endless trove.
74. Mark Twain, http://www.goodreads.com/quotes/404897-keep-away-from-people-who-try-to-belittle-your-ambitions, accessed September 23, 2017.
75. Eckhart Tolle, "Ego Relationship versus Real Love," segment of *The Power of Now*, audiobook, published on YouTube, May 27, 2017, https://www.youtube.com/watch?v=AGVLjcVR4uY, accessed September 24, 2017.
76. From the teachings of Dr. David R. Hawkins.
77. Paul Tough, "What If the Secret to Success Is Failure?" *New York Times Magazine*, September 14, 2011.
78. David McCullough Jr., "You Are Not Special," graduation speech, Wellesley High School, 2012, as quoted in *Time* staff's "The 'You Are Not Special' Graduation Speech Is Just as Relevant Today," time.com, November 17, 2015, http://time.com/4116019/david-mccullough-jr-graduation-speech-wellesley-high/, accessed September 24, 2017.
79. Fictional story based on quotes and excerpts from Billy Ray Cyrus interview, *GQ*, February 9, 2011.
80. "Mork Meets Robin Williams," *Mork and Mindy*, aired February 19, 1981, as quoted in "Robin Williams Examined the Dark Side of Fame 33 Years Ago on 'Mork and Mindy,'" Dashiell Bennet, *The Wire*, August 11, 2014, https://www.theatlantic.com/entertainment/archive/2014/08/robin-williams-examined-the-dark-side-of-fame-33-years-ago-on-mork-and-mindy/375907/, accessed September 24, 2017. The ending segment of the episode is also published on YouTube, https://www.youtube.com/watch?v=HzVbh4IULog.

81. Dr. David R. Hawkins, *Healing and Recovering* (Sedona, AZ: Veritas, 2015).

82. Teenage Girls Targeted for Sweet-Flavored Alcoholic Beverages: Polls Show More Teen Girls See "Alcopop" Ads than Women Age 21–44," press release, American Medical Association, December 16, 2004, http://www.alcoholpolicymd.com/pdf/alcopops_release_final_2.pdf , accessed September 24, 2017.

83. Ibid.

84. Ibid.

85. From Jim Carrey interview with Steve Kroft, *60 Minutes*, aired November 21, 2004, as quoted in "Carrey: Life Is Too Beautiful," Rebecca Leung, CBSnews.com, November 18, 2004, http://www.cbsnews.com/news/carrey-life-is-too-beautiful/, accessed September 24, 2017.

86. "The Tragic Stories of the Lottery's Unluckiest Winners: Billy Bob Harrell, Jr.," Time.com, November 27, 2011, http://newsfeed.time.com/2012/11/28/500-million-powerball-jackpot-the-tragic-stories-of-the-lotterys-unluckiest-winners/slide/billie-bob-harrell-jr/, accessed October 17, 2017.

87. From the "Serenity Prayer" by American theologian Reinhold Niebuhr.

88. Paul McCartney, "Paul McCartney: Musician," in *The Right Words at the Right Time*, Marlo Thomas ed. (New York: Atria Books, 2002), 217.

89. Ibid, 218.

90. Ibid, 218.

91. From a lecture by philosopher Allan Watts.

92. Ibid.

93. Naomi Long Madgett, "Woman with Flower," *Star by Star* (Harlo Press, 1965). Reprinted with permission.

94. See Matthew 6:22.

95. See Matthew 7:3.

96. Allan Watts, http://quoteaddicts.com/1386174, accessed September 24, 2017.

97. Dr. David R. Hawkins, *Truth versus Falsehood: How to Tell the Difference* (Toronto: Axial, 2005).

98. Paraphrased from the teachings of David. R. Hawkins, *I: Reality and Subjectivity* (Sedona, AZ: Veritas, 2003).

99. Original Gandhi quote can be found in Ramashray Roy and Ravi Ranjan, *Essays on Modernism, Democracy and Well-being: A Gandhian Perspective* (New Delhi: Sage, 2016), 223.

100. Lecture by Dr. David R. Hawkins.

101. Dr. David R. Hawkins, *I: Reality and Subjectivity* (Sedona, AZ: Veritas, 2003).

102. "Am" signifies beingness. The ultimate truth is beyond is-ness, or any intransitive verb. "I" signifies the radical subjectivity of the state of

realization. It is in itself the complete statement of Reality. Dr. David Hawkins, *I: Reality and Subjectivity* (Sedona, AZ: Veritas, 2003).

103. Neville Goddard, *Prayer: The Art of Believing* (Eastford, CT: Martino, 2009).
104. Matthew 13:12.
105. Neville Goddard, *Prayer: The Art of Believing* (Eastford, CT: Martino, 2009).
106. Gregg Braden, "Feeling Is the Prayer," published on YouTube, December 11, 2016, https://www.youtube.com/watch?v=wJ0O1FTn9RQ, accessed September 24, 2017.
107. Luke 12:7.
108. Matthew 17:20.
109. Helen Schucman, *A Course in Miracles* (Mill Valley, CA: Foundation for Inner Peace, 1976).
110. Joe Simpson, *Touching the Void* (New York: Harper Collins, 1988).
111. Ibid.
112. Ibid.
113. This is advice Tony Robbins often gives in his lectures.
114. This saying is commonly attributed to yogi Paramahansa Yogananda, https://www.goodreads.com/author/quotes/14650.Paramahansa_Yogananda, accessed on September 24, 2017.
115. Joel Osteen, *The Power of I Am: Two Words That Will Change Your Life Today* (New York: Hatchette Book Group, 2016).
116. Often attributed to Gandhi, http://www.goodreads.com/quotes/24499-be-the-change-that-you-wish-to-see-in-the, accessed September 24, 2017.
117. Neville Goddard, *The Feeling Is the Secret* (Seattle: Pacific Publishing Studio, 2010).
118. Ibid.
119. Paul Tough, "What If the Secret to Success Is Failure?" *New York Times Magazine*, September 14, 2011.
120. Larry Smith expresses this so well. Check out his Tedx Talk, "Why You Will Fail to Have a Good Career," given at the University of Waterloo, Canada, November 2011, https://www.ted.com/talks/larry_smith_why_you_will_fail_to_have_a_great_career, accessed September 24, 2017.
121. This idea about discouraging fear is borrowed from Regina Dugan's Ted Talk "From Mach 20 Glider to Hummingbird Drone," given at the TED Conference, New York University, March 2012, https://www.ted.com/talks/regina_dugan_from_mach_20_glider_to_humming_bird_drone#t-105949, accessed September 24, 2017.
122. Henry David Thoreau, *Walden* (Boston: Houghton Mifflin Company).
123. Text of J. K. Rowling's speech, "The Fringe Benefits of Failure, and the Importance of the Imagination," *Harvard Gazette*, June 8, 2011, http://news.harvard.edu/gazette/story/2008/06/text-of-j-k-rowling-speech/, accessed July 8, 2017.

124. For more about quitting and refocusing, see Seth Godin, *The Dip: A Little Book that Teaches You When to Quit (and When to Stick)* (New York: Portfolio, 2007).

125. From a Tony Robbins lecture; this is a point he often makes.

126. Jim Carrey, Commencement Speech 2014, given at Maharishi University of Management, published on YouTube by Maharishi University, May 30, 2014, https://www.youtube.com/watch?v=V80-gPkpH6M, accessed September 24, 2017.

127. Helen Schucman, *A Course in Miracles* (Mill Valley, CA: Foundation for Inner Peace, 1976).

128. Based on teachings of Dr. David R. Hawkins.

129. Attributed to Swami Muktananda.

130. Dr. David R. Hawkins, *Healing and Recovering* (Sedona, AZ: Veritas, 2015).

131. Descriptions of the four "floors" are from Dr. David R Hawkins, *Healing and Recovering* (Sedona, AZ: Veritas, 2015).

132. Ibid.

133. Based on teachings of Dr. David R. Hawkins.

134. Dr. David R. Hawkins *Transcending the Levels of Consciousness* (Sedona, AZ: Veritas, 2006).

135. From the teachings of Dr. David R. Hawkins.

136. Dr. David R. Hawkins, *Transcending the Levels of Consciousness* (Sedona, AZ: Veritas, 2006).

137. A paraphrase of a quote of Paul Tillich found in Elizabeth Gilbert's *Big Magic* (New York: Riverhead Books, 2015).

138. Helen Schucman, *A Course in Miracles* (Mill Valley, CA: Foundation for Inner Peace, 1976).

139. Ibid.

140. Ibid.

141. Based on Dr. David R. Hawkins, Map of Consciousness, www.veritaspub.com.

142. Henry David Thoreau, *Walden* (Boston: Houghton Mifflin).

143. Helen Schucman, *A Course in Miracles* (Mill Valley, CA: Foundation for Inner Peace, 1976).

Morgan James
Speakers Group

www.TheMorganJamesSpeakersGroup.com

We connect Morgan James published authors with live and online events and audiences whom will benefit from their expertise.

Morgan James makes all of our titles available
through the Library for All Charity Organization.

www.LibraryForAll.org

CPSIA information can be obtained
at www.ICGtesting.com
Printed in the USA
LVHW08s2022060718
582995LV00003B/13/P